ATHANASIUS AND DIDYMUS

Works on the Spirit

T0335272

ST VLADIMIR'S SEMINARY PRESS
Popular Patristics Series
Number 43

The Popular Patristics Series published by St Vladimir's Seminary Press provides readable and accurate translations of a wide range of early Christian literature to a wide audience—students of Christian history to lay Christians reading for spiritual benefit. Recognized scholars in their fields provide short but comprehensive and clear introductions to the material. The texts include classics of Christian literature, thematic volumes, collections of homilies, letters on spiritual counsel, and poetical works from a variety of geographical contexts and historical backgrounds. The mission of the series is to mine the riches of the early Church and to make these treasures available to all.

Series Editor
BOGDAN BUCUR

Associate Editor
IGNATIUS GREEN

* * *

Series Editor
1999–2020
JOHN BEHR

Works on the Spirit

ATHANASIUS AND DIDYMUS

Athanasius'
Letters to Serapion on the Holy Spirit
and Didymus'
On the Holy Spirit

Translated, with an Introduction and Annotations, by

MARK DELCOGLIANO,
ANDREW RADDE-GALLWITZ,
and LEWIS AYRES

ST VLADIMIR'S SEMINARY PRESS
YONKERS, NEW YORK
2011

Library of Congress Cataloging-in-Publication Data

Works on the Spirit : Athanasius's letters to Serapion on the Holy Spirit, and, Didymus's On the Holy Spirit / Athanasius and Didymus ; translated, with an introduction and annotations, by Mark DelCogliano, Andrew Radde-Gallwitz, and Lewis Ayres.

    p. cm. — (Popular patristics series ; no. 43)
    Includes bibliographical references and index.
    ISBN 978-0-88141-379-3
    1. Holy Spirit—Early works to 1800. 2. Athanasius, Saint, Patriarch of Alexandria, d. 373. Epistolae ad Serapionem. 3. Didymus, the Blind, ca. 313–ca. 398. De Spiritu Sancto. 4. Athanasius, Saint, Patriarch of Alexandria, d. 373.—Correspondence. 5. Serapion, of Thmuis, Saint—Correspondence. I. DelCogliano, Mark. II. Radde-Gallwitz, Andrew. III. Ayres, Lewis. IV. Athanasius, Saint, Patriarch of Alexandria, d. 373. Epistolae ad Serapionem. English. V. Didymus, the Blind, ca. 313–ca. 398. De Spiritu Sancto. English.

    BT121.3.W6813 2011
    231'.309015—dc23

                      2011032049

ST VLADIMIR'S SEMINARY PRESS
575 Scarsdale Road, Yonkers, NY 10707
1-800-204-2665
www.svspress.com

ISBN 978-088141-379-3
ISSN 1555-5755

PRINTED IN THE UNITED STATES OF AMERICA

Contents

Preface

This volume is the fruit of a happy collaboration that originated during the years 2006–2007 when the three of us were at Emory University in Atlanta, Georgia. Our partnership began when Lewis Ayres suggested that we translate Didymus's *On the Holy Spirit* with a view to publication. It was truly a joint effort. Each week the three of us prepared translations of a predetermined amount of text. At weekly meetings we then went through the Latin line-by-line, discussing the meaning and producing a collaborative translation that incorporated the best elements from each of our efforts. The translation of Athanasius's *Letters to Serapion on the Holy Spirit* is principally the work of Mark DelCogliano, though major sections were completed in collaboration with Andrew Radde-Gallwitz. All three of us carefully went through both translations in the autumn of 2007 in preparation for a weekend of meetings in January 2008, during which each was substantially revised. Two further years of tinkering with the translations on the part of all three of us have produced the versions that appear in this volume. Each section of the General Introduction has a primary author, whose work was critiqued by his two collaborators. Mark DelCogliano wrote the brief survey of pre-fourth century pneumatology and the Introduction to Athanasius's *Letters to Serapion on the Holy Spirit*, and Andrew Radde-Gallwitz the Introduction to Didymus's *On the Holy Spirit*. Lewis Ayres wrote the sections, "Athanasius's Argument" and "Didymus's Argument," within these two Introductions.

Abbreviations

General Introduction

By the Word of the Lord the heavens were established,
by the Spirit of his mouth all their power [Ps 32.6 LXX].

You send forth your Spirit, and they are created,
and you renew the face of the earth [Ps 103.30 LXX].

Who is the Holy Spirit, especially in relation to the Father and the Son? What is the role of the Holy Spirit in the life of the church and in the life of individual Christians? Broadly speaking, these two questions animated reflection upon the Holy Spirit in early Christianity.[1] Athanasius's *Letters to Serapion* and Didymus's *On the Holy Spirit* are among the earliest Christian texts dedicated exclusively to the Holy Spirit, reflecting the pneumatological debates of the mid fourth century. Although the Holy Spirit only became the object of sustained theological reflection in the fourth century, there were earlier Christian pneumatologies. In fact, the pneumatological developments of the fourth century constitute what can be considered a *third* stage in the history of the theology of the Spirit.[2]

---

[1]For standard accounts of the history of the theology of the Holy Spirit, see H. B. Swete, *The Holy Spirit in the Ancient Church* (London: MacMillan, 1912; repr. Eugene: Wipf and Stock, 1996); J. Patout Burns, and Gerald M. Fagan, *The Holy Spirit*, Message of the Fathers of the Church 3 (Wilmington: M. Glazier, 1984; repr. Eugene: Wipf and Stock, 2002).

[2]See Lewis Ayres and Michel René Barnes, "Pneumatology: Historical and Methodological Considerations," *Augustinian Studies* 39 (2008): 163–236, a collection of four papers, with an Introduction and Conclusion, originally delivered at the annual meeting of the North American Patristics Society in 2005. The individual contributions are cited below.

In the first and second centuries there was no single Christian pneumatology, but rather a variety of continuations and developments of diverse, pre-existing Jewish pneumatologies.[3] The most important of these is Spirit as Creator pneumatology, according to which the Holy Spirit was identified as co-Creator on the basis of texts such as Psalms 32.6 and 103.30. Athenagoras, Theophilus, and Irenaeus are adherents of this pneumatological tradition.[4] Other early Jewish-Christian pneumatologies identified the Spirit as an Angel, as Wisdom, as the Consort of God, and so forth. Angelic pneumatology is particularly relevant for our purposes since both Athanasius and Didymus were compelled to refute a fourth-century version of it.

The second stage, beginning in the third century, sees the end of this "high" pneumatology. In this period significant figures such as Tertullian and Origen abandoned earlier Jewish-Christian pneumatologies in response to a variety of doctrinal pressures.[5] Monarchians, who viewed Christ and the Spirit as identical with the Father, differing only in name and in their mode of manifestation, may have been particularly important. For Tertullian and Origen, monarchian accounts threatened the priority and uniqueness of God, the Father of Jesus Christ and Creator of all things. In response they tried to

[3]Michel René Barnes, "The Beginning and End of Early Christian Pneumatology," *Augustinian Studies* 39 (2008): 169–86 at 171–80. On Jewish-Christian pneumatologies, see Jean Daniélou, *The Theology of Jewish Christianity*, translated by John A. Baker (London: Darton, Longmann & Todd; Chicago: The Henry Regnery Company, 1964); Marie E. Isaacs, *The Concept of Spirit: A Study of Pneuma in Hellenistic Judaism and its Bearing on the New Testament*, Heythrop Monographs 1 (London: Heythrop College, 1976); John Levinson, "The Angelic Spirit in Early Judaism," *SBL 1995 Seminar Papers*, 464–92; Alan F. Segal, *Two Powers in Heaven: Early Rabbinic Reports about Christianity and Gnostics* (Leiden: Brill, 1977; repr. 2002); idem, "Two Powers in Heaven and Early Christian Thinking," in Stephen T. Davis, Daniel Kendall, and Gerald O'Collins, eds., *The Trinity: An Interdisciplinary Symposium on the Doctrine of the Trinity* (Oxford and New York: Oxford University Press, 2000), 73–95.

[4]On Irenaeus's pneumatology, see J. Armitage Robinson, *St. Irenaeus: Demonstration of Apostolic Preaching* (London: SPCK; New York: MacMillan, 1920), 24–68; and Michel René Barnes, "Irenaeus's Trinitarian Theology," *Nova et Vetera* 7 (2009): 76–106.

[5]Barnes, "The Beginning and End of Early Christian Pneumatology," 180–6.

distinguish the Son and the Spirit from the Father with greater clarity and order. As part of this shift, they neglected scriptural passages about the "Spirit" as Creator (such as Psalms 32.6 and 103.30) and reinterpreted other key scriptural passages about the "Spirit" (such as Luke 1:35), so that they were no longer understood as statements about the Holy Spirit, but about the pre-incarnate Son.[6] Scriptural texts about the Wisdom of God were reinterpreted in a similar way. Such neglect of some passages and reinterpretations of others thus undercut the exegetical basis for the "high" Jewish-Christian Spirit as Creator pneumatology. In these "low" pneumatologies of the third century the Holy Spirit was considered subordinate to the Son, largely on the basis of John 1:3, *All things came to be through him*, i.e. the Word.[7] Such subordination is in fact a key feature of the anti-monarchian Trinitarian theology of Tertullian and Origen, who employed the idea of Trinitarian order (*gradus* or *taxis*) to understand the unity and diversity of the three: Father, Son, and Spirit, while distinct, are unified in an ontological hierarchy. As Michel Barnes notes, while this new emphasis on Trinitarian order resulted in "a curtailment of previous pneumatological options," it contained "its own tensions and possibilities that were played out in subsequent centuries."[8] Indeed, no one in the fourth century questioned this hierarchical Trinitarian order as such, though its meaning and significance was heavily contested.[9]

The third stage covers the mid to late fourth century and is characterized by the continuation, retrieval, and clash of older pneumatologies and their reconfiguration within the new context of Pro-Nicene Trinitarian theology.[10] A comparison of the creeds of Nicaea

[6]For example, see Tertullian, *Against Praxeas* 26.

[7]For example, see Origen, *Commentary on the Gospel according to John* 2.73–88.

[8]Lewis Ayres and Michel René Barnes, "Conclusions," *Augustinian Studies* 39 (2008): 235–6 at 235.

[9]Barnes, "The Beginning and End of Early Christian Pneumatology," 186.

[10]Lewis Ayres, "Innovation and *Ressourcement* in Pro-Nicene Pneumatology," *Augustinian Studies* 39 (2008): 187–206. For a survey of other theories why controversy about the divinity of the Holy Spirit broke out at this time, see Michael A. G. Haykin, *The Spirit of God* (Leiden: Brill, 1994), 1–3.

in 325 and Constantinople in 381 gives a sense of the development of pneumatological doctrine in the mid forth century:

Nicene Creed (325)	Nicene-Constantinopolitan Creed (381)
We believe . . . in the Holy Spirit.	We believe . . . in the Holy Spirit, the Lord and the Giver of Life, who proceeds from the Father, who is worshipped and glorified together with the Father and the Son, who spoke through the prophets.

By the time of the Council of Constantinople in 381, the original Nicene pronouncement was deemed no longer sufficient and was expanded in the light of the Pro-Nicene clarifications about the Holy Spirit that had developed in the interim. Pro-Nicene Trinitarian theology viewed the Father, Son, and Holy Spirit as three irreducible agents who share or constitute one indivisible divine nature or power and operate inseparably.[11] Most significantly, this new context led to a recovery of pneumatology which emphasized the Spirit's status as Creator within the inseparable and unmediated creative activity of God.

This new Pro-Nicene theology of the Holy Spirit was, however, resisted by those who still adhered to the ontologically subordinated Trinitarian order developed by the anti-monarchians, by those who believed that the Holy Spirit was a creature. Such theologians appealed to the fact that scripture itself lacked clear support for the claim that the Holy Spirit was God, and drew upon a variety of older Jewish-Christian pneumatologies to establish their position for the created status of the Holy Spirit. For example, they retrieved Angelic pneumatology but rejected Spirit as Creator pneumatology, resulting in a "low" Angelic pneumatology in contrast to its earlier "high" Jewish-Christian precedent. These theologians may also have

[11]On the meaning of "Pro-Nicene," see Lewis Ayres, *Nicaea and its Legacy* (Oxford: Oxford University Press, 2004), 236–40.

been influenced by wider currents in Homoian doctrine of the late 350s—the ecclesial alliance out of which the Heteroousians would emerge.[12] The subordinationist impulse of Homoian theology was surely extended to the Spirit, and the Heteroousians followed this impulse to its logical conclusion by completely depriving the Spirit of divinity.[13] And so, we may posit a dual context for those who opposed Pro-Nicene pneumatology: (1) the continued presence of some older Jewish-Christian pneumatologies filtered through the low pneumatology of the anti-monarchians, and (2) the vitalization of these pneumatologies by Homoians and Heteroousians. The writings of Athanasius and Didymus on the Holy Spirit are the first Pro-Nicene writings directed against such groups, refuting both older (Jewish-Christian and anti-monarchian) and recent (Homoian and Heteroousian) pneumatological themes.

Introduction to Athanasius's Letters to Serapion

Life and Legacy

Narratives of the fourth-century Trinitarian debates have, until quite recently, been dominated by the figure of Athanasius. Traditional accounts of these debates corral its participants into two competing camps: the beleaguered Athanasius and his supporters, who formulate an unalterable theological vision enshrined in the Creed of Nicaea in 325, and the Arians, who maliciously oppose Nicene theology at every chance in order to promote their shameless heresy. These two parties battle it out through the fourth century, with Athanasius bravely and resolutely at the helm of the ship of orthodoxy, however rocked by Arian waves it may be. Efforts on the part of the

---

[12]On the Homoians and Heteroousians, see Ayres, *Nicaea and its Legacy*, 138–9 and 144–9.

[13]See Eunomius, *Apology* 25–26.

Nicenes to defend their theology are made all the more difficult by various Arian emperors who thwart them at every step. The denouement of this war-drama occurs at the Council of Constantinople in 381, where Nicene Orthodoxy—as defended by the Cappadocian Fathers who inherited the legacy of Athanasius—finally triumphs and is given imperial sanction. Ancient fourth- and early-fifth-century church polemicists and historians such as Gregory Nazianzen, Epiphanius, Socrates, Sozomen, and Theodoret preserved this narrative. Hence from shortly after his death Athanasius has been hailed as the unflinching Champion of Nicene Orthodoxy, "the Holy Luminary of Egypt,"[14] "the Pillar of the Church."[15]

Athanasius continues to fascinate, but modern scholarship has approached him more critically, less hagiographically. Athanasius still has strident defenders, but has acquired a legion of harsh critics. His character and methods have been scrutinized and found suspect.[16] Athanasius's polemical polarization between his own orthodoxy and "Arianism" that he developed in the 330s and ceaselessly promoted thereafter has been deconstructed as a fiction.[17] His theological influence upon the Cappadocians and his contributions to Pro-Nicene orthodoxy have been called into question.[18]

---

[14]Evagrius of Pontus, *Gnostikos* 46 (ed. A. Guillaumont and C. Guillaumont, *Évagre le Pontique. Le gnostique ou à celui qui est devenu digne de la science*, SChr 356 (Paris: Éditions du Cerf, 1989), 182).

[15]Gregory Nazianzen, *Oratio* 21.26.

[16]See R. P. C. Hanson, *The Search for the Christian Doctrine of God* (Edinburgh: T&T Clark, 1988), 239–40, for a summary of the different opinions on Athanasius's character and methods. Duane W.-H. Arnold, *The Early Episcopal Career of Athanasius of Alexandria* (Notre Dame: University of Notre Dame Press, 1991), stands out as one of his modern defenders; Eduard Schwartz, *Zur Geschichte des Athanasius, Gesammelte Schriften* III (Berlin: De Gruyter, 1959), and Timothy D. Barnes, *Athanasius and Constantius* (Cambridge: Harvard University Press, 1993), epitomize 20th century scholarship on the unsavory aspects of Athanasius. See also David Brakke, *Athanasius and the Politics of Asceticism* (Oxford: Clarendon Press, 1995).

[17]David M. Gwynn, *The Eusebians. The Polemic of Athanasius of Alexandria and the Construction of the Arian Controversy* (Oxford: Oxford University Press, 2007).

[18]E.g. Marina Silvia Troiano, "Il *Contra Eunomium* III di Basilio di Cesarea e le *Epistolae ad Serapionem* I-IV di Atanasio di Alessandria: nota comparativa," *Augustinianum* 41.1 (2001), 59–91; Mark DelCogliano, "Basil of Caesarea on Proverbs

In particular, the influence of Athanasius's pneumatology upon subsequent Pro-Nicene theologians such as Basil of Caesarea and Gregory of Nazianzus must not be overestimated.[19] At the same time, Athanasius has also been studied as a theologian significant in his own right, one with a distinct theological vision.[20] Though Athanasius may have lost some of his luster in the eyes of scholars, his theological achievements are considerable, his tenacity in pursuit of orthodoxy remarkable, and the esteem in which Pro-Nicenes held him undeniable. While much work remains to be done on Athanasius, we now have a clearer, more accurate portrait of the man and his thought, a man who for many remains a profoundly important Saint and Father of the Church.

When conflict erupted around 318 between Alexander, the bishop of Alexandria, and a popular presbyter named Arius over the relation between the Father and the Son, Athanasius, then a young dea-

8:22 and the Sources of Pro-Nicene Theology," *Journal of Theological Studies* n.s. 59 (2008): 183–90; idem, "Basil of Caesarea, Didymus the Blind, and the Anti-Pneumatomachian Exegesis of Amos 4:13 and John 1:3," *Journal of Theological Studies* n.s. 61 (2010): 644–58. On the issue more generally, see Hanson, *The Search*, 678–9; Ayres, *Nicaea and its Legacy*, 221; Stephen M. Hildebrand, *The Trinitarian Theology of Basil of Caesarea: A Synthesis of Greek Thought and Biblical Truth* (Washington D.C.: Catholic University of America Press, 2007), 80 n. 10.

[19] In the past Athanasius's influence in pneumatology was exaggerated; see, for example, Swete, *The Holy Spirit in the Ancient Church*, 220; Haykin, *The Spirit of God*, 7. For recent reassessments of the influence of Athanasius's pneumatology upon the Cappadocians, see the studies of Troiano and DelCogliano in n. 18 above, as well as Christopher A. Beeley, *Gregory of Nazianzus on the Trinity and the Knowledge of God* (New York: Oxford, 2008), 277–83.

[20] E.g. E. P. Meijering, *Orthodoxy and Platonism in Athanasius. Synthesis or Antithesis?*, 2nd ed. (Leiden: Brill, 1975); Charles Kannengiesser, *Athanase d'Alexandrie. Évêque et Écrivain: Une lecture des traités contra les Ariens* (Paris: Beauschesne, 1983); J. Rebecca Lyman, *Christology and Cosmology: Models of Divine Activity in Origen, Eusebius, and Athanasius* (Oxford: Clarendon Press, 1993); Peter Widdicombe, *The Fatherhood of God from Origen to Athanasius* (Oxford: Clarendon Press, 1994); Khaled Anatolios, *Athanasius: The Coherence of his Thought* (London and New York: Routledge, 1998); idem, *Athanasius* (London: Routledge, 2004); Xavier Morales, *La théologie trinitaire d'Athanase d'Alexandrie* (Paris: Institut d'Études Augustiniennes, 2006); Thomas G. Weinandy, *Athanasius: A Theological Introduction* (Aldershot: Ashgate, 2007).

con, wholeheartedly supported his bishop.[21] After a series of failed attempts to reconcile the feuding factions within the Alexandrian church, in 325 the emperor Constantine convened a council at Nicaea to resolve the controversy—now spread throughout the churches of the east—once and for all. The council ratified a creed designed to exclude the theology of Arius and secured his excommunication. Athanasius attended the council as a member of Alexander's entourage. When Alexander died a few years later, Athanasius succeeded him, though not without steep resistance from the Melitians.

Though Athanasius wrote theological tracts against "Arianism" (as he perceived it) from ca. 339 onwards,[22] nothing much is heard from him on the Nicene Creed as the standard of orthodoxy until the early 350s.[23] In the meantime Athanasius was charged with violence and other crimes, tried and convicted at the Council of Tyre in 335, and exiled to Gaul. For the remainder of his ecclesiastical career, these charges would dog Athanasius, rendering him suspect and tainted in the eyes of many eastern bishops. Before his death in 373, Athanasius would spend five periods of exile outside of Alexandria, about seventeen years in total. By the time of his death, however, a viable Pro-Nicene alliance had emerged which viewed the Nicene Creed as a cipher for a Trinitarian theology in which the three, the Father, Son, and Holy Spirit, are irreducible and one nature, power, and will. Gaining impetus in the late 350s in the face of the splintering of the old Eusebian alliance[24] into several mutually opposed alli-

---

[21]For accounts of the fourth-century Trinitarian controversies, see Hanson, *The Search*; Ayres, *Nicaea and its Legacy*; and John Behr, *The Nicene Faith* (Crestwood: St Vladimir's Seminary Press, 2004).

[22]His three genuine *Orations against the Arians* are dated to 339–346.

[23]Lewis Ayres, "Athanasius' Initial Defense of the Term Ὁμοούσιος: Rereading the *De decretis*," *Journal of Early Christian Studies* 12 (2004): 337–59.

[24]"Eusebian' is a problematic term, as recently discussed by Gwynn, *The Eusebians*. Here 'Eusebian' is used in contrast to the Athanasian usage deconstructed by Gwynn and in line with other recent usage to name the *ad hoc* alliance of eastern bishops and theologians initially formed around the figures of Eusebius of Nicomedia and Eusebius of Caesarea that lasted from ca. 320 to ca. 355. For a definition of the category, see Ayres, *Nicaea and its Legacy*, 52; and Joseph T. Lienhard, *Contra Marcellum. Marcellus of Ancyra and Fourth-Century Theology* (Washington, D.C.: The

ances (the Heteroousians, the Homoiousians, and the Homoians), in subsequent decades the Trinitarian theology of the Pro-Nicene alliance finally received imperial sanction at the Council of Constantinople in 381.

The Context of the Letters

Athanasius wrote three letters on the Holy Spirit.[25] He addressed his letters to Serapion, the bishop of Thmuis in Lower Egypt since the late 330s at the latest.[26] A former monk and monastic superior,[27] Serapion was one of Athanasius's most trusted agents in the promotion of his ecclesiastical policies and theology. For example, in the late 330s Athanasius relied on Serapion to help him maintain control of his see during exile.[28] Athanasius also entrusted him with a delicate mission in 353, placing him at the head of a delegation to

Catholic University of America Press, 1999), 34–5. On the theological and ecclesio-political cohesiveness of the Eusebians, see Mark DelCogliano, "Eusebian Theologies of the Son as Image of God," *Journal of Early Christian Studies* 14 (2006): 459–84; "The Eusebian Alliance: The Case of Theodotus of Laodicea," *Zeitschrift für Antikes Christentum* 12 (2008): 250–66; and "George of Laodicea: A Historical Reassessment," *Journal of Ecclesiastical History* 62 (2011): 667–92.

[25]Four letters are preserved in the manuscripts, and appear thus in Maurist edition. But it is now generally accepted that those traditionally called the second and third letters were originally a single letter. See Joseph Lebon, *Athanase d'Alexandrie: Lettres à Sérapion sur la divinité du Saint-Esprit.* SChr 15 (Paris: Cerf, 1947), 31–39; C. R. B. Shapland, *The Letters of Saint Athanasius concerning the Holy Spirit.* (London: Epworth Press, 1951), 11–13; and Dietmar Wyrwa and Kyriakos Savvidis, *Athanasius Werke I/1. Die dogmatischen Schriften. 4. Lieferung. Epistulae I-IV ad Serapionem* (Berlin / New York: Walter de Gruyter, 2010), 385. The new *Athanasius Werke* edition, on which our translation is based, reconstitutes the second and third letters as Letter Two. This has necessitated a new system for numbering the sections of the letters; see pp. 48–49 below. Note that in the manuscripts an independent treatise was attached to the three letters at a later date (now known as *Serap. 4*).

[26]On Serapion's life and writings, see Klaus Fitschen, *Serapion von Thmuis: Echte und unechte Schriften sowie die Zeugnisse des Athanasius und anderer*, Patristische Texte und Studien 37 (Berlin and New York: De Gruyter, 1992). Fitschen discusses Athanasius's letters to Serapion on pp. 135–47.

[27]Athanasius, *Letter to Dracontius 7.*

[28]Athanasius, *Festal Letter 12*; see Barnes, *Athanasius and Constantius*, 190–1.

Emperor Constantius.[29] Besides the *Letters to Serapion*, Athanasius sent him a letter on the death of Arius (*Ep.* 54) to prove that Arius had not died in communion with the church. Hence Athanasius and Serapion were partners in the various struggles facing the Egyptian church. A few of Serapion's own writings survive: a treatise *Against the Manichees*,[30] a letter to the disciples of Antony after his death,[31] and a letter of consolation to a bishop.[32] Serapion was also an intimate of Antony the Great.[33] On his deathbed (ca. 356) Antony bequeathed one of his two sheepskins to Serapion; the other went to Athanasius.[34] Jerome notes that Serapion was considered worthy of the appellation *Scholasticus* (that is, a man of culture and erudition) on account of his meticulous scholarship,[35] and Evagrius of Pontus called him "the Angel of the Church of Thmuis."[36]

From the *Letters to Serapion* we learn that Athanasius was responding to a letter that he had received from Serapion himself.[37] In his letter to Athanasius (no longer extant), Serapion reported that certain people had "set their minds against the Holy Spirit, claiming not only that he is a creature but also that he is one of *the ministering spirits* [Heb 1.14] and is different from the angels only in degree" (*Serap.* 1.1.2) and asked Athanasius to refute them. Athanasius obliged Serapion with a long letter (Letter One) that sought to correct those who held this "low" variety of Angelic pneumatology, whom Athanasius calls "Tropikoi" (the meaning of which is dis-

---

[29]*Historia acephala* 1.7; Sozomen, *h.e.* 4.9.6.

[30]R. P. Casey, *Serapion of Thmuis against the Manichees* (Cambridge: Harvard University Press, 1931).

[31]René Draguët, "Une lettre de Sérapion de Thmuis aux disciples d'Antoine (A.D. 356) en version syriaque et arménienne," *Le Muséon* 64 (1951): 1–25; there is an English translation by Rowan A. Greer in Tim Vivian and Apostolos N. Athnassalis, *Athanasius of Alexandria: The Life of Antony* (Kalamazoo: Cistercian Publications, 2003), 39–47.

[32]PG 40.924–925. Serapion's authorship of a *Letter to Monks* attributed to him (PG 40.925–941) is disputed.

[33]*Life of Antony* 82.3.

[34]*Life of Antony* 91.8–9.

[35]Jerome, *On Illustrious Men* 99.

[36]Evagrius of Pontus, *Gnostikos* 47.

[37]See *Serap.* 1.1.

cussed below). Apparently the length of the letter was daunting to some members of Serapion's church and Serapion passed along their request for an epitome. They sought a summary of the first letter "so that they might have a brief and readily accessible arsenal from which they can both answer those who ask questions about our faith and refute the impious" (*Serap.* 2.1.1). Hence it seems that within the church of Thmuis there was still ongoing dialogue between the Tropikoi and the orthodox. And so, Athanasius obliged them with a second letter (Letter Two). Yet the Tropikoi persisted in their opinions, for Athanasius was prompted to write a third letter to Serapion after their obstinacy had been reported to him. In this third and final letter (Letter Three), Athanasius's tone is no longer conciliatory. The intransigence of the Tropikoi had robbed him of his hope for a resolution based on persuasive arguments.

Athanasius uses the label "Tropikoi" without any explanation, seemingly assuming that Serapion would be familiar with it.[38] The appellation seems to be based from the fact that he thinks their "mode of exegesis" (*tropos*) fallacious when interpreting certain passages of scripture.[39] Indeed, the bulk of Athanasius's rebuttal is conducted on an exegetical basis. Thus one might translate "Tropikoi" as "Misinterpreters."[40] Athanasius also refers to the Tropikoi as those who are "fighting against the Spirit" (πνευματομαχοῦντες; *Serap.* 1.32.2 and 3.1.2). Athanasius's description will later evolve into a label for those who deny the divinity of the Holy Spirit: οἱ πνευματομάχοι, the "Pneumatomachians" or "Spirit-fighters."

The ecclesiastical origins of the Tropikoi are obscure,[41] but Athanasius reports how Serapion described them: "you wrote that

---

[38]*Serap.* 1.10.4, 1.17.4–5, 1.21.4, 1.30.3 and 1.32.1. See Haykin, *The Spirit of God*, 20 n. 50.

[39]See *Serap.* 1.2.2, 1.3.2, 1.7.2, and 1.10.4. See Haykin, *The Spirit of God*, 20 n. 50 a survey of the scholarly views on the label.

[40]In the ancient Armenian version of the letters, the epithet is translated as "changers" or "changers of the original." See George A. Egan, *The Armenian Version of the Letters of Athanasius to Bishop Serapion Concerning the Holy Spirit*, Studies and Documents 37 (Salt Lake City: University of Utah Press, 1968).

[41]For an attempt to identify them, see Shapland, *The Letters*, 18–34. See Haykin,

certain ones who have withdrawn from the Arians on account of their blasphemy against the Son of God have nonetheless set their minds against the Holy Spirit" (*Serap.* 1.1.2). Recall that "Arianism" is a polemical construct of Athanasius (and his supporters) that strives to link his opponents to the heretic Arius. We have no way of knowing whether the Tropikoi had formerly subscribed to the view that Athanasius labeled "Arian." They most likely arose within the dual context mentioned above.[42]

The Structure of the Letters

The three letters have a clear structure. Athanasius begins the first letter with a counter-exegesis of the scriptural passages on which the Tropikoi based their pneumatological claims. He traces the claim that the Holy Spirit is a creature to a misinterpretation of Amos 4.13, and the claim that the Holy Spirit is one of the ministering spirits different from the angels only in degree to a misinterpretation of 1 Timothy 5.21. The first is refuted in *Serap.* 1.3.1–10.3 and the second in *Serap.* 1.10.4–14.7 Athanasius next reports the Tropikoi's objections to the Nicene teaching that the Spirit was not a creature:

> If the Spirit is not a creature, nor one of the angels, but proceeds from the Father, then is he also a son? And are the Spirit and the Word two brothers? And if he is a brother, how is the Word only-begotten? How can they not be equal, but the one is named after the Father and the other after the Son? If the Spirit is from the Father, why isn't it also said that he has been begotten and is a son, but is simply called Holy Spirit? If the Spirit is of the Son, then is the Father the grandfather of the Spirit? (*Serap.* 1.15.1–2).

The Spirit of God, 20 n. 52 for references to additional literature.
[42]See p. 15.

Athanasius's arguments against these objections reduce them to absurdity and accuse the Tropikoi of a defective understanding of how the language of "Father" and "Son" is applied to God (*Serap.* 1.15–21). The first letter concludes with an extended demonstration that the Spirit is unlike creatures based on both scriptural proofs (*Serap.* 1.22–27) and Trinitarian arguments (*Serap.* 1.28–31). In this first letter, Athanasius underscores how the belief that the Spirit is a creature destroys the Christian concept of God as Trinity. Letter Two, meant to be an epitome of Letter One, begins with a demonstration that the Son is not a creature (*Serap.* 2.1–8), which has no parallel with the previous letter, but concludes with a summary of *Serap.* 1.22–31, recapitulating the earlier arguments for the Spirit's not being a creature (*Serap.* 2.10–16). Letter Three is a renewed treatment of the Tropikoi's objections first dealt with in *Serap.* 1.15–21, a section omitted for the epitome in Letter Two.

Athanasius's Argument

Throughout these letters Athanasius consistently emphasizes the interrelationship of Son and Spirit, and the dependence of the latter on the former. Alongside other scriptural designations of the Spirit Athanasius speaks frequently of "the Spirit of the Son." But by linking the Spirit firmly to the Son Athanasius sees himself necessarily linking the Spirit also to the Father. Throughout the text Athanasius makes use of his earlier anti-"Arian" arguments in this new controversy. Right at the beginning of the first letter Athanasius writes:

> For just as Arians by denying the Son also deny the Father, so too these people by disparaging the Holy Spirit also disparage the Son. And these two groups divide between themselves the opposition to the truth, so that, with some setting their minds against the Word and others against the Spirit, they might hold the same blasphemy against the Holy Trinity. (*Serap.* 1.1.3).

The link between anti-"Arian" polemic and these new controversies over the Spirit can be seen particularly clearly in Letter Two, the first half of which is devoted to proving that the Son is not a creature (*Serap.* 2.1–8) and the second half to proving the same about the Spirit (*Serap.* 2.10–16). Athanasius explains the structure of this letter in this way: "Thus it is with good reason that we speak and write about the Son of God first, so that from our knowledge of the Son we may be able to have true knowledge of the Spirit" (*Serap.* 2.10.2).

Athanasius's linking of the Spirit and the Son should not be read, however, as entirely reactive: from this linking he develops themes long fundamental to his account of creation and redemption. These may be seen clearly in a brief discussion of the second half of the first letter.[43] At *Serap.* 1.19–20 Athanasius shows that Father, Son, and Spirit are accorded a series of parallel titles by scripture (e.g. each is named as "light"), but that this naming of the three also brings with it an order and progression (συστοιχία) which begins with the Father, leads us to the Son, and then to the Spirit. We are drawn toward God by the Spirit leading us to the Son who leads us to the Father; thus (continuing with the example of light) the Spirit enlightens us and enables us to see the Son in the Spirit, but the Son is the radiance of the Father. In his discussions of this ordering Athanasius hints toward an account of the relative roles of Son and Spirit in the work of redemption (and in the Godhead) that he never fully developed. At least in part, the inchoate quality of this account of relative roles must stem from the difficulty of separating them in a context where Father, Son, and Spirit mutually indwell and are all present whenever one is present (again see *Serap.* 1.19–20). For example, at *Serap.* 1.23.4–7 Athanasius speaks of the Son anointing us with the Spirit, but emphasizes that the Son is anointing us with *his own* Spirit. The Spirit draws us necessarily into union with Son and Spirit. This interrelationship of Son and Spirit is extended also to the Incarnate

---

[43]For more extended discussions of Athanasius's doctrine of the Holy Spirit in the *Letters to Serapion*, see Lebon, *Athanase d'Alexandre*, 52–77; Shapland, *The Letters*, 34–43; and Haykin, *The Spirit of God*, 59–103.

Christ, with Athanasius emphasizing the importance of the Spirit in forming the Incarnate Christ and shaping his ministry.

The same relationship between Father, Son and Spirit also governs Athanasius's account of the Trinity's work of creation.[44] Athanasius insists that the Son is the Father's own and that the Spirit, who is the Spirit of God and the Spirit of the Son, must be proper to the substance of the Son and hence ranked with the creating triad not the creation (see *Serap.* 1.25). This observation points in two directions. First, while Athanasius only hints at the role of the Spirit in creation, he is clear *that* the Spirit is intimately involved with God's creating activity, and that the Father continues to work through the Son and in the Spirit. The latter is stated as a general principle at *Serap.* 1.24.6 and 1.28.3, while the former is clear in his use of Psalms 32.6 and 147.18 at *Serap.* 1.31.3. In the latter section we also find "there is nothing which is not brought into being and actualized through the Word in the Spirit" (1.31.2). Second, if the Spirit is one with Father and Son, then the Spirit is unchangeable, present everywhere, and that in which things participate but which participates in nothing (see *Serap.* 1.23 and 27). In particular, the Spirit sanctifies and gives life to those who participate in him, who is an immutable, perfect source of life and sanctification. We will meet this argument, which has a long pedigree in Alexandrian thought, developed at far greater length in Didymus.

The Date of the Letters

Most scholars date the exchange of letters between Athanasius and Serapion to 358–359.[45] They are a product of Athanasius's third exile,

---

[44]On this theme see Anatolios, *The Coherence*, esp. pp. 114–5; on the Spirit and the Incarnation see pp. 158–9.

[45]See Haykin, *The Spirit of God*, 59–60, for a comprehensive list of scholarly opinions on the date. The text's most recent editors prefer to date the correspondence from 357/358 to 358/359; see Wyrwa and Savvidis, *Athanasius Werke I/1*, 449–50, 537, and 567.

which lasted from February 356 until February 362. After an initial flight, he hid in the suburbs of Alexandria until December 358 when a crackdown on his supporters on the part of the authorities necessitated that he withdraw to the Egyptian deserts to hide among the monks of Nitria and the lower Thebaid.[46] In the opening line of his first letter, he reports that Serapion's letter had "reached him in the desert" (*Serap.* 1.1.1), indicating that the exchange of letters began during or after December 358, the *terminus a quo*.[47]

Determining the *terminus ante quem* is more difficult.[48] The so-called *Tomus ad Antiochenos*, a letter written by the Council of Alexandria in 362 to persuade the Nicene factions in Antioch to reconcile, offers what amounts to a summary of the doctrine presented in the *Letters to Serapion*.[49] Athanasius and his fellow bishops write that those who wish to reconcile ought

> to anathematize the Arian heresy, confess the faith confessed
> by the holy fathers at Nicaea, and anathematize those who
> claim that the Holy Spirit is a creature and separate him from

[46]See Barnes, *Athanasius and Constantius*, 119. The main evidence that Athanasius hid in Alexandria is *Index of Festal Letters* 28–32; see Annik Martin, *Histoire ‹acéphale› et index syriaque des lettres festales d'Athanase d'Alexandrie* (Paris: Cerf, 1985), 256–60.

[47]See Haykin, *The Spirit of God*, 59 n. 5. In contrast to most scholars, Wyrwa and Savvidis, *Athanasius Werke I/1*, 449, downplay the significance of Athanasius's initial seclusion in the suburbs of Alexandria. They date the correspondence to 357/358 because they claim the letters reflect not only an early stage of the debate with the Tropikoi but also the controversy caused by Aetius and Eunomius in Egypt since 356. Since Athanasius is the earliest witness to the Tropikoi, and thus to the earliest stage of debate with them, it is hard to see how this fact can be used to date the letters. On the issue of Eunomius and the dating of the correspondence, see below pp. 28–29.

[48]As Shapland (*The Letters*, 16) argued, the argument for the *terminus ante quem* based on the fact that a certain Ptolemaeus is listed as the bishop of Thmuis at the Council of Seleucia in late September 359 (Epiphanius, *Panarion* 73.26) is inconclusive. Nonetheless, Wyrwa and Savvidis, *Athanasius Werke I/1*, 449–50, adopt a *terminus ante quem* based on this fact. Their *terminus ante quem* is also based on the claim that Didymus, whose *Spir.* they date to 362, borrowed from Athanasius; as we discuss below p. 37–42, this is doubtful.

[49]For further discussion of the *Tomus*, see p. 41 below.

the substance of Christ. For a complete repudiation of the loathsome heresy of the Arians consists in this: not dividing the Holy Trinity and not claiming one of the Trinity is a creature. For those who pretend to confess the faith confessed at Nicaea while daring to utter blasphemies against the Holy Spirit do nothing more than deny the Arian heresy verbally while retaining it mentally.[50] ... The Holy Spirit is not a creature, nor is he foreign to the substance of the Son and the Father, but rather he is proper to it and inseparable from it.[51]

Even if Athanasius was not the primary author of the *Tomus*, it is evident that the bishops who drew up this synodal document were influenced by the pneumatological teaching of Athanasius in the *Letters to Serapion*. The *Letters* must consequently date to 362 or earlier.

There are also internal indications of the *terminus ante quem*. At the end of the third letter, Athanasius attributes pneumatological views similar to those of the Tropikoi to the "the Eunomiuses, and the Eudoxiuses, and the Eusebiuses" (*Serap.* 3.5.4) and "the bishop of Caesarea and the bishop of Scythopolis" (*Serap.* 3.7.1)—Acacius of Caesarea in Palestine and Patrophilus of Scythopolis. The mention of these Homoian and Heteroousian figures suggests some connection between them and the Tropikoi. Since the 330s Athanasius had polemically labeled his opponents "Eusebians" (οἱ περὶ Εὐσέβιον) in an attempt to define a long-standing conspiracy against him and his orthodoxy.[52] Eudoxius, Acacius and Patrophilus were leaders among the eastern Homoian bishops with whom Athanasius struggled in the late 350s, and all three figure prominently in his *De synodis* from the autumn of 359.[53] Patrophilus had been a Eusebian opponent of Athanasius since the 330s. Eudoxius, formerly bishop of Germanicia,

---

[50] *Tomus ad Antiochenos* 3.

[51] *Tomus ad Antiochenos* 5.

[52] See Gwynn's monograph, *The Eusebians*.

[53] See especially *De synodis* 1.3, 12.5 and 37.2, where all three are mentioned together.

become bishop of Antioch in late 357 or early 358, and, after a series reversals and counter-reversals, became the influential bishop of Constantinople in January 360. Acacius was the powerful leader of the Homoian alliance from late 359 to roughly the early 360s. Athanasius's mention of all three at the conclusion of his third letter squares well with the traditional date of 358–359.

But his mention of "the Eunomiuses" may not. In the late 340s Eunomius became a disciple of Aetius in Alexandria. Active there for only a few years, in the early 350s they relocated to Antioch, and after the accession of Eudoxius, became members of his circle.[54] In 358 Eunomius was banished along with Eudoxius and Aetius through the machinations of Basil of Ancyra, though all were rehabilitated in time for the Council of Seleucia in the fall of 359.[55] During the 350s, however, Eunomius was involved in the theological debates of the era not as one of its driving forces but as a disciple of his master Aetius. He came into prominence only at the Council of Constantinople in 360, when Aetius was condemned and exiled and he was awarded the bishopric of Cyzicus. Here it was that Eunomius probably delivered the address that would be issued later that year or the next as the *Apology*.[56] As Richard Vaggione writes, this "marks the point at which he began to step out from the shadow of his teacher and become a public figure in his own right."[57] Therefore, it seems as if it was only from 360 that Eunomius could be considered the leader of the Heteroousians, such that his name could be used as a shorthand for an entire movement. Eunomius surely was known by name at least to some of the opponents of Eudoxius and Aetius before 360, including possibly by Athanasius, but it would have been unusual (though admittedly not impossible) for him to be singled

[54]For these dates, see Thomas A. Kopecek, *A History of Neo-Arianism* (Philadelphia: The Philadelphia Patristic Foundation, 1979), 105 and 111.

[55]Sozomen, *h.e.* 4.13.4–14.7; Philostorgius, *h.e.* 4.8. Hanson, *The Search*, 357.

[56]For dating the *Apology*, see Richard Vaggione, ed. and trans., *Eunomius: The Extant Works* (Oxford: Clarendon Press, 1987), 5–9.

[57]Richard Paul Vaggione, *Eunomius of Cyzicus and the Nicene Revolution* (Oxford: Oxford University Press, 2000), 232.

out as a source of error before his elevation to the episcopacy. Thus, Athanasius's mention of "Eunomiuses" may indicate that the third letter to Serapion (Letter Three) dates to 360 or afterward.

Therefore, if we base our estimates on the earliest possible dates, we suggest that the entire exchange could with reasonable likelihood be dated from December 358 (when Athanasius left Alexandria) through the middle of 360 (when Eunomius first became prominent). But if we account for the time it must have taken for Athanasius to settle into his hiding-place in the deserts of Egypt and for the notoriety of Eunomius to reach him in those same deserts, then the *Letters to Serapion* are more plausibly dated to 359–361.

Greek Text

A new edition of the *Letters to Serapion* for the *Athanasius Werke* series was planned in the 1930s but abandoned as a result of the death of Hans Georg Opitz in the second world war. Therefore, when we began to translate the *Letters to Serapion*, we used the Greek text of the Benedictine edition established by the Maurist scholar Bernard de Montfaucon in 1698, which was republished with additions in 1777 and reprinted by J. P. Migne in his *Patrologia graeca* in 1857 (PG 26.529–638).[58] At the Fifteenth International Patristics Conference at Oxford in 2007 we learned that the *Athanasius Werke* edition of the letters had been revived when we attended a communication by Dietmar Wyrwa which reported on the current status of the project.[59] When the new *Athanasius Werke* edition was published in 2010, we revised our translation to reflect this most recent text. Hence, the present translation of the *Letters to Serapion* is the first to be based upon this new edition.

[58]See Lebon, *Athanase d'Alexandre*, 17–22; Shapland, *The Letters*, 11–16 and 43–47; and Wyrwa and Savvidis, *Athanasius Werke I/1*, 385–440, for further information on the Greek text, manuscripts, and editions.

[59]Dietmar Wyrwa, "Zum Editionsprojekt: Athanasius, Epistulae ad Serapionem (*Athanasius Werke* I,1,4. Lieferung)" given on August 8, 2007.

In the course of revising our initial translation, we were able to confirm Joseph Lebon's view of Montfaucon's edition: "the text of the Benedictine edition hardly seems to call for important corrections; in fact, it does not appear to contain a lacuna, an interpolation, an insoluble puzzle, or a difficulty that affects the meaning."[60] Though the *Athanasius Werke* edition is based upon more manuscript evidence than Montfaucon's text, and furthermore takes into account the ancient Armenian translation (dated between the early 5th century and the 8th century and a witness to the original Athanasian text that is independent of the known Greek traditions), we found that the new edition differed only in minor ways from the old edition in approximately eighty-six places (excluding alternative word orders). Only rarely have we departed from the *Athanasius Werke* edition and preferred another reading; these are signaled and explained in the footnotes. In three cases the editors of the *Athanasius Werke* edition chose to insert words into the main body of the text based on evidence found in the Armenian translation but which are not found in any Greek manuscript (see *Serap.* 1.33.5, 2.2.1, 2.8.1). In two cases the editors chose to surround these additions with curved braces {}, indicating uncertainty over whether they are original to Athanasius. We have thought it best to relegate these three insertions to footnotes.

Our translation has benefited greatly from Shapland's version, which, though excellent, is not without occasional mistakes in translation, questionable word choices, infelicities in style, and digressions from good, idiomatic English prose. It goes without saying that we hope to have avoided these imperfections. May our rendition be honored and useful for as long as Shapland's has. If we may be allowed to slightly modify an oft-repeated expression attributed to the 12th century Bernard of Chartres: *vere nani gigantis humeris insidentes sumus,* "truly we are dwarves sitting on the shoulders of a giant."

[60]Lebon, *Athanase d'Alexandre*, 20–1.

Introduction to Didymus's
On the Holy Spirit

Life and Writings

In comparison with Athanasius, contemporary sources on Didymus are scarce. What we do have reveals a man renowned throughout the Mediterranean Christian world of his day as a teacher and interpreter of scripture. He was born in Alexandria, most likely in 313, and died in 398.[61] Disease blinded him at age four, before he could receive any schooling.[62] Yet this did not prevent him from learning. One of his disciples, Rufinus, records that Didymus had texts read to him which he would retain by memory. Late in the night after his weary lectors would succumb to sleep, he would stay awake, silently rehearsing what had been read, "like a clean animal chewing its cud."[63]

According to Rufinus, he received training in dialectic, geometry, astronomy, and arithmetic. Rufinus portrays him as stunning philosophers who brought questions from these arts.[64] He claims that these disputations were recorded by stenographers, though none survive. Yet it must be noted that his praise of Didymus echoes formulaic praise of great teachers, such as Athanasius's descriptions of Antony (who is said to have paid Didymus the honor of a visit).[65] Jerome's assessment of Didymus in the preface to *On the Holy Spirit* emphasizes the uncultivated style of the work, reproducing another commonplace: the opposition between artless philosophy, committed solely to truth, and flowery rhetoric, concerned more with style than substance.[66] Recently, Richard Layton has argued that Didymus probably did not receive advanced training beyond what one

[61] See Gustave Bardy, *Didyme L'Aveugle* (Paris: Beauchesne, 1910), 3–4.

[62] Disease: Socrates, *h.e.* 4.25; Age four: Palladius, *Lausiac History* 4.

[63] Rufinus, *h.e.* 11.7.

[64] Ibid.

[65] Athanasius, *Life of St Antony* 74–80; visit: Rufinus, *h.e.* 11.7; Palladius, *Lausiac History* 4.

[66] See below, p. 141.

would receive from a grammarian and that his obvious knowledge of classical philosophy—especially Aristotle's *Organon* and aspects of Stoic ethics—was likely gained as part of an ecclesiastical education. In other words, Didymus learned philosophy as a handmaiden to exegesis.[67]

Didymus's reputation for erudition and virtue attracted some of the brightest students of the time. In addition to Rufinus, Palladius, best known as the author of the *Lausiac History*, spent time studying with him.[68] So too did Jerome. It is possible that Gregory of Nazianzus knew him.[69] Evagrius praised him as "the great and gnostic teacher."[70] According to Rufinus's continuation of Eusebius's *Ecclesiastical History*, Didymus played a key role in the ecclesiastical school in Alexandria: "Thus in a short time, with God as his teacher, he arrived at such expert knowledge of things divine and human that he became a teacher in the church school (*scholae ecclesiasticae doctor*), having won the high esteem of Bishop Athanasius and the other wise men in God's church."[71] Some take this to suggest that the official catechetical school, formerly headed by Origen, continued to exist in fourth century Alexandria.[72] However, it is not clear that the school Didymus taught in was quite as official as Rufinus suggests or that it was the direct successor of Origen's. Nor is it clear what exact role Didymus played in the school: whereas Rufinus merely calls him "teacher" (*doctor*) in this school, a generation later the Greek historian Sozomen more expansively calls him "president of the school

[67]See Richard A. Layton, *Didymus the Blind and His Circle in Late-Antique Alexandria: Virtue and Narrative in Biblical Scholarship* (Urbana and Chicago: University of Illinois Press, 2004), 137–43.

[68]*Lausiac History* 4: four times over a period of ten years.

[69]See John A. McGuckin, *St. Gregory of Nazianzus: An Intellectual Biography* (Crestwood, N.Y.: SVS Press, 2001), 44–5.

[70]Evagrius, *Gnostikos* 48 (ed. A. Guillaumont and C. Guillaumont, *Évagre le Pontique. Le gnostique ou à celui qui est devenu digne de la science*, SChr 356 (Paris: Éditions du Cerf, 1989), 186).

[71]Rufinus, *h.e.* 11.7 (Amidon trans., altered in light of Layton); cf. Sozomen, *h.e.* 3.15.

[72]See, e.g., Christopher Haas, *Alexandria in Late Antiquity: Topography and Social Conflict* (Baltimore and London: The Johns Hopkins University Press, 1997),

of sacred learning in Alexandria" (προϊστάμενος ἐν Ἀλεξανδρείᾳ τοῦ διδασκαλείου τῶν ἱερῶν μαθημάτων).[73] Didymus's role as teacher is not without significance for the interpretation of *On the Holy Spirit*, since, as we shall see in a moment, the work was written for certain "brothers" whom Didymus presumes are familiar with his previous writings—in other words, it is probably written for his students. We know from elsewhere that Didymus's writings were frequently prompted by requests from disciples, whether present or not. Learned Christians of the day sought his opinion on such vexed questions as why infants die prematurely, a topic on which Jerome says he wrote a treatise at the behest of Rufinus.[74] For Jerome, he wrote two multi-volume works on Old Testament books.[75]

Less clear than Didymus's status as an illustrious teacher is the issue of his relationship with the episcopal hierarchy in Alexandria. While Didymus was instrumental in articulating the divinity of the Spirit and other key tenets of Pro-Nicene orthodoxy, he was condemned by contemporaries and by posterity as an "Origenist"—someone who followed his predecessor too closely in such areas as allegorical exegesis and the pre-existence of the soul.[76] No less than the Fifth Ecumenical Council (in Constantinople, AD 553) anathematized him for being "Origenist." It is imperative, however,

229. Edeltraut Staimer goes so far as to refer to it as a "episcopal academy" (*bischöfliche Hochschule*) and Didymus as its "director" (*Leiter*): "Die Schrift 'De Spiritu Sancto' von Didymus dem Blinden von Alexandrien," (Ph.D. diss., München, 1960), 119.

[73]Sozomen, *h.e.* 3.15. Chester D. Hartranft, trans. in *Socrates, Sozomenus: Church Histories* (Peabody, MA: Hendrickson, 1999 [orig. pub. 1894]) NPNF 2nd series, vol. 2, p. 294. Joseph Bidez, ed, Günther Christian Hansen, rev. *Sozomen: Kirchengeschicte*, GCS Neue Folge, 4 (Berlin: Akademie Verlag, 1995), 125.

[74]This has not survived. Didymus's answer to Rufinus's query was that the infants who die sinned only a little in their pre-incarnate state, making the briefest contact with the flesh sufficient punishment. Jerome, *Against Rufinus* 3.28.

[75]Jerome, *Against Rufinus* 3.28; *On Famous Men* 109; *Commentary on Zechariah*, preface.

[76]For studies of the label "Origenism" in Didymus's day, see Jon Dechow, *Dogma and Mysticism in Early Christianity: Epiphanius of Cyprus and the Legacy of Origen*, Patristic Monograph Series, no. 13 (Macon, GA: Mercer University Press, 1988); and Elizabeth A. Clark, *The Origenist Controversy: The Cultural Construction of an Early Christian Debate* (Princeton: Princeton University Press, 1992).

in approaching *On the Holy Spirit*, to bracket later controversies over Origen. In this treatise, Didymus shows no interest in the themes which may have led to his condemnation. Many of his arguments are similar to those of Athanasius, who according to Rufinus favored him. There is no good reason to doubt this, even if the "Origenist" Rufinus would have had reason to emphasize *Athanasius's* support for Didymus as a subtle criticism of the great Archbishop's successors, who grew increasingly suspicious of all hints of "Origenism". Whatever Rufinus's motives, there would have been reasons for Athanasius, working before the rise of the "Origenist" specter, to endorse an independent scholar whose doctrinal agenda dovetailed with his own and whose writings emphasized episcopal authority. In particular, Layton points to a common opposition by Athanasius and Didymus to followers of Hieracas—like Didymus, an independent Christian scholar and teacher—as well as their support for the Council of Nicaea.[77] We might add their united front, beginning in the late 350s and early 360s, against those in the region of Alexandria who were associating the Spirit with the angelic realm.

While the discovery of more of Didymus's works at Tura has brought to light his exegetical labors (showing him to be a follower of Origen in this area), it has also led to an unfortunate neglect of Didymus's contributions to Trinitarian doctrine. Didymus the Origenist has eclipsed Didymus the dogmatician.[78] Though subtlety is not something one typically associates with Jerome, it is perhaps time we reconsider his appraisal of this man who was *both* (in Jerome's

---

[77]Layton, *Didymus the Blind*, 15–8.

[78]To some extent, this neglect has resulted from uncertainty over the authenticity of the three books *On the Trinity* attributed (rightly, we believe) to Didymus. *On the Trinity* has been shown to be most probably by Didymus. For a succinct presentation of the argument for its authenticity, see Alasdair Heron's analysis of its sources: "Some sources used in the *De Trinitate* ascribed to Didymus the Blind," in Rowan Williams, ed., *The Making of Orthodoxy: Essays in Honour of Henry Chadwick* (Cambridge: Cambridge University Press, 1989), 173–81; more fully, idem, "Studies in the Trinitarian Writings of Didymus the Blind: his Authorship of the Adversus Eunomium IV-V" (Ph.D. diss., Tübingen, 1972); cf. Jürgen Hönscheid, ed. and trans., *Didymus der Blinde: De trinitate, Buch I*, Beiträge zur Klassischen Philologie 44 (Meisenheim am Glan: Verlag Anton Hain, 1975), 6–7.

loaded language) "Catholic as regards the Trinity" *and* a successor to Origen on such doctrines as the pre-existence of souls, which might be less palatable to subsequent generations.[79] The variety of Didymus's writings—and the interplay of doctrine, exegesis, and philosophy in these works—is clear from the list of works attributed to him, even in those cases where only a title survives.

In his work *On Famous Men* from 392/93, Jerome lists the following works by Didymus: "Commentaries *On all the Psalms*, commentaries *On the Gospels of Matthew and John*, *On the Doctrines*, also two books *Against the Arians*, and one book *On the Holy Spirit*, which I translated into Latin, eighteen volumes *On Isaiah*, three books of commentaries *On Hosea*, addressed to me, and five books *On Zechariah*, written at my request, also commentaries *On Job*, and many other things."[80] Jerome conspicuously does not mention the extant work *On the Trinity*, which might suggest that it was written between 392 and Didymus's death in 398, if it is authentic, as we believe it to be.[81] There are indeed other reasons for placing it late in Didymus's life.[82] Also not mentioned is the short, partially extant work *Against the Manichees*. From other sources, we have more titles of works which have not survived: *On the Sects*, *On the Son*, *On Virtue and Vice*, a *Defense of Origen*, *To a Philosopher*, *On the Incorporeal*, as well as works on Galatians and Ephesians and possibly an exposition of the seven Catholic Epistles. Of the works named by Jerome, *On the Holy Spirit* is extant in Jerome's Latin translation, while, thanks to the discovery at Tura, all of the *Commentary on Zechariah* and portions of the works on Job and the Psalms are extant in Greek. We have fragments of his exegetical works on the Gospel of John, the Acts of the Apostles, and 1 and 2 Corinthians. There are also fragments

---

[79] Jerome, *Apology against Rufinus* 2.16.

[80] *On Famous Men* 109; trans. by W.H. Fremantle in *Theodoret, Jerome, Gennadius, Rufinus: Historical Writings, etc.*, ed. by Philip Schaff and Henry Wace, NPNF, 2nd series, volume 3 (Peabody, MA: Hendrickson, 1994 [orig. pub. 1892]), 381 (altered).

[81] For the authenticity of *On the Trinity*, see n. 78 above.

[82] See Alasdair Heron, "The Two Pseudo-Athanasian Dialogues Against the Anomoeans," *Journal of Theological Studies* n.s. 24 (1973): 101–22, at 121.

of his apologetically-motivated commentary on Origen's *On First Principles*, mentioned by Socrates[83] and Jerome[84] and preserved in catenae and in John of Damascus's *Sacra Parallela*.

It has also been claimed that he authored the works that come down to us as Basil of Caesarea's fourth and fifth books *Against Eunomius*, the seven pseudo-Athanasian dialogues, the pseudo-Athanasian works *On the Trinity and the Holy Spirit* and *On the Incarnation and Against the Arians*, the treatise *Against Arius and Sabellius*, frequently ascribed to Gregory of Nyssa,[85] and an unattributed treatise *On the Vision of the Seraphim*.[86] Of these extant pseudonymous works, *Against Eunomius* 4–5 and the pseudo-Athanasian *On the Trinity and the Holy Spirit* and *On the Incarnation and Against the Arians* are the most likely ones to have been written by Didymus, but scholars remain divided.[87]

[83]Socrates, *h.e.* 4.25.

[84]Jerome, *Apology against Rufinus* 2.16.

[85]Karl Holl attributed this text to Didymus in 1904: "Über die Gregor von Nyssa zugeschriebene Schrift 'Adversus Arium et Sabellium,'" *Zeitschrift für Kirchengeschicte* 25 (1904): 380–98. Many remain unconvinced. Some prefer not to assign the work definitively to any known author: see Bardy, *Didyme L'Aveugle*, 17–9, 71–3, 113–4; Reinhard Hübner, "Gregor von Nyssa und Markell von Ankyra," in Marguerite Harl, ed., *Écriture et Culture Philosophique dans la Pensée de Grégoire de Nysse*, Acts du Colloque de Chevetogne (Leiden: Brill, 1971), 199–229, at 211, n. 1; and Joseph T. Lienhard, *Contra Marcellum: Marcellus of Ancyra and Fourth-Century Theology* (Washington, DC: CUA Press, 1999), 232–9. Gregorian authenticity is maintained by Jean Daniélou ("L'*Adversus Arium et Sabellium* de Grégoire de Nysse et l'Origénisme cappadocien," *Recherches de science religieuse* 54 (1966): 61–6) and Friedrich Müller (*Gregorii Nysseni Opera Dogmatica Minora, Pars I* (Leiden: Brill, 1958), lxi). Regardless of one's position, Holl's premise that the work must have been written before 358 is certainly false.

[86]See Johannes Quasten, *Patrology, Vol. III: The Golden Age of Greek Patristic Literature from the Council of Nicaea to the Council of Chalcedon* (Notre Dame, IN: Christian Classics, 1993), 90.

[87]For discussion of these pseudo-Athanasian works, see Alasdair Heron, "The Pseudo-Athanasian Works *De Trinitate et Spiritu Sancto* and *De Incarnatione et Contra Arianos*: A Comparison," in G. D. Dragas, ed., *Aksum-Thyateira: A Festschrift for Archbishop Methodios of Thyateira and Great Britain* (Athens and London: Thyateira House, 1985), 281–98; cf. Heron, "Some Sources."

The Date of On the Holy Spirit

The text translated here is unquestionably by Didymus. With respect to the question of when Didymus wrote *On the Holy Spirit*, only one thing is absolutely firm: it was written before Ambrose of Milan used it in writing his own treatise on the same subject in 381. The work clearly responds to contemporaries who claimed, on the basis of Amos 4.13 and John 1.3, that the Spirit is to be associated with the angelic order. The first evidence we have for a group like this outside of this treatise comes from the other work translated in this volume, though it is important to note certain differences: Athanasius's opponents made much use of 1 Timothy 5.21 and Hebrews 1.14. While Didymus does not record an opponent's argument based on Hebrews 1.14, he spends enough time on the verse to suggest that he might be attempting to reclaim it from his adversaries. But whereas Athanasius devotes an entire section to 1 Timothy 5.21, it is not mentioned in *On the Holy Spirit*. Nor do Athanasius's terms of abuse for his opponents, "Tropikoi" and "Pneumatomachians" (that is, "Spirit-fighters"), appear in Didymus's text. So it is likely that Didymus and Athanasius were responding to different currents of a broad movement. With respect to the question of dating, Athanasius demonstrates no awareness of Didymus and emphasizes the novelty of his opponents; thus, we should not expect Didymus's work to be significantly earlier than Athanasius's.

By comparing the treatise itself to other, more easily datable works, we can further specify its date. It was once common to assign it to the middle of the 370s, around the time when Basil of Caesarea wrote his own *On the Holy Spirit*. But the arguments for this are weak, relying on a sense that Didymus's treatise, with its developed pneumatology, could not have preceded Basil's by many years. Subsequent work has shown that the two treatises deal with rather different currents of opposition to the Spirit's divinity.[88]

---

[88]Staimer, "Die Schrift 'De Spiritu Sancto,'" 127–32; Heron, "Studies in the Trinitarian Writings of Didymus the Blind," 169–70.

Returning to the question of possible parallels between Athanasius and Didymus, one must be careful not to overstate the case.[89] Louis Doutreleau, the editor of Jerome's Latin translation of Didymus, points to five similarities in the pneumatological polemics of Athanasius and Didymus, suggesting that they indicate the latter's dependence on the former.[90] Yet, for Doutreleau, the fact that Didymus handles the five themes differently shows a considerable gap between the two authors in time and overall disposition, Didymus being more "serene" and less polemically-driven. The five areas of overlap Doutreleau points to are:

1. Both draw a clear distinction between the Spirit and angels.

2. Both argue from the presence of the definite article: when it appears, scripture is referring to the *Holy* Spirit and not merely a created spirit.

3. Both worry over interpreting Amos 4.13 ("I [God] am the one who . . . creates spirit") rightly.

4. Both distinguish various uses of the word "spirit" in scripture.

5. Both respond to the *reductio* that, if the Father has a Son who in turn has a Son called 'Spirit', then the Father is in fact a Grandfather.

However, Doutreleau is wrong to conclude that the concurrence of these themes in the two demonstrates Athanasius's influence upon Didymus. Numbers 1 and 4 appear in Cyril of Jerusalem's *Catecheses*, which were delivered in 348 or 350, before either of Athanasius's or Didymus's writings and indeed before the likely rise of the Alex-

[89]The argument here deals only with the relation between Didymus's *On the Holy Spirit* and Athanasius's *Letters to Serapion*. We will bracket the question of the influence of other Athanasian works upon Didymus's treatise.

[90]Louis Doutreleau, ed. and trans., *Didyme L'Aveugle: Traité du Saint-Esprit*, SChr 386 (Paris: Cerf, 1992), 33–6.

andrian Pneumatomachians.[91] Moreover, when Athanasius argues against the Tropikoi on point 1, he makes clear that they base their association of the Spirit with angels on 1 Timothy 5.21 ("In the presence of God and Jesus Christ and the elect angels … "), but Didymus never alludes to the verse. Point 2 is implicit in Cyril's contrast between "spirit without qualification" (*pneuma haplôs*) and the Holy Spirit, where he uses the same terminology we find in Athanasius and Didymus.[92] Cyril also takes pains to argue that there is no "second Father" in the Trinity alongside the Father, a point not unlike number 5; he further parallels Didymus and Athanasius in his concern to deny that the Spirit is a second Son.[93] It is true that Cyril does not concern himself with recovering Amos 4.13 (point 3).[94] However, as we shall see shortly, the parallel between Didymus and Athanasius on this point is only partial. So, in sum, with the exception of the exegesis of the Amos passage, the parallels Doutreleau invokes between Didymus and Athanasius can be found in another work of Greek theology from the time. Consequently, he has given us no reason to believe Didymus used Athanasius's text in composing his own work. Indeed, in a major study of Didymus's treatise, Edeltraut Staimer argued that *On the Holy Spirit* was surely written *before* Athanasius's letters—a proposal which gives one pause, even though it has not met with general acceptance.[95]

But perhaps Doutreleau has not noted all possible parallels between the two works. One is the appeal by both Athanasius and Didymus to the idea that the Spirit is capable of being participated in, but does not participate in the Father.[96] For both authors, this

[91]For point 1, see Cyril, *Catecheses* 16.23, and cf. 16.13. For point 4, see *Catecheses* 16.13–15.

[92]*Catecheses* 16.13; cf. Didymus's use of *simpliciter* with *spiritus* (or Greek *pneuma*) in *Spir.* 8 and 246.

[93]*Catecheses* 16.3. Cf. Staimer, "Die Schrift 'De Spiritu Sancto,'" 121; Heron, "Studies in the Trinitarian Writings of Didymus the Blind," 170.

[94]Cyril's only reference to Amos 4.13 deals only with the phrase, "and announces his Christ to humanity," and does not mention the Spirit: *Catecheses* 10.15.

[95]Staimer, "Die Schrift 'De Spiritu Sancto,'" 123ff.; cf. Heron, "Studies in the Trinitarian Writings of Didymus the Blind," 170.

[96]Athanasius, *Serap.* 1.23, 1.27; Didymus, *Spir.* 10–19, 54ff., 265.

places the Spirit unequivocally on the far side of an absolute division between what is created and what is uncreated. The specific language used is not exactly commonplace and might suggest one author has used the other. However, Lewis Ayres has shown that this language comes from Origen, and is much more central to Didymus than to Athanasius.[97] Didymus explicitly states that he has already made this point in his (lost) work *On the Sects* (*Spir.* 19). One cannot, therefore, argue that he must have drawn the idea from Athanasius's *Letters to Serapion* or that Athanasius must have taken it from *On the Holy Spirit*. In sum, then, we have no firm grounds for believing that either author knew the other's work, let alone that either used the other as a source.

Further light can be shed upon the treatise's occasion by asking how *On the Holy Spirit* relates to three pieces of evidence roughly from this period. First, Lewis Ayres has shown that, in *On the Holy Spirit*, Didymus responds to Eunomius's *Apology*, which was most likely delivered at the Council of Constantinople in January 360 and published in that year or the next.[98] As mentioned above, by the middle of 360, Eunomius had established quite a reputation around the eastern Mediterranean.[99] In the *Apology*, for the first time in extant works by opponents of Nicene theology, Eunomius appeals to John 5.19 ("The Son can do nothing on his own, but only what he sees the Father doing"). Eunomius uses this to show the difference between the Father and the Son, and proceeds to explain the difference between the Spirit and the Son by alluding, most likely, to John 16.14.[100] Didymus addresses these verses together.[101] Since they were

---

[97]Lewis Ayres, "The Holy Spirit as Undiminished Giver: Didymus the Blind's *De Spiritu Sancto* and the Development of Nicene Pneumatology," in Janet Rutherford and Vincent Twomey, eds., *The Holy Spirit in the Fathers of the Church* (Dublin: Four Courts Press, 2011), 57–72. For further discussion of this doctrine see pp. 45–47 below.

[98]Ayres, "The Holy Spirit as Undiminished Giver." For dating the *Apology*, see n. 56 above.

[99]See pp. 28–29.

[100]*Apology* 20 (Vaggione 60); cf. the use of John 5:19 at *Apology* 26 (Vaggione 70).

[101]*Spir.* 160–164.

first connected by Eunomius, it would appear he is responding to his *Apology*, which gives us a reasonably firm *terminus post quem* of 360. Thus, *On the Holy Spirit*, or at least one section of it, is the first work in a long career of opposing Eunomius, a polemical agenda for which Didymus had gained a reputation by 392.[102]

Second, there is the Synod of Alexandria in 362 and the resultant *Tomus ad Antiochenos*. The *Tomus* sought to reconcile those Melitians in Antioch who taught three hypostases but a single deity with those older Nicenes around Paulinus who held only one hypostasis, equating the term with *ousia* as the Council of Nicaea had done. The pneumatology of the *Tomus* resembles that of Athanasius's *Letters to Serapion*.[103] Following Staimer, Heron suggested that "the doctrine of the Trinity in [*On the Holy Spirit*] is still in an early and undeveloped state as compared with the position after the Synod of Alexandria and the *Tomus ad Antiochenos*."[104] For Staimer and Heron, the *Tomus* provides a *terminus ante quem* for *On the Holy Spirit*. However, this document certainly did not have the effect Staimer and Heron ascribe to it: it was not immediately viewed as a "neo-Nicene Renaissance" rendering works like *On the Holy Spirit* obsolete.[105] Moreover, since its target is Antioch rather than Alexandria, it helps very little for dating Alexandrian theology. So, the *Tomus* does not help us to fix a date for *On the Holy Spirit*.

Third, it has recently been shown by Mark DelCogliano that there are striking parallels between Didymus's treatment of Amos 4.13 together with John 1.3 and Basil's brief remarks on the same verses in his *Against Eunomius* 3.7, which can be dated to 364 or 365. The verses appear together in both works and not in Athanasius. In a number of ways, Basil and Didymus interpret the verses similarly,

---

[102]Jerome, *On Famous Men* 120. The anti-Eunomian agenda is carried forward in the Pseudo-Athanasian works *On the Incarnation and Against the Arians* and *On the Trinity and the Holy Spirit*, which are possibly by Didymus, since they are very closely related to *On the Trinity*; see n. 87 above.

[103]See also pp. 26–27 above.

[104]Heron, "Studies in the Trinitarian Writings of Didymus the Blind," 169.

[105]See esp. Staimer, "Die Schrift 'De Spiritu Sancto,'" 132–3.

while differing from Athanasius's treatment of the verse in the *Letters to Serapion*. Given the way in which Basil appears to compress Didymus's fuller treatment, it is most likely Basil has read Didymus, rather than vice-versa.[106]

The cumulative force of the evidence suggests that *On the Holy Spirit* should be dated to 360–365 and not to the mid-370s.[107] This fits nicely with our comments about the relative chronology of this work with the *Letters to Serapion*, since Didymus's tome is likely not to have been much later than Athanasius's letters. Heron, who proposed a range of 355–362, notes that the matter of dating has broader significance for interpreting Didymus: "This incidentally also means that [*On the Holy Spirit*] is the first systematic treatment of the subject, and that Didymus must be recognized as having been a much more original and pioneering spirit [than] had been thought."[108]

[106]Mark DelCogliano, "Basil of Caesarea, Didymus the Blind, and the Anti-Pneumatomachian Exegesis of Amos 4:13 and John 1:3," *Journal of Theological Studies* n.s 61 (2010): 644–58.

[107]The dating of 358/59 proposed by Hauschild and followed by Sieben ignores Didymus's use of Eunomius's *Apology*. Hauschild also dates Athanasius's *Letters to Serapion* to 358/9. See Wolf-Dieter Hauschild, "Die Pneumatomachen: Eine Untersuchung zur Dogmensgeschicte des vierten Jahrhunderts "(Ph.D., Hamburg, 1967), 10–1, 34; and Hermann Josef Sieben, ed., *Didymus der Blinde: De Spiritu Sancto/Über den Heiligen Geist*, Fontes Christiani 78 (Turnhout: Brepols, 2004), 39–41.

[108]Heron, "Studies in the Trinitarian Writings of Didymus the Blind," 169. In his "Zur Theologie der 'Tropici' in der Serapionbriefe des Athanasius. Amos 4,13 als Pneumatologische Belegstelle," *Kyrios: Vierteljahresschrift für Kirchen- und Geistesgeschichte Osteuropas* 14 (1974): 3–24, Alasdair Heron reverted to the traditional dating of ca. 370. See DelCogliano, "Basil of Caesarea, Didymus the Blind, and the Anti-Pneumatomachian Exegesis," 657 n. 50, for a critique of this reassessment. In our opinion, here Heron demonstrates (*contra* Staimer; see n. 95 above) that Didymus's treatise was *not necessarily* written *before* Athanasius's letters, but does not offer compelling evidence that it *must* have been written *after* Athanasius's letters (nor after Basil's *Contra Eunomium*).

The Context of On the Holy Spirit

From the treatise, we can glean some hints as to *why* Didymus wrote it. In his preface, he refers to unnamed pneumatological rabble-rousers:

> some have raised themselves up to investigate heavenly matters by a kind of recklessness rather than by living rightly, and they brandish certain things concerning the Holy Spirit which are neither read in the Scriptures nor taken from any one of the old ecclesiastical writers. And so, we are compelled to acquiesce to the oft-repeated exhortation of the brothers that we set forth our opinion on the Holy Spirit by means of proof-texts from the Scriptures, lest those who hold contrary opinions deceive people through their lack of familiarity with so great a doctrine and instantly drag them away into the opinion of their enemies without careful reflection (*Spir.* 2).

While the passage does not identify Didymus's opponents, it does reveal that the immediate impetus for the work was given not by the "enemies" but by "the brothers" who have exhorted Didymus to respond to the current chatter. It also reveals the method of the treatise, which is of course not peculiar to Didymus: the citation and discussion of relevant "proof-texts." Throughout the course of the work, Didymus's principal authority is the text of scripture. He does, nonetheless, point the "brothers" to his earlier works *On the Sects* (*Spir.* 19 and 93) and *On Dogmas* (*Spir.* 145), neither of which is extant or datable. He also expects them to recognize his frequent teaching—does he refer to oral instruction?—on how to interpret passages where the Son is called the hand, the arm, and the right hand of the Father (*Spir.* 87). It would be unusual to cite one's work in a treatise addressed to one's opponent. So despite the obvious polemical intentions of the work, it was clearly written for a group of like-minded students.

As for the errors Didymus opposes in the work, some have already been mentioned: the association of the Spirit with the angelic order; the notion that Amos 4.13 proves that the Spirit is created; the same inference from John 1.3; the objection that ascribing divinity to the Spirit would make the Father a Grandfather. To these we must add one which does not appear in Athanasius or in Cyril of Jerusalem: the doctrine that the Spirit is an activity of God and not a substantial reality (*Spir.* 97). Eunomius also argues against this doctrine in a highly compressed passage.[109] As with Eunomius, Didymus's response to this is evidently dependent on a fragment of Origen's *Commentary on John*.[110] So in arguing that the Spirit is a substantial reality—an agent and not merely an act—Didymus is not opposing a contemporary group, but is using Origen's argument to mark out an extreme position to be avoided.[111]

The Structure of On the Holy Spirit

The structure of Didymus's text may be described thus: after a brief introduction (*Spir.* 1–9), Didymus discusses the Spirit's nature (*Spir.* 10–73); the Spirit's activity (*Spir.* 74–109); the Spirit's sending, procession, and proper names (*Spir.* 110–131); scriptural testimonies on the Spirit (*Spir.* 132–230). He concludes with various reflections: he offers a proof that the Spirit shares the substance of the Father and

---

[109] *Apology* 25.

[110] Frag. 37 (Erwin Preuschen, ed., *Origenes Werke, IV: Der Johanneskommentar*, GCS 10 (Leipzig: J.C. Hinrichs, 1903), 513–4). Given his fuller treatment of the issue, Didymus appears to draw his argument directly from the Origen fragment rather than from Eunomius. Still, he does modify Origen's argument.

[111] See Andrew Radde-Gallwitz, "The Holy Spirit as Agent, not Activity: Origen's Argument with Modalism and its Afterlife in Didymus, Eunomius, and Gregory of Nazianzus," *Vigiliae Christianae* 65 (2011): 227–248. The discussion of the date of *On the Holy Spirit* in this introduction revises the one found on pp. 235–6 of this article.

the Son from the Spirit's role along with them in making believers good and holy (*Spir.* 231–237), discusses the various senses of the term "spirit" in scripture (*Spir.* 237–256), analyzes the unique way in which the Spirit is said to "fill" believers substantially (*Spir.* 257–268), and dismisses talk of the Spirit as the Father's brother or the Son's son (*Spir.* 269–271). This is followed by a short conclusion which reiterates the danger of blasphemy against the Spirit (*Spir.* 272–277). Didymus's treatise is thus complex and at times appears to have no overarching organization.

Didymus's Argument

Despite this confusion, however, one fundamental argument provides a theological foundation to the work. Didymus argues that the Spirit is the boundless source of all sanctification in which Christians (and all angels) participate, and thus *a priori* cannot be a created reality participating in goodness:

> Nor is it possible to find in the Holy Spirit any strength which he receives from some external activity of sanctification and virtue, for a nature such as this would have to be mutable. Rather, the Holy Spirit, as all acknowledge, is the immutable sanctifier, the bestower of divine knowledge and all goods. To put it simply, he himself subsists in those goods which are conferred by the Lord (*Spir.* 11).

For Didymus, as for Athanasius before him, if the Spirit may be described in these terms, then the Spirit must be one with the Father and the Son:

> Now because he is good, God is the source and principle of all goods. Therefore he makes good those to whom he imparts himself; he is not made good by another, but is good.

Hence it is possible to participate in him but not for him to participate (*ideo capabilis, et non capax*) (18) ... the Father and the Son are possessed rather than possessors, but the creature possesses while not being possessed (*Spir.* 17–18).

Didymus's use of the undiminished giver parallels Athanasius's in some respects, but shows independent development. For example, Didymus strongly emphasizes that only when we understand the Spirit to give without loss and to be immutable and omnipresent can we understand what it means for the Spirit to "fill" the apostles and Christians. In the same context, as we saw in the quotation from *Spir.* 11 above, Didymus places much emphasis on the Spirit being the substance of the gifts he is said to give, emphasizing the unmediated transforming presence of the Spirit. At the same time, this account of the Spirit's presence is placed in the framework of Didymus's strong insistence on the inseparability of Father, Son and Spirit: there is, for example, "a single reception of the Trinity" (*Spir.* 75).

The doctrine of the undiminished giver has a long history. Initial hints toward it in Plato are developed in Hellenistic thought and appear at Wisdom 7.27 and in Philo. Clement and Origen make use of it, as do a number of non-Christian Platonists.[112] In the fourth century the same doctrine crops up on different sides of the Trinitarian controversies. Eusebius of Caesarea, for example, uses a version of the doctrine to argue that the Spirit gives to those "below" but also receives from the Word who, in turn, receives from the Father. The Father alone is the true undiminished giver.[113] Cyril of Jerusalem uses the doctrine to speak of the Father and the Spirit but without clearly indicating the relations between them.[114] With Athanasius and Didymus, we see this doctrine used in order to assert the unity of Father, Son and Spirit. As we have already noted, Didymus may well

---

[112]See e.g. Philo, *De opificio mundi* 6.23, *De gigantibus* 25–7; Clement, *Stromata* 7.2.5; Origen, *Contra Celsum* 6.63–4. For further discussion of the doctrine's history, see Ayres, "The Holy Spirit as Undiminished Giver," 59–65.

[113]Eusebius, *Praeparatio evangelica* 7.15.

[114]Cyril of Jerusalem, *Catecheses* 6.7; 17.14.

know Athanasius's *Letters to Serapion*, but he also demonstrates an independent engagement with a variety of sources, especially Origen. The doctrine then appears in the Cappadocians, perhaps with some debt to our two Alexandrian authors—although this question lies outside the scope of this introduction.

One of the other distinctive features of this text is Didymus's willingness to speak of the Trinity as *homoousios*—rather than of the Son as *homoousios* with the Father in the manner most common in Athanasius. "Therefore, the fact that there is a single grace of the Father and the Son perfected by the activity of the Holy Spirit demonstrates that the Trinity is of one substance" (*Spir.* 76). Didymus does not make use of a formal terminology of *ousia* or *physis* and *hypostaseis* or *prosopa* (and in this he parallels Athanasius among others), expressing the unity of the irreducible Father, Son and Sprit in other striking ways. With specific reference to the Spirit, he reflects in intriguing fashion on what it means for the Spirit to be "the Spirit of Wisdom and Truth," a phrase he perhaps took from Athanasius. Didymus argues that Father, Son and Spirit each subsist as Wisdom and Truth. Because the Spirit shares this status the Spirit "possesses the same circle of unity and substance as the Son and, moreover, . . . the Son is not divided from the substance of the Father" (*Spir.* 94). This phrase poses many questions for the interpreter but it shows Didymus reflecting in far more detail than Athanasius on ways of imagining Father, Son, and Spirit as irreducible and yet in a unique unity of substance.

Jerome's Latin Translation of Didymus's On the Holy Spirit

The Greek original of *On the Holy Spirit* is lost. All we have is Jerome's Latin translation from 385, which is the text translated here from the critical edition prepared by Louis Doutreleau, SJ. In this work, Jerome is a literal and indeed rather wooden translator, though the dryness of the prose might be attributable to Didymus himself, if we follow Jerome's backhanded reference in the preface to the Alexandrian's simplicity of style. Jerome's translation has some peculiarities, however, which the reader must bear in mind. First, when the argument depends upon features of the Greek, as in the dispute over the definite article which Latin lacks, Jerome provides both the Greek and a Latin rendering (*Spir.* 8 and 73). Jerome also provides the Greek for the technical terms ὁμοούσια and ἑτεροούσια, while also translating them. In these cases, we have kept the Greek, as Jerome does, while of course rendering his Latin into English. In one case, he provides a Greek title for the book of Wisdom (Πανάρετος) without translating it; we have provided the Greek and an English translation (*All-Perfect*) (*Spir.* 118). Finally, Jerome occasionally provides explanatory asides which are not part of Didymus's original text (*Spir.* 55, 70, and 223). Like Doutreleau, we have indented these paragraphs. Some of this is explained by Jerome's need to use Latin terms he does not use elsewhere in his corpus to convey difficult, but important Greek terms as [τὸ] μεθεκτόν, which he renders both with the unusual *capabilem* (*Spir.* 51 and 55–56) and, more expansively, with *quod capiatur participatione* (*Spir.* 265).

A NOTE ON THE TRANSLATIONS

In the Benedictine edition, Athanasius's three letters to Serapion are subdivided into numbered sections, and in the new *Athanasius Werke* edition these numbered sections are further subdivided into subsections. In contrast, Didymus's treatise is divided into 277 short sections. These section and subsection numbers are signaled in each translation. For Athanasius's letters, the numbers of the letter, section, and subsection are provided; for example, 1.4.4 indicates the fourth subsection of the fourth section of the first letter. While influenced by the section and subsection divisions of the editors, our paragraphization in both translations is based upon the author's flow of thought and follows modern English practice. The part and section subtitles in both translations are our own and are intended to facilitate a fruitful reading of the texts.

Italics are used in the translation for scriptural citations or reminiscences; these are always followed by the scriptural reference in square brackets, for example [Jn 1.1]. References to scriptural allusions are given in the footnotes. Note that the Psalms are referenced according to the Septuagint version. On rare occasions words are inserted in square brackets to improve the sense.

In line with scholarly consensus, the editors of the *Athanasius Werke* edition treat what the manuscripts call the second and third letters as a single letter, Letter Two. In addition, they divide what the manuscripts call the fourth letter into two separate documents (the first is Letter Three, the second is a short treatise on Mt 12.32).[115] This has necessitated the adoption of a new numbering system for the *Letters to Serapion*. Here is a comparison of the old and new systems:

old	new
Serap. 1.1–33	*Serap.* 1.1–33 (no change)
Serap. 2.1–9	*Serap.* 2.1–9 (no change)
Serap. 3.1–7	*Serap.* 2.10–16
Serap. 4.1–7	*Serap.* 3.1–7
Serap. 4.8–23	*Serap.* 4.1–16

Since all scholarship on the *Letters to Serapion* has hitherto employed the old numbering system, at the appropriate places the old reference numbers are provided in curved braces—e.g. {4.4} indicates the beginning of the fourth section of the fourth letter according to the old numbering (now numbered as 3.4).

Finally, in our numbering of the subsections of the *Letters to Serapion* we have corrected two misprints in the *Athanasius Werke*

[115]See p. 19 n. 25 above.

edition. There are two subsections labeled 1.7.4: the second is renumbered 1.7.5 and consequently 1.7.5 of the AW edition appears here as 1.7.6. There are two subsections labeled 1.20.4: the second is renumbered 1.20.5 and consequently 1.20.5 and 1.20.6 of the AW edition are respectively renumbered 1.20.6 and 1.20.7.

LETTERS TO SERAPION
ON THE HOLY SPIRIT

Letter One

INTRODUCTION [1.1–2]

1.1.1. {1.1} The letter of Your Sacred Kindness has reached me in the desert.[1] Even if the persecution leveled against us is somewhat bitter and the pursuit by those looking to kill us is intense, nonetheless *the Father of mercies and the God of all consolation* [2 Cor 1.3] has used your letter to comfort us. For when I called to mind Your Kindness and all my friends, it seemed to me that you and they were present with me at that time.

1.1.2. So then, I was overjoyed to receive your letter. But as I read it, once again I began to lose heart because of those who formerly aimed to fight against the truth. For you were clearly upset, my beloved and truly most dear friend, and you wrote that certain ones who have withdrawn from the Arians on account of their blasphemy against the Son of God have nonetheless set their minds against the Holy Spirit, claiming not only that he is a creature but also that he is one of *the ministering spirits* [Heb 1.14] and is different from the angels only in degree.[2]

1.1.3. But this amounts to a feigned battle against the Arians, while their real dispute is with the pious faith. For just as Arians

---

[1]Athanasius addresses Serapion with a title of courtesy, a common feature in fourth-century epistolary writing. Letter One is transmitted in the mss. with the following title: "Bishop St. Athanasius of Alexandria's Letter to Bishop Serapion on the Holy Spirit."

[2]Thus there are two elements of the Tropikoi's heretical teaching on the Spirit, that the Holy Spirit is a creature and that he has angelic status. Athanasius traces the first to the Tropikoi's misinterpretation of Am 4.13 and refutes this in *Serap.* 1.3.1–1.10.3, and the second to their misinterpretation of 1 Tim 5.21, refuting this in *Serap.* 1.10.4–1.14.7.

by denying the Son also deny the Father,[3] so too these people by disparaging the Holy Spirit also disparage the Son. And these two groups divide between themselves the opposition to the truth, so that, with some setting their minds against the Word and others against the Spirit, they might hold the same blasphemy against the Holy Trinity.[4]

1.1.4. So then, observing these matters and giving them careful consideration, I came to lose heart because once again the devil has found players to stage his madness. While I had decided to keep silent at this time, nonetheless, at the behest of Your Sincerity and due to their heterodoxy and diabolical presumption, I wrote this letter, brief as it is, though I am scarcely capable of such a thing. But take this letter as an opportunity to add what still needs to be said, as seems best to your understanding. And so, thus will the refutation of this impious heresy become complete.

How the teaching of the Tropikoi amounts to Arianism

1.2.1. {1.2} So then, on the one hand, this kind of thinking is not foreign to the Arians. For having once denied the Word of God, it is natural for them also to disparage his Spirit in the same way. Thus we don't need to say anything more against them. For what we have already said against them is sufficient.[5] **1.2.2.** But on the other hand, in order to respond to those who have been deceived about the Spirit through a certain "mode of exegesis" (as they themselves would say),[6] it would be fitting for us to subject a few of their tenets

---

[3] See 1 Jn 2.22–23.

[4] Throughout the letter Athanasius adopts the polemical strategy of assimilating the views of the Tropikoi to those of the Arians.

[5] Athanasius maintains that his anti-Arian writings should suffice for the refutation of the Tropikoi, whose views, he claims, are fundamentally similar to those of the Arians.

[6] Athanasius uses the label "Tropikoi" (see *Serap.* 1.10.4) for his opponents in his letters to Serapion, which seems to be derived from the fact that they employ a fallacious "mode of exegesis" (*tropos*).

to a careful examination. Indeed, one should marvel at their stupidity! For if they do not wish the Son of God to be a creature—and in this matter at any rate their thinking is sound—then how are they content to countenance that the Spirit of the Son is a creature?

1.2.3. For even if on account of the unity of the Word with the Father they do not wish the Son to be one of the things that have come into existence, but—as is truly the case—they think that he is the Creator of things that are made, why do they say that the Holy Spirit, who has the same unity with the Son as the Son has with the Father, is a creature? Why hasn't it dawned on them that, just as by not dividing the Son from the Father they preserve the unity of God, so too, by dividing the Spirit from the Word they no longer preserve the divinity in the Trinity as one, but rupture it, and mix with it a nature that is foreign to it and different in kind, and reduce it to the level of creatures? **1.2.4.** This in turn renders the Trinity no longer one but compounded of two distinct natures, because the Spirit, as they imagine among themselves, is different in substance.

So then, what sort of theology is this, which makes God a compound of Creator and creature? For either there is not a Trinity, but a dyad plus a creature, or, if there is a Trinity—as in fact there is—then how can they rank the Spirit of the Trinity with the creatures who come after the Trinity? For once again this amounts to dividing and dissolving the Trinity. **1.2.5.** Therefore, because of their faulty thinking about the Holy Spirit, not even their thinking about the Son is sound. For if they were to think correctly about the Word, they would also think soundly about the Spirit, *who proceeds from the Father* [Jn 15.26] and, being proper to the Son, is given by him to the disciples and to all who believe in him. **1.2.6.** Erring in this way they do not even have sound faith about the Father. For those who oppose the Spirit, as the great martyr Stephen said,[7] also deny the Son, and those who deny the Son do not even have the Father.[8]

[7]See Acts 7.51.
[8]See 1 Jn 2.23.

On the Correct Interpretation
of Amos 4.13 [1.3.1–1.10.3]

The Tropikoi base their claim that Holy Spirit
is a creature on Amos 4.13

1.3.1. {1.3} Now where did you find a pretext for such great audacity, that you do not fear what was said by the Savior: *Whoever blasphemes against the Holy Spirit has no forgiveness either in this age or in the age to come* [Mt 12.32]? For the Arians, though they did not understand the incarnate presence of the Word and the things said by him when he was present,[9] nevertheless found a pretext for their own heresy in what he said, and thus were condemned as *fighters against God* [Acts 5.39] and in truth *babblers uttering sounds from the earth* [Is 8.19]. **1.3.2.** But as for you, what misled you? What teaching of theirs have you countenanced? What mode of exegesis[10] is responsible for this great error of yours? As you write: "We have read," say our opponents, "in the Prophet Amos, where God says: *Therefore I am the one who gives strength to thunder and who creates spirit and who proclaims his Christ to humanity, who makes the dawn and foggy mist, and who mounts upon the high places of the earth: Lord God Almighty is his name!* [Am 4.12–13]. And on this basis the Arians have persuaded us when they say that the Holy Spirit is a creature." **1.3.3.** So you've read the passage from Amos.

Yet the Tropikoi correctly interpret Proverbs 8.22

But there's a passage in Proverbs: *The Lord created me as the beginning of his ways for his works* [Prov 8.22]. Have you or have you not read this? And you interpret this passage correctly, in not

---

[9]That is, Christ's displays of weakness, which according to Athanasius the Arians interpreted as precluding him from truly being God.

[10]Gr. τρόπος. See n. 6 above.

saying that the Word is a creature. But as for the passage in the Prophet, isn't it true that you did not interpret it, but upon hearing of an unmodified "spirit" you immediately thought that the Holy Spirit was being called a creature? **1.3.4.** Even though in Proverbs it is clearly Wisdom who says: *he created me*, yet you do what is right and interpret the passage such that you do not classify the creative Wisdom with the creatures. But the passage of the Prophet gives no indication that it concerns the Holy Spirit, but speaks in an unqualified way about "spirit." **1.3.5.** So then, even though the Scriptures contain a great variety of uses of "spirit" and the passage of Amos can have a proper meaning that is correct, why do you—either out of love of contention or because you have been poisoned by the bite of the Arian serpent—think that Amos is speaking about the Holy Spirit? The only reason must be that you do not want to stop thinking that he is a creature.

When "spirit" is unqualified in the Scriptures, it does not refer the Holy Spirit

1.4.1. {1.4} Tell me: have you found any passage in the Divine Scriptures where the Holy Spirit is called "spirit" without qualification, without being modified with either "of God," or "of the Father," or "my," or "his," or "of Christ" and "of the Son," or "from me," that is, from God, or with the definite article[11] (such that he is not called "spirit" without qualification but "the Spirit"), or the very term "the Holy Spirit," or "Paraclete," or "of Truth" (that is, of the Son, who says: *I am the Truth* [Jn 14.6])—any passage in which, when you hear "spirit" without any qualification, you assume that it is the Holy Spirit?

For the moment, exclude from consideration those instances in which people who have already received the Spirit are mentioned again, and those passages where readers, after having already

[11]See Didymus, *Spir.* 8, 73, and 246.

learned about the Holy Spirit, are not unaware about whom they are hearing when later, in cases of repetition and reminder, mention is made of only "the Spirit," especially since in these cases "spirit" is said with the definite article.[12] **1.4.2.** In general, if "spirit" is said without the definite article or without one of the aforementioned modifiers, it cannot be the Holy Spirit who is signified.

Such is what Paul writes to the Galatians: *Only this do I want to learn from you: have you received the Spirit from works of the Law or by faith in what you have heard?* [Gal 3.2]. What did they receive if not the Holy Spirit, who is given to those who believe and are *reborn* [1 Pet 1.23] *through the washing of regeneration* [Titus 3.5]? And when he wrote to the Thessalonians: *Do not quench the Spirit* [1 Thess 5.19], he was speaking to those who also knew what they had received, so that through carelessness they would not quench the grace of the Spirit that had been kindled within them.

1.4.3. And in the Gospels, when the Evangelists speak of the Savior in a human way on account of the flesh that he assumed: *Jesus, being full of the Spirit, returned from the Jordan* [Lk 4.1], and: *Then Jesus was driven by the Spirit into the desert* [Mt 4.1], it has the same sense. For Luke had previously said: *And it happened that after many people had been baptized, and after Jesus had been baptized and was praying, the heavens were opened, and the Holy Spirit descended upon him in bodily form, like a dove* [Lk 3.21–22]. It is clear that when "the Spirit" is mentioned, the Holy Spirit is signified.

1.4.4. So then, in those passages where it is the Holy Spirit, it is not ambiguous that the Holy Spirit is signified even if only "the Spirit" is said without a modifier added to it, especially since it has the definite article.

---

[12]For the present moment Athanasius suggests leaving aside two sets of scriptural texts which employ the term "spirit" without any further qualification: (1) those which mention recipients of the Holy Spirit that have already been mentioned, and (2) those in which it is clear from the context that the reference is to the Holy Spirit. In the examples that follow, those from Paul correspond to the first set, whereas those from the Gospels to the second set.

Testimonies of qualified usages of "spirit" that refer to the Holy Spirit

1.5.1. {1.5} Answer the question set before you, whether anywhere in the Divine Scriptures you have found the Holy Spirit called "Spirit" without qualification, without one of the aforementioned modifiers added to it (excluding the cases mentioned above). But you will not be able to provide an answer, since you will find nothing like that written in Scripture.

On the contrary, in Genesis it is written: *And the Spirit of God was moving over the water* [Gen 1.2]. And a little after this: *My Spirit shall not abide in these people because they are flesh* [Gen 6.3].

1.5.2. In Numbers Moses says to the son of Nun: *Are you jealous for my sake? Would that all the people of the Lord were prophets, when the Lord bestows his Spirit upon them!* [Num 11.29].

1.5.3. And in Judges it is said of Othniel: *And the Spirit of the Lord came upon him, and he judged Israel* [Judg 3.10]. And again: *And the Spirit of the Lord came upon Jephthah* [Judg 11.29]. Concerning Sampson it says: *The child grew, and the Lord blessed him. And the Spirit of the Lord began to stir him* [Judg 13.24–25]. And: *The Spirit of the Lord sprung upon him* [Judg 15.14].

1.5.4. And David sings in the psalm: *Do not take your Holy Spirit away from me!* [Ps 50.13]. And again in Psalm 142: *Your good Spirit shall guide me on level ground for your name's sake, Lord* [Ps 142.10–11].

1.5.5. In Isaiah it is written: *The Spirit of the Lord is upon me, because he has anointed me* [Is 61.1]. Before this he said: *Woe to you, rebellious children! Thus says the Lord: "You have carried out a plan, but not with me; you have made covenants, but not with my Spirit, adding sins to sins."* [Is 30.1]. And again: *Listen to these things: I have not spoken in secret from the beginning; when it took place, I was there. And now the Lord has sent me, and his Spirit* [Is 48.16]. **1.5.6.** And a little further on he speaks the following words: *This is my covenant with them, said the Lord, my Spirit which is upon you* [Is 59.21]. And again in a subsequent passage he adds: *Neither a legate nor an angel, but the Lord himself saved them because he loved them and he spared them. He redeemed them and took them and raised them in all the days of the age. But they did not believe and they enraged his Holy Spirit, and he turned to them in animosity* [Is 63.9–10].

1.5.7. Ezekiel speaks these words: *And the Spirit took me, and he led me into the land of the Chaldaeans, into captivity, in a vision, in the Spirit of God* [Ezek 11.24]. And in Daniel: *God aroused the Holy Spirit of a young man whose name was Daniel, and he cried out with a loud shout: "I am innocent of the blood of this woman!"* [Dan 13.45].

1.5.8. And Micah says: *The house of Jacob provoked the Spirit of the Lord* [Micah 2.7]. And through Joel God says: *And it shall come to pass after these things that I will pour out upon all flesh from my Spirit* [Joel 3.1]. And again, through Zechariah the voice of God says: *But receive my words and my laws, which I have enjoined by my Spirit upon my servants, the prophets* [Zech 1.6]. A little further on, the Prophet said in rebuke of the people: *And they made their hearts disobedient in order not to obey my law, and the words which the almighty Lord had sent by his Spirit by the hands of the prophets of long ago* [Zech 7.12].

These are passages we have collected from the Old Testament; we have recorded only a few of them here.

1.6.1. {1.6} Also investigate for yourselves the contents of the Gospels and the writings of the Apostles. You will see how even there, inasmuch as there is a great difference among spirits, the Holy Spirit is not typically called "Spirit" without qualification but with one of the modifiers we have mentioned.

1.6.2. So then, as I said above, when the Lord was baptized in human fashion on account of the flesh which he bore, it is said that *the Holy Spirit descended upon him* [Lk 3.22; Jn 1.32–33]. And when the Lord gave him to his disciples, he said: *Receive the Holy Spirit* [Jn 20.22]. And he taught them: *But the Paraclete, the Holy Spirit, whom the Father will send in my name, he will teach you all things* [Jn 14.26]. And a little after this, he said about the same: *But when* the Paraclete comes, whom I will send you from the Father, the Spirit of Truth, who proceeds from the Father, he will bear witness about me [Jn 15.26]. **1.6.3.** And again: *For it is not you who speak but it is the Spirit of your Father who is speaking in you* [Mt 10.20]. And a little after this: *But if it is by the Spirit of God that I cast out demons, then the reign of God has come upon you* [Mt 12.28]. And perfecting all our knowledge of God and our baptismal initiation, by which he joins us to himself and, through him, to the Father, the Lord enjoined upon his disciples: *Go, make disciples of all nations, baptizing them in the name of the Father, and of the Son, and of the Holy Spirit* [Mt 28.19].

1.6.4. When the Lord promised to send him to them: *He commanded them: "Do not depart from Jerusalem"* [Acts 1.4], and after a few days: *When the time for Pentecost had been fulfilled, they were all together in one place. And suddenly a sound came from heaven like a mighty wind rushing, and it filled the whole house where they were sitting. And there appeared to them tongues divided as of fire, and they rested on each one of them. And they were all filled with the Holy Spirit and began to speak in different tongues, as the Spirit enabled to utter* [Acts 2.1–4]. **1.6.5.** Later on, the Holy Spirit was given to those who were born again when Apostles laid their hands on them.[13] A certain Agabus prophesied through him, saying: *Thus says the Holy Spirit* [Acts 21.11]. **1.6.6.** And Paul: . . . *the flock in which the Holy Spirit has set you as overseers to shepherd the church of God, which he acquired through his own blood* [Acts 20.28]. And when the eunuch was baptized, *the Spirit of the Lord snatched Philip* [Acts 8.39].

And Peter wrote: *You obtain as the goal of faith the salvation of souls. The prophets who prophesied about the grace for you searched and inquired about this salvation; they inquired into what time or which circumstance was being indicated by the Spirit of Christ in them, when he was predicting the sufferings reserved for Christ and the glories that would follow after* [1 Pet 1.9–11]. And John wrote in his letter: *By this we know that we remain in him, and he in us, because he has given to us from his Spirit* [1 Jn 4.13].

[13]See Acts 8.17–18.

And Paul wrote to the Romans: *You are not in the flesh but in the Spirit, if in fact the Spirit of God dwells in you.* **1.6.7.** *But if anyone does not have the Spirit of Christ, he does not belong to Christ. But if Christ is in you, although your body is dead because of sin, the Spirit is alive because of righteousness. But if the Spirit of him who raised Jesus from the dead dwells in you, he who raised Jesus Christ from the dead will give life even to your mortal bodies through his Spirit who dwells in you.* [Rom 8.9–11].

1.6.8. To the Corinthians: *For the Spirit scrutinizes all things, even the depths of God. For who knows the things that belong to a human being except the human spirit that is in him? So too no one knows the things that belong to God except the Spirit of God. But we have not received the spirit of the world, but the Spirit that comes from God, that we might know the gifts bestowed on us by God* [1 Cor 2.10–12]. And after a little bit: *Do you not know that you are a temple of God, and that the Spirit of God dwells in you?* [1 Cor 3.16]. **1.6.9.** And again: *But you were washed, you were sanctified, you were justified in the name of our Lord Jesus Christ, and in the Spirit of our God* [1 Cor 6.11]. And after a little bit: *But one and the same Spirit works all these, apportioning to each as he wills* [1 Cor 12.11]. And again: *The Lord is the Spirit, and where the Spirit of the Lord is, there is freedom* [2 Cor 3.17].

1.6.10. See how he writes also in the letter to the Galatians, saying: *That the blessing of Abraham might come through Christ Jesus, that we may receive the promise of the Spirit through faith* [Gal 3.14]. And again: *Since you are sons, God has sent the Spirit of his Son into your hearts, crying out, "Abba, Father!" The result is that you are no longer a servant, but a son. And if a son, then an heir of God through Christ* [Gal 4.6–7].

1.6.11. To the Ephesians he spoke these words: *Do not sadden the Holy Spirit in whom you have been sealed for the day of redemption* [Eph 4.30]. And again: *Be eager to maintain the unity of the Spirit in the bond of peace* [Eph 4.3].

To the Philippians he boldly wrote: *What then? Only that in every way, whether in pretense or in truth, Christ is proclaimed, and in this*

I rejoice, but I will also continue to rejoice. For I know that this will lead to my salvation through your prayers and through the support of the Spirit of Jesus Christ, according to which my expectation and hope that in nothing shall I be ashamed [Phil 1.18–20]. **1.6.12.** And again: *For we are the circumcision, who worship by the Spirit of God, and glory in Christ Jesus* [Phil 3.3].

And to the Thessalonians he testifies: *The one who rejects does not reject a human being, but God who gave his Holy Spirit to you* [1 Thess 4.8].

1.6.13. And to the Hebrews: *By this the Holy Spirit reveals that the way into the sanctuary was not yet made manifest so long as the first tabernacle was still standing* [Heb 9.8]. And again: *How much worse punishment do you think will be deserved by the man who has despised the Son of God, and regarded as profane the blood of the covenant by which he was sanctified, and outraged the Spirit of grace?* [Heb 10.29]. And again: *For if the blood of bulls and goats and the ashes of a heifer, when sprinkled on unclean persons, sanctifies for the purification of the flesh, how much more shall the blood of Christ, who through the eternal Spirit offered himself unblemished to God, purify your conscience from dead works?* [Heb 9.13–14].

And to the Thessalonians: *And then the lawless one will be revealed, whom the Lord Jesus will slay with the Spirit of his mouth and destroy by the manifestation of his coming* [2 Thess 2.8].

The various scriptural senses of "spirit" when not qualified as described above

1.7.1. {1.7} See how the Holy Spirit is recognized in all the Divine Scriptures! So, did you observe something like this in the Prophet?[14] For the "spirit" mentioned by the Prophet does not even have the definite article to give you a pretext. **1.7.2.** Out of sheer audacity

[14]That is, Am 4.13.

you have invented your own modes of exegesis[15] and claim that the "spirit" said to be created is nothing other than the Holy Spirit. Yet from scholars you could have learned about the difference among spirits.

1.7.3. For the spirit of a human being is called a "spirit," as David sings in the psalm: *At night I mused within my heart, and my spirit questioned* [Ps 76.7]. Baruch prayed in these words: *The soul in anguish and the spirit of weariness had cried out to you* [Bar 3.1]. And in Daniel it is written: *Spirits and souls of the just, bless the Lord!* [Dan 3.86]. **1.7.4.** The Apostle writes: *The Spirit himself gives testimony with our spirit that we are children of God. And if children, then also heirs* [Rom 8.16–17]. And again: *No one knows the things that belong to a human being except the human spirit that is in him* [1 Cor 2.11]. In the letter to the Thessalonians he prays in these words: *May your spirit and soul and body be kept sound and blameless at the coming of our Lord Jesus Christ* [1 Thess 5.23].

1.7.5. Also, wind is called "spirit," as in Genesis: *And God brought a spirit upon the earth, and the water abated* [Gen 8.1]. As for Jonah: *And the Lord stirred up a spirit upon the sea, and a great wave arose on the sea, and the ship was in danger of shattering* [Jon 1.4]. And in Psalm 106 it is written: *He spoke, and a gust of spirit rose up, and the waves of sea were tossed* [Ps 106.25]. **1.7.6.** And in Psalm 148: *Praise the Lord from the earth, monsters of the sea and all deeps, fire and hail, snow and ice, gust of spirit, all that obey his word!* [Ps 148.7–8]. And in Ezekiel, in the Lament for Tyre: *In the heart of the sea, in great water your rowers brought you; the spirit of the south wind has shattered you* [Ezek 27.25–26].

1.8.1. {1.8} If you read the Divine Scriptures, you will also find that "spirit" is used for the meaning which is in the divine words themselves, as Paul writes: *He has made us to be fit ministers of the new covenant, not of its letter but of its spirit. For the letter kills, but the spirit gives life* [2 Cor 3.6]. For that which can be uttered is characterized by the letter, but the meaning in it is called its "spirit." Thus too,

---

[15]Gr. τρόπος. See n. 6 above.

the law is spiritual [Rom 7.14], as he says again, *so that we may serve not in the oldness of the letter but in the newness of the spirit* [Rom 7.6]. And the same is said in thanksgiving: *So then, I serve the law of God with my mind, but with my flesh the law of sin. So now there is no condemnation for those in Christ Jesus. For the law of the spirit of life in Christ Jesus has liberated me from the law of sin* [Rom 7.25–8.2].

1.8.2. When Philip wanted to turn the eunuch from the letter to the spirit, he said: *Do you understand what you are reading?* [Acts 8.30]. In Numbers it is testified that Caleb had a spirit like this, when God said: *But as for my servant Caleb, because another spirit came to be in him, and he has followed me, I shall lead him into the land into which* he was called [Num 14.24].[16] **1.8.3.** For *he pleased God* [Wis 4.10] by speaking with an understanding that differed from that of others. It was such a heart that God exhorted the people to have, when he said through Ezekiel: *Make yourself a new heart and a new spirit* [Ezek 18.31].

The word "spirit" in Amos 4.13 is to be interpreted as "the wind"

1.8.4. Now in light of these considerations, and inasmuch as we have shown the great difference among spirits, you would have done better, if when you heard of a "spirit" that was created, you had thought of one of the aforementioned spirits.[17] Such a spirit was written about in Isaiah: *Aram has come to agreement with Ephraim, and his soul was amazed and the soul of his people, in the way that the trees of the woods are shaken by spirit* [Is 7.2]. **1.8.5.** And such a spirit is mentioned here: *the Lord stirred up a spirit upon the sea* [Jon 1.4] because of Jonah. For the spirits of the wind follow upon the thunder, as with the rains that fell against Ahab, when it is written:

---

[16]The LXX reads *into which he went*. One family of mss. corrects the text of Athanasius here.

[17]I.e. in Am 4.12–13.

And it came to pass in a little while that the heaven grew black with clouds and spirit [1 Kg 18.45].

The Tropikoi's objection to this interpretation, and a response

1.9.1. {1.9} "But since the oracle mentions Christ," our opponents say, "it follows that what is called 'spirit' must be understood as nothing other than the Holy Spirit." So you have observed that the Holy Spirit is named together with Christ. But you have not learned that by nature he is different and separated from the Son. Why is it that Christ you do not call a creature, but the Holy Spirit you do call a creature? **1.9.2.** Furthermore, it is absurd to name together and glorify together things that are by nature unlike. For what sort of commonality or what sort of likeness is there between a creature and the Creator? You are determined to classify and join together with the Son the creatures brought into existence by the Son.

An alternative interpretation of "spirit" in Amos 4.13 as "the human spirit"

1.9.3. So then, it would be sufficient, as we have said, to understand what has been written[18] as about the spirit of winds. But since you appeal to the fact that Christ is mentioned in this passage as the pretext for your claims, we must subject what is said to a precise analysis, to see if we can find a more suitable understanding of the "spirit" which is said to be created. **1.9.4.** So what does it mean when *he proclaims his Christ to humanity* [Am 4.13]? Nothing other than that he becomes human. It is equivalent to saying: *Behold! The virgin shall conceive and bear a son, and they shall call his name Emmanuel* [Is 7.14; Mt 1.23], and as many other things which were written about his sojourn. But if it is the incarnate presence of the Word that is

[18]I.e. Am 4.12–13.

proclaimed, then how must the created "spirit" be understood, if not as the recreated and renewed spirit of human beings?

1.9.5. For this is what God proclaims through Ezekiel, saying: *A new heart I shall give you, and a new spirit I shall give you; and I shall take out of your flesh the stony heart and give you a fleshy heart; and I shall put my Spirit within you* [Ezek 36.26–27]. When was this fulfilled, if not when the Lord came and renewed everything by his grace? **1.9.6.** See too how in this passage the difference among spirits is indicated: our spirit is renewed, whereas the Holy Spirit is not a spirit without qualification, but God says he is his Spirit, in whom our spirits are renewed. As the Psalmist sings in Psalm 103: *You take away their spirit, and they die, and return to the dust from which they came. You send forth your Spirit, and they are created, and you renew the face of the earth* [Ps 103.29–30]. If we are renewed by the Spirit of God, then when the spirit in this passage is said to be created, it is not the Holy Spirit but our spirit. **1.9.7.** Indeed, if you rightly think that the Son is not a creature because all things came into existence through the Word,[19] how is it not blasphemous for you to call the Spirit a creature, in whom the Father through the Word perfects and renews all things?

1.9.8. And if they have imagined that the Holy Spirit is meant when it is written that a "spirit" without qualification is created, they still ought to be persuaded that it is not the Holy Spirit who is created, but that it is our spirit which is renewed by him. David prayed about this spirit when he sang in the psalm: *A pure heart create for me and renew an upright spirit within me* [Ps 50.12]. **1.9.9.** Here God is said to "create" a spirit. But Zechariah says that God first "formed" it: *He stretched out the heavens, and founded the earth, and formed the spirit of man in him* [Zech 12.1]. When the spirit he first formed had fallen, the Word remade it by coming among the creatures when he became flesh,[20] so that, as the Apostle says, *he might make the two into one new man, who according to God was created in righteousness*

[19]See Jn 1.3.
[20]See Jn 1.14.

and holiness of truth [Eph 2.15 + 4.24]. **1.9.10.** Here it is not as if he were saying that another man had been created, other than the man who from the beginning was made according to the Image, but he is advising them to adopt the mind that was recreated and renewed in Christ. This is once again clarified through Ezekiel, when he says: *Make yourselves a new heart and a new spirit. Why will you die, house of Israel? For I do not want the death of the one that dies, says the Lord God* [Ezek 18.31–32].

An interpretation of the "thunder" in Amos 4.13 as the unshaken law of the Spirit

1.10.1. {1.10} So then, if this is how the created spirit is to be understood, it would be appropriate to take the *thunder to which he gives strength* [Am 4.13] as that saying which is sure[21] and that law of the Spirit which cannot be shaken.[22] The Lord wanted James and John to be ministers of this when he called them *"Boanerges," that is, "sons of thunder"* [Mk 3.17]. **1.10.2.** John, at least, truly rumbled from heaven: *In the beginning was the Word, and the Word was with God, and God was the Word* [Jn 1.1]. Earlier *the law had a shadow of the good things to come* [Heb 10.1], but when Christ was proclaimed to humanity and came near, saying: *I who speak am here* [Is 52.6; Jn 4.26], then, in the words of Paul, *his voice shook the earth, as he promised long ago: "Yet once more I shall shake not only the earth, but also the heavens." The phrase "once more" indicates the removal of what can be shaken so that what cannot be shaken may remain. Therefore, let us be grateful for receiving a kingdom that cannot be shaken, through which we offer acceptable worship to God* [Heb 12.26–28]. **1.10.3.** As for that kingdom which Paul says cannot be shaken, David says that it has been given strength when he sings in the psalm: *The Lord reigns, he has robed himself with majesty. The Lord has clothed*

---

[21]See 2 Tim 2.11.
[22]See Heb 12.28.

and girded himself with power. For he has given strength to the world, which will not be shaken [Ps 92.1]. And so, the utterance of the Prophet signifies the coming of the Savior, by which we are renewed and the law of the Spirit remains unshaken.

On the Correct Interpretation of 1 Timothy 5.21 [1.10.4–1.14.7]

The Tropikoi claim the Holy Spirit has angelic status based on 1 Timothy 5.21

1.10.4. But the Tropikoi, true to their name, who reached an agreement with the Arians and divided between themselves the blasphemy against the divinity (such that the latter call the Son a creature and the former the Spirit a creature), have once again dared, as they themselves would admit, to come up with their own modes of exegesis[23] and to misinterpret that saying of the Apostle which he flawlessly wrote to Timothy, saying: *In the presence of God and Jesus Christ and the elect angels, I charge you to observe these things without prejudice, doing nothing out of partiality* [1 Tim 5.21]. Because Paul listed the angels only after he mentioned God and Christ, our opponents claim that the Spirit must be classified with the angels, and he belongs to their order and is an angel that is greater than the others.

This teaching is really based on Valentinus, not the Scriptures

1.10.5. First of all, this invention smacks of the impiety of Valentinus, and they have not been able to conceal that they repeat his ideas.[24] For he said that, when the Paraclete was sent, the angels who

---

[23]Gk. τρόπους. See n. 6 above.

[24]The second-century theologian and exegete Valentinus was born and educated

were his contemporaries were sent together with him.[25] So, when our opponents bring the Spirit down to the level of the angels, they rank all the angels with the Trinity. **1.10.6**. For if the angels come after the Father and Son, as our opponents claim, it is clear that the angels are whatever the Trinity is. No longer are they *ministering spirits sent to minister* [Heb 1.14], nor are they sanctified but they themselves sanctify others.

1.11.1. {1.11} What makes our opponents spout such great nonsense? Where in the Scriptures have they found the Holy Spirit called an angel? I must repeat the points I've already made. He is called "Paraclete,"[26] "Spirit of adopted sonship,"[27] "Spirit of sanctification,"[28] "Spirit of God,"[29] and "Spirit of Christ."[30] Nowhere is he called "angel," or "archangel," or "ministering spirit," as are the angels. On the contrary, together with the Son he is himself ministered to by Gabriel when he says to Mary: *The Holy Spirit will come upon you, and the Power of the Most High will overshadow you* [Lk 1.35]. **1.11.2.** If the Scriptures do not call the Spirit an angel, what sort of defense can our opponents offer for such irrational audacity? For even Valentinus, who sowed this kind of evil thinking among them, called the Spirit "Paraclete" and the angels "angels," though at the same time he very foolishly ranks the Spirit as a contemporary of the angels.

---

in Alexandria but taught in Rome. His doctrines were condemned by certain of his contemporaries as Gnostic, and by the fourth century a charge of imitating Valentinus was a common polemical jab.

[25] Athanasius's description of Valentinus's teaching here appears to be based on Irenaeus, *Adversus haereses* 1.4.5: "Christ, having returned to the Pleroma, probably because he shrank from a second descent, sent her [sc. the mother of Achamoth] the Paraclete, that is, the Savior, whom the Father endowed with all his power. . . . The Paraclete was sent to her together with the angels who were his contemporaries."

[26] See Jn 14.16, 14.26, 15.26, 16.27.

[27] See Rom 8.15.

[28] See Rom 1.4.

[29] See e.g. Mt 3.16.

[30] See Rom 8.9 and 1 Pet 1.11.

Refutation of the Tropikoi's appeal to Zechariah 4.5

"But look," our opponents say, "in the Prophet Zechariah it is written: *Thus says the angel who speaks within me* [Zech 4.5]. It is clear that the angel who speaks within him is the Spirit." **1.11.3.** Now they would not have said this if they had been attentive to the reading.[31] Upon seeing the vision of the lampstand, Zechariah said: *And the angel who speaks within me answered, and said: "Don't you know what these things are?" And I said: "No, lord." And he answered, and said to me, saying: "This is the word of the Lord to Zerubbabel, saying: 'Not by great power, nor by strength, but by my Spirit, says the Lord Almighty'."* [Zech 4.5–6]. **1.11.4.** It is obvious that the angel who spoke within the Prophet was not the Holy Spirit. For the angel was an angel, but the spirit was the Spirit of Almighty God, to whom the angel ministers and who is inseparable from the divinity and proper to the Word.

The Scriptures are careful to distinguish between the Holy Spirit and angels

Since they want to base their claim on the passage of the Apostle because it lists the elect angels after Christ,[32] they will need to answer some questions. Who from among all the angels is to be ranked with the Trinity? For indeed they are all of them not one in number! Which of them descended to the Jordan in the form of a dove?[33] For the ministering angels are *a thousand thousands* and *ten thousand times ten thousand* [Dan 7.10]. When the heavens were opened,[34] why didn't it say, "one of the elect angels descended," but, *the Holy Spirit descended* [Lk 3.22]? **1.11.5.** Why did the Lord himself distin-

---

[31]Cf. 1 Tim 4.13.
[32]I.e., 1 Tim 5.21.
[33]See Lk 3.22.
[34]See Lk 3.21.

guish between them, when he discussed the end of the world with his disciples? For on the one hand he said: *The Son of man will send his angels* [Mt 13.41]. And before this he said: *The angels ministered to him* [Mt 4.11]. And again he says: *The angels will come out* [Mt 13.49]. **1.11.6.** But on the other hand, when he gave the Spirit to his disciples, he said: *Receive the Holy Spirit* [Jn 20.22]. And when he sent them, he said: *Go, make disciples of all nations, baptizing them in the name of the Father, and of the Son, and of the Holy Spirit* [Mt 28.19]. **1.11.7.** He did not rank an angel with the divinity, nor was it through a creature that he joined us to himself and to the Father, but through the Holy Spirit. And when Lord promised him, he did not say that he would send an angel, but *the Spirit of Truth, who proceeds from the Father* [Jn 15.26] and from him receives and is given.[35]

    1.12.1. {1.12} Moses also knows that the angels are creatures, but that the Holy Spirit is united to the Son and the Father. For when God says to him: *Go up from this place, you and your people, whom you have led up from the land of Egypt into the land which I swore to Abraham, Isaac, and Jacob, saying: "To your seed I will give it. And I will send my angel before you, and he will drive out the Canaanite."* [Ex 33.1–2], he refused, saying: *If you yourself do not go along with us, do not lead me up from this place!* [Ex 33.15]. For he did not want a creature to lead the people, lest they should learn *to worship the created order instead of the one who created* all things, God [Rom 1.25]. **1.12.2.** Indeed, when he refused the angel, he begged God himself to guide them. But God had made the following promise, saying to him: *And this word of yours that you have spoken, I will do it. For you have found favor before me, and I know you above all* [Ex 33.17], and in Isaiah it is written: *Where is the one who brought the shepherd of the sheep up from the land, the one who places the Holy Spirit in them, the one who leads Moses up by his right hand?* [Is 63.11–12]. And he says a little after this: *The Spirit came down from the Lord and guided them. In this way you led your people, to make your name glorious* [Is 63.14].

[35]See Jn 16.14.

1.12.3. Who cannot perceive the truth from these passages? For when God promised to guide them, note that he no longer promised to send an angel, but his Spirit who is superior to the angels, and he guides the people. And he shows that the Spirit is neither one of the creatures, nor an angel, but superior to the created order and united to the divinity of the Father. **1.12.4.** For God himself through the Word in the Spirit guided the people. Hence, all through Scripture he says: *I led you up out of the land of Egypt: you are witnesses, if there was a foreign god among you besides me* [Lev 11.45; Judg 6.8; Is 44.8; Is 45.21; Hos 13.4]. And the saints declare unto God: *You guided your people like sheep* [Ps 76.21], and: *The Lord guided them with hope, and they were not afraid* [Ps 77.53]. To him they also offered up a hymn, singing: *To him who led his people through the desert, for his mercy endures forever* [Ps 135.16]. **1.12.5.** And the great Moses unceasingly proclaimed: *The Lord God who goes before your face* [Deut 1.30]. And so, the Spirit of God cannot be an angel, nor a creature, but is proper to his divinity. For when the Spirit was among the people, God was among them through the Son in the Spirit.

The absence of any reference to the Spirit in 1 Timothy 5.21 has scriptural warrant

1.13.1. {1.13} "But even granting this," say our opponents, "why did the Apostle not list the Holy Spirit, but rather the elect angels, after Christ?" We could ask them the same thing. Why did Paul only list the elect angels, but not archangels, nor cherubim, nor seraphim, nor dominions, nor thrones, or anything else? **1.13.2.** Because he does not list all these, are the angels archangels, or are they only angels, and neither seraphim, nor cherubim, nor archangels, nor dominions, nor thrones, nor principalities, nor anything else? But this is nothing other than to ask the Apostle why he wrote as he did and not in some other way; it bespeaks ignorance of the Divine Scriptures and thus divergence from the truth.

1.13.3. For look at what was written in Isaiah: *Draw near to me, and listen to these things: I have not spoken in secret from the beginning; when it took place, I was there. And now the Lord has sent me, and his Spirit* [Is 48.16]. And in Haggai: *And now take courage, Zerubbabel, says the Lord. And take courage, Joshua, son of Jehozadak, the high priest, says the Lord. And take courage, all you people of the land, says the Lord. And work, for I am with you, says the Lord Almighty. . . . And my Spirit abides in the midst of you* [Hag 2.4–5]. Now in both Prophets mention is made only of the Lord and Spirit.

1.13.4. So, what will our opponents say about this? They rank the Spirit among the angels because Paul, after listing Christ, omitted the Spirit and mentioned the elect angels. Therefore, when they read these passages of the Prophets, they will argue with even greater audacity about the one who was omitted. **1.13.5.** If they were to say that the Lord is the Son, what would they say about the Father? But if they were to say that the Lord is the Father, what would they say about the Son? No one should even ponder the blasphemy which they say follows from this. For he who was omitted must either be said not to exist or be classified with the things that are made.

1.14.1. {1.14} What would our opponents say if they also hear the Lord saying: *In a certain place there was a judge who neither feared God nor respected man* [Lk 18.2]. Because a man is listed after God, is the Son the man whom the unjust judge does not respect? Or, because the man is listed after God, is the Son third after the man and the Holy Spirit fourth? **1.14.2.** What if they also hear the Apostle when he says again in the same letter: *I charge you before God who gives life to all things, and before Jesus Christ who witnessed to a good confession in the time of Pontius Pilate, that you keep the commandment without spot, blameless* [1 Tim 6.13–14]. **1.14.3.** Because now he omits the angels and the Spirit, will our opponents have doubts about whether the Spirit exists and about whether the angels exist? Yes, they have doubts, even to the point of being well practiced in uttering such blasphemies against the Spirit! **1.14.4.** If they hear the Scripture when it says in Exodus: *The people feared the Lord, and* *believed in God and in Moses, his servant* [Ex 14.31], will they then classify Moses with God? Will they think of only Moses, and not of the Son, as coming after God? **1.14.5.** What if they also hear the patriarch Jacob when he blessed Joseph and said: *O God who has sustained me from my youth until this day, the angel who rescued me from all evils, bless these children* [Gen 48.15–16]? Because an angel is mentioned after God, is the angel prior to the Son? Or is the Son classified with angels? **1.14.6.** Yes again, this is what they think, for their hearts are corrupted.

But this is not the apostolic faith, nor can a Christian even possibly tolerate such things. For the holy and blessed Trinity is indivisible and united in itself. When the Father is mentioned, with him are both his Word and the Spirit who is in the Son. If the Son is named, the Father is in the Son, and the Spirit is not external to the Word. For there is one grace from the Father which is perfected through the Son in the Holy Spirit. And there is one divinity, and one God who is *over all, and through all, and in all* [Eph 4.6]. **1.14.7.** Thus Paul too, when he said: *I charge you in the presence of God and Jesus Christ* [2 Tim 4.1], knew that the Spirit had not been divided from the Son, but was in Christ, as the Son is in the Father.

Why Paul mentioned the elect angels in 1 Timothy 5.21

Nonetheless, it was appropriate for him to mention the elect angels, so that the disciple to whom his charge was directed would realize that what is said by God is said through Christ in the Spirit, but that angels minister to our affairs, overseeing the actions of each person, and thus would keep the exhortations of his teacher, as there were witnesses who observe what is said. Or perhaps, because the angels *always behold the face of the Father who is in heaven*, Paul charges them on behalf of *the little ones* in the Church [Mt 18.10], so that the disciple would realize who it is that guards the people and not neglect the exhortations of the Apostle.

EVEN IF THE SPIRIT IS NOT A CREATURE, HE IS NOT A SON [1.15–21]

*An objection: if the Spirit is from the Father
yet not a creature, he must be a son*

1.15.1. {1.15} So then, it appears to me that this is the meaning of the Divine Oracles, and it refutes the blasphemy which our irrational[36] opponents utter against the Spirit. Yet still defiant in their struggle against the truth, as you write, they make another claim. But this time it is no longer based on the Scriptures (since they do not find it there) but belched up *from the surfeit of their own heart* [Mt 12.34; Lk 6.45]:[37] "If the Spirit is not a creature, nor one of the angels, but proceeds from the Father, then is he also a son? And are the Spirit and the Word two brothers? **1.15.2.** And if he is a brother, how is the Word only-begotten? How can they not be equal, but the one is named after the Father and the other after the Son? If the Spirit is from the Father, why isn't it also said that he has been begotten and is a son, but is simply called Holy Spirit? If the Spirit is of the Son, then is the Father the grandfather of the Spirit?" Such are the mockeries of these dishonorable men who out of idle curiosity want to search into *the depths of God*, which *no one knows, except the Spirit of God* [1 Cor 2.10–11]—the very Spirit whom they blaspheme. **1.15.3.** Therefore, we ought not continue to respond to them, but in accordance with the Apostle's precept, after they have been admonished by what has already been said, to avoid them as heretics.[38]

---

[36]The adjective "irrational" (τῶν ἀλόγων), also implies "deprived of the Word."
[37]See *Serap.* 3.5.4.
[38]See Titus 3.10. See *Serap.* 3.1.1 and 3.6.7.

The invalidity of the objection is shown
by reducing it to absurdity

Or perhaps we should ask them questions on par with those they ask us, and demand an answer from them that corresponds to the answer they demand from us.[39] So then, tell us: if the Father is from a father, and if another has been begotten along with him, and they are brothers from that same one, then what are their names? And who is the father and grandfather of this one?[40] Who are their ancestors? But they will say that there are none. **1.15.4.** So then, let them tell us this: how can the Father be a father if he did not come from a father? Or how could he have the Son if he himself had not been previously begotten as a son? I know that this line of questioning is impious. But our justification for this mockery of those who utter such mockeries is that such an absurd and impious line of questioning lets them perceive their own foolishness. For what they are saying is not true. God forbid! Nor is it appropriate to pursue such a line of questioning in the case of the divinity. For *God is not like a human being* [Num 23.19], such that someone can dare to ask human questions about God.

Only when used of the divinity are the
terms "father" and "son" stable

1.16.1. {1.16} So then, as I said before, we ought to keep silent on these matters and not waste our time on such people. But lest our silence serve as a pretext for their shamelessness, we have to say something to them. Just as it is impossible to say that the Father has a father, so too it is impossible to say that the Son has a brother. **1.16.2.** As written above, there is no God other than the Father;[41]

---

[39] Athanasius uses the same tactic in *Serap.* 3.5–6.

[40] Here we read τούτου instead of τούτων (PG 26.568b; AW I/1.491), following some mss. and Shapland (98 n. 15[13]).

[41] See Is 43.10.

there is no other Son, for he is only-begotten. Hence the one and only Father is the Father of the one and only Son, and only in the case of the divinity have the names "Father" and "Son" always been stable and always are. **1.16.3.** But among human beings, if someone is called a father, he is nonetheless another man's son; and if someone is called a son, he is nonetheless another man's father. Hence among human beings the names "'father" and "son" are not preserved in their proper senses. **1.16.4.** For example, Abraham was the son of Nahor and became the father of Isaac.[42] And Isaac was the son of Abraham and became the father of Jacob. And this is the way things are for human nature. For human beings are parts of one another, and each son, when begotten, has a part of his father, so that he too can become another's father.

1.16.5. But this is not how things are for the divinity. For *God is not like a human being* [Num 23.19]. Nor does he have a nature that is divisible into parts. Hence he does not beget the Son by being divided into parts, so that the Son may also become the father of another, for he himself is not from a father. Nor is the Son a part of the Father. Hence he does not beget as he has himself been begotten, but is whole from whole, *Image* [Col 1.15; 2 Cor 4.4] and *Radiance* [Heb 1.3]. **1.16.6.** And in the case of the divinity the Father is a father in the proper sense and the Son a son in the proper sense. In their case the Father's name has always been "Father" and the Son's name always "Son." And just as the Father could never have been a son, so too the Son could never become a father. And just as the Father will never cease to be only a father, so too the Son will never cease to be only a son. **1.16.7.** Therefore, it would be sheer insanity to imagine a brother for the Son and to apply the name "grandfather" to the Father. In the Scriptures the Spirit is never called a son, lest he be

---

[42]We read Ναχώρ with some mss. and Shapland (102 n. 16[6]) instead of Montfaucon's corrective emendation Θάρρου (PG 29.569a) or the Θάρρα of Wyrwa and Savvidis (AW I/1.492). Note however that Athanasius is mistaken here: Nahor was Abraham's grandfather; Terah the son of Nahor was Abraham's father (see Gen 11.24–28). As Athanasius makes the same mistake in *Serap.* 3.6.5 this is the correct reading here.

considered a brother. Nor is he called a son of the Son, lest the Father be thought of as a grandfather. Instead, the Son is called the Son of the Father, and the Spirit is called the Spirit of the Father, and thus in the Holy Trinity there is one divinity and one faith.

> *The insolence of speculation about*
> *what is beyond human knowledge*

1.17.1. {1.17} It is also insanity to call the Spirit a creature for the following reason: if he were a creature, he would not be ranked with the Trinity. For the whole Trinity is one God. Now it is sufficient to know that the Spirit is not a creature, nor classified with things that have been made. For nothing foreign to the Trinity is mixed with it, but it is indivisible and self-consistent.[43] These considerations are sufficient for believers. This is as far as human knowledge can go. At this point the cherubim spread the covering of their wings.

1.17.2. Whoever seeks to know more than this and wants to inquire further disobeys the one who said: *Do not seek much wisdom, lest you be stupefied* [Eccl 7.16]. For the traditions of the faith are not appropriately understood by human wisdom but by *hearing with faith* [Gal 3.2]. What sort of rational account could worthily interpret what surpasses the nature that has come into existence? Or what sort of ears could possibly understand things *it is not lawful for human beings* either to hear or *to speak* [2 Cor 12.4]? **1.17.3.** This is how Paul spoke of what he heard, but when he spoke of God himself, he said: *How unsearchable are his ways! For who has known the mind of the Lord? Or who has been his counselor?* [Rom 11.33–34]. Certainly, Abraham did not conduct futile investigations, nor did he question the one who spoke to him, but *he believed, and it was reckoned to him as righteousness* [Rom 4.3]. **1.17.4.** So too was Moses called the *faithful servant* [Heb 3.5].

---

[43] Gk. ὁμοία ἑαυτῇ, lit. "like itself." See *Serap.* 1.28.2.

But as for those whose minds are with Arius, into whose *wicked and scheming souls wisdom will not enter* [Wis 1.4], if they can neither understand nor believe in the indivisible and holy Trinity, let them for this reason not also pervert the truth, nor claim that what they cannot understand cannot be.[44] They have backed themselves into the most absurd corner. Because they cannot understand how the Holy Trinity is indivisible, the Arians make the Son one with the created order, and the Tropikoi themselves classify the Spirit with the creatures. **1.17.5.** It would be best for them either to keep silent when they do not understand anything at all—the Arians not ranking the Son with the creatures and the Tropikoi not ranking the Spirit with the same—or else for them to acknowledge what is written, joining the Son with the Father and not dividing the Spirit from the Son, so as to preserve the truth of the Holy Trinity's indivisibility and sameness of nature.

If they were to learn such things, there would be no need for them to be so audacious, nor to ask contentious questions about how these things could be; and if the one being asked such questions is at a loss for words, there would be no need for them to dream up evil notions according to their own lights. **1.17.6.** For none of the things that have come into existence, least of all us human beings, can speak worthily about what is ineffable. So again, it is much more audacious, when we cannot speak of these matters, to invent novel terms other than those in the Scriptures. And this present attempt above all is insanity, both on the part of the one who asks the questions and on the part of the one who would even consider giving an answer. For not even someone who asked such questions about the things which have come into existence would be considered to be in his right in mind.

---

[44]See *Serap.* 2.1.2.

We do not understand the mysteries of nature, let alone the mysteries of God

1.18.1. {1.18} Or let these opponents of ours, who have an easy answer for everything, dare to answer the following: How is the heaven formed and from what sort of materials?[45] Or how are they combined? Or how is the sun formed? What about each of the stars? Is it any wonder that we can refute their foolishness on the basis of realities set above us, when we do not even understand what the nature of the trees here below is like, or how the waters were gathered together[46] and how living things were constructed and constituted? But they won't be able to answer these questions. **1.18.2.** For even Solomon, who had a greater share of wisdom than all, realized that it was impossible for human beings to discover such things, and said: *And he has given every heart a whole lifetime, lest humanity discover the work which God has done from the beginning to the end* [Eccl 3.11]. **1.18.3.** So then, since they cannot discover[47] these things, will they claim that these things cannot be? Yes, they will make this claim since their minds are corrupted.

Therefore, it would be with good reason if we say to them: "You are so stupid and utterly reckless. Instead, why don't you drop your futile investigations of the Holy Trinity and simply believe that he exists? In this matter you have the Apostle as your teacher, when he says: *One must first believe that God exists and that he rewards those who seek him* [Heb 11.6]. For he did not say, "how God exists," but simply, *that God exists.*" **1.18.4.** But if they are not overcome by this argument, let them state how the Father exists, so that from this they may also learn how the Word of the Father exists. "But it is absurd," they will say, "to ask questions about the Father in this manner." Let them realize that it is also absurd to ask questions about his Word in this manner.

---

[45]For a similar argument, see *Serap.* 2.1.3; Basil, *Against Eunomius* 1.12 and 3.6; and Gregory of Nazianzus, *Oration* 31.8.

[46]See Gen 1.10.

[47]Here we prefer to read the "discover" (εὑρεῖν) found in several important mss. rather than "say" (λέγειν) (*Serap.* 1.18.3, 10; AW I/1.497).

*Scriptural examples of the order among
Father, Son, and Holy Spirit*

1.19.1. {1.19} And so, since this present attempt surpasses the utmost insanity, no one should ask such questions any more, but only study what is in the Scriptures. For the examples on this subject found therein are sufficient and fitting. The Father is called Fountain and Light. For it says: *They have forsaken me, the Fountain of living water* [Jer 2.13]. **1.19.2.** And again in Baruch: *Why is it, O Israel, that you are in the land of your enemies? You have forsaken the Fountain of wisdom* [Bar 3.10+12]. And according to John: *Our God is Light* [1 Jn 1.5]. But the Son, as if in reference to the Fountain, is called River: *The River of God is filled with waters* [Ps 64.10]. And in reference to the Light, he is called Radiance, as Paul says: *He is the Radiance of his glory, and the Character of his Subsistence* [Heb 1.3]. **1.19.3.** Thus the Father is Light and his Radiance is the Son—for in particular one must not hesitate to affirm the same things about them many times[48]—and so we are also permitted to see in the Son the Spirit in whom we are enlightened. For it says: *may he give you the Spirit of Wisdom and of revelation in the knowledge of him, having the eyes of your hearts enlightened* [Eph 1.17–18]. **1.19.4.** But when we are enlightened in the Spirit, it is Christ who enlightens us in him. For it says: *He was the true Light who enlightens every human being coming into the world* [Jn 1.9]. And again, the Father is the Fountain and the Son is called the River, and so we are said to drink of the Spirit. For it is written: *we were all made to drink of the one Spirit* [1 Cor 12.13]. But when we drink of the Spirit, we drink of Christ. For *they drank of the spiritual Rock that followed them, and the Rock was Christ* [1 Cor 10.4].

1.19.5. And again, Christ is the true Son, and so when we receive the Spirit, we are made sons. For it says: *you did not receive the spirit of slavery leading you back into fear, but you have received the Spirit*

---

[48]See *Serap.* 1.27.1 and 3.4.1.

of adopted sonship [Rom 8.15].[49] But when we are made sons in the Spirit, it is clear that we are called children of God in Christ. For *however many received him, to them he gave the power to become children of God* [Jn 1.12]. **1.19.6.** Then, the Father is, as Paul said, *the only wise* [Rom 16.27], and so the Son is his Wisdom. For *Christ is the Power of God and the Wisdom of God* [1 Cor 1.24]. The Son is Wisdom itself, and so when we receive *the Spirit of Wisdom* [Eph 1.17], we possess the Son and become wise in him. For so it is written in Psalm 145: *The Lord sets prisoners free; the Lord gives Wisdom to the blind* [Ps 145.7–8].

1.19.7. And when the Spirit is given to us—the Savior said: *Receive the Holy Spirit* [Jn 20.22]—God is in us. For this is what John wrote: *If we should love one another, God remains in us. In this we know that we remain in him, and he in us, because has given us of his Spirit* [1 Jn 4.12–13]. But when God is in us, the Son is also in us. For the Lord himself said: *I and the Father will come and make our home with him* [Jn 14.23]. **1.19.8.** Next, the Son is life—for he said: *I am the life* [Jn 14.6]—and so we are said to be given life in the Spirit. For it says: *the one who raised Christ Jesus from the dead will also give life to your mortal bodies through his Spirit who dwells in you* [Rom 8.11]. But when we are given life in the Spirit, Christ himself is said to live in us. For it says: *I am crucified with Christ. It is no longer I who live, but Christ who lives in me* [Gal 2.19–20].

1.19.9. And again, the Son said that the works he did were accomplished by the Father. For he says: *The Father who remains in me does his works. Believe me, that I am in the Father and the Father is in me. Otherwise, believe me because of the works themselves* [Jn 14.10–11]. Likewise, Paul said that the works that he accomplished in the power of the Spirit were Christ's. *For I will not dare to speak anything other than what Christ has worked through me to win obedi-*

[49]Gr. υἱοθεσία. The word literally means "adopting as a son" (υἱός), a nuance that the normal English translation, "adoption," does not capture. For Athanasius and many other Greek fathers, the title "Spirit of adopted sonship" shows Spirit's intimate connection with the Father's adoption of sons in Christ.

*ence from the gentiles, in word and in deed, in the power of signs and
wonders, in the power of the Holy Spirit* [Rom 15.18–19].

1.20.1. {1.20} Seeing that there is such an order and unity in the
Holy Trinity, who could separate either the Son from the Father, or
the Spirit from the Son or from the Father himself? Who could be
so audacious as to say that the Trinity is unlike itself and different in
nature?[50] Or that the Son is foreign to the Father in substance?[51] Or
that the Spirit is estranged from the Son? 1.20.2. How could such
things be possible?

Again, suppose some inquisitive person were to ask: "When the
Spirit is in us, how is the Son said to be in us? And when the Son
is in us, how is the Father said to be in us? Or since it is entirely a
Trinity, how is the Trinity indicated by only one of them? Or when
just one of them is in us, how is the Trinity said to be in us?" First
let him divide the Radiance from the Light or the Wisdom from the
Wise One, or else tell us how these things are possible. 1.20.3. But
if this cannot be done, much more is it the audacity of the insane
to ask such questions about God. For the divinity is not handed
down through logical demonstration and arguments, as has been
said, but by faith and by pious reasoning joined with reverence. If
Paul preached the saving cross *not in the wisdom of words, but in
the demonstration of spirit and power* [1 Cor 2.4], and *he heard secret
words* in paradise *which it is not possible to speak* [2 Cor 12.4], then
who can make declarations about the Holy Trinity?

1.20.4. Nevertheless, such a great puzzle can be solved primarily
by faith, and then by using the examples mentioned above, I mean,
the Image and the Radiance, the Fountain and the River, the Subsistence and the Character. For as the Son is in the Spirit as in his own
Image, so too is the Father in the Son. And in fact, the Divine Scripture, in order to palliate our inability to explain and comprehend
these matters with words, gave us examples such as these. And so, in
combating the disbelief of our audacious opponents, it is possible, if

---

[50]Gk. ἀνόμοιον καὶ ἑτεροφυῆ.
[51]Gk. ἀλλοτριοούσιον.

we use such examples, to speak more simply, to speak without danger, to think without fault, and to believe that there is one holiness which comes from the Father through the Son in the Holy Spirit.

1.20.5. Indeed, just as the Son is the only-begotten offspring, so too is the Spirit, who is given and sent from the Son, also one and not many, nor one of many, but the only Spirit. Since there is one living Word, there must be one perfect and complete living activity and gift whereby he sanctifies and enlightens. This is said to proceed from the Father, because the Spirit shines forth, and is sent, and is given from the Word, who is confessed to be from the Father. **1.20.6.** Indeed, the Son is sent from the Father. For he says: *God so loved the world that he sent his only-begotten Son* [Jn 3.16]. But the Son sends the Spirit. For he says: *If I go away, I will send you the Paraclete* [Jn 16.7]. And the Son glorifies the Father, saying: *Father, I have glorified you* [Jn 17.4]. But the Spirit glorifies the Son. For he says: *He will glorify me* [Jn 16.14].[52] And the Son says: *I declare to the world what I heard from the Father* [Jn 8.26]. But the Spirit receives from the Son. For *he shall receive from what is mine and announce it to you* [Jn 16.14]. **1.20.7.** And the Son came in the name of the Father,[53] but the Son says: *the Holy Spirit whom the Father will send in my name* [Jn 14.26].

If the Spirit is a creature, the Son must also be a creature

1.21.1. {1.21} And so, if the Spirit's rank and nature vis-à-vis the Son corresponds to the Son's vis-à-vis the Father, how can anyone who claims that the Spirit is creature not be compelled to think the same about the Son? For if the Spirit is a creature of the Son, it would be consistent to claim that the Word is a creature of the Father. In fact, it was by imagining such things that the Arians fell into the

---

[52]From the context it is clear that the subject of the verse is "the Spirit of Truth."

[53]See Jn 5.43.

Judaism of Caiaphas. **1.21.2.** But if those who are making such claims about the Spirit protest that they do not subscribe to what Arius believed, then they should abandon the teachings of that man and not be impious toward the Spirit. **1.21.3.** For just as the Son, who is in the Father and the Father in him, is not a creature but is proper to the substance of the Father—now this is purportedly what you claim—, so too it is incorrect for the Spirit, who is in the Son and the Son in him, to be ranked with creatures or to be separated from the Word, thereby destroying the perfection of the Trinity.

Conclusion to this section and transition to the next

1.21.4. So then, since they have falsified the meaning of the sayings of both the Prophet and the Apostle[54] in a display of self-delusion, these considerations are sufficient to refute the slander to which the ignorance of the Tropikoi gives rise. But we still need to examine, one by one, each passage in the Divine Scriptures that speaks about the Holy Spirit. Like good bankers,[55] we need to judge whether the Spirit has anything that is proper to creatures or whether he is proper to God. In this manner we will be able to determine whether to call him a creature or something other than creatures and proper to and one of the divinity in the Trinity. Perhaps they will be ashamed by this exercise, when they learn the extent to which they have invented blasphemies that are out of harmony with the Divine Oracles.

[54]I.e. Am 4.13 and 1 Tim 5.21.
[55]This common aphorism referring to the skill of distinguishing the good from the bad or the true from the false is based on the opinion that a good banker was skilled at distinguishing genuine from counterfeit coinage.

THE SPIRIT IS UNLIKE CREATURES AND PROPER TO THE SON: TESTIMONIES FROM SCRIPTURE [1.22–27]

Creatures are from nothing, whereas the Spirit is from God

1.22.1. {1.22} So, creatures came into existence from nothing; they have a beginning to their coming into existence. For *in the beginning God made the heaven and the earth* and all that is in them [Gen 1.1]. But the Holy Spirit is said to be from God: *No one knows the things that belong to a human being except the human spirit that is in him. Thus also no one knows the things that belong to God except the Spirit of God. Now we have not received the spirit of the world but the Spirit that is from God* [1 Cor 2.11–12]. Based on this, what sort of kinship does the Spirit have with creatures? For creatures did not exist. But God is *"He Who Is"* [Ex 3.4], and the Spirit is from him. The one who is from God cannot be from nothing, nor can he be a creature—unless they think that the one from whom the Spirit comes is also a creature! **1.22.2.** But who then would tolerate such fools, who say in their hearts that God does not exist?[56] Indeed, just as *no one knows the things that belong to a human being except the spirit that is in him*, so too *no one knows the things that belong to God except the Spirit* in him [1 Cor 2.11]. If this is the case, how then is it not blasphemous to claim that the Spirit in God, who searches *even the depths of God* [1 Cor 2.10], is a creature? For if someone were to maintain this viewpoint, he would take from these passages that the human spirit is external to the human being and that the Word in the Father is a creature.

[56]See Ps 13.1.

Creatures are sanctified and renewed, whereas the Spirit sanctifies and renews

1.22.3. Again, the Spirit is and is said to be the Spirit of sanctification and renewal. For Paul writes: *who designated the Son of God in power according to the Spirit of sanctification on the basis of his resurrection, Jesus Christ our Lord* [Rom 1.4]. **1.22.4.** And again he says: *But you were sanctified, you were justified in the name of our Lord Jesus Christ and in the Spirit of our God* [1 Cor 6.11]. When writing to Titus, he said: *When the goodness of God our Savior and his love of humanity appeared, not because of works of righteousness done by us but on account of his mercy he saved us through the washing of the second regeneration and the renewal of the Holy Spirit, whom he has poured forth upon us abundantly through Jesus Christ our Savior, so that we might be justified by his grace and become heirs[57] of eternal life in hope* [Titus 3.4–7]. **1.22.5.** But creatures are sanctified and renewed: *You send forth your Spirit, and they are created* [Ps 103.30].[58] And Paul says: *For it is impossible for those who were once enlightened, who have tasted the heavenly gift, and who have become partakers of the Holy Spirit . . .* [Heb 6.4]. **1.23.1.** {1.23} So, he who is not sanctified by another, nor participates in sanctification, but is himself the one who is participated in, the one in whom all creatures are sanctified: how can he be one of the *all things* [Jn 1.3] and proper to those who participate in him? For those who claim this would also have to say that the Son, through whom *all things* came to be, is one of the *all things*.

---

[57]Here the word "heirs" is missing from the best mss., but we include it since the meaning of the sentence is obscure without it.

[58]Here some mss. continue the quotation: *and you renew the face of the earth.*

Creatures receive life, whereas the Spirit gives life

1.23.2. The Spirit is said to be life-giving: *The one who raised Christ from the dead will also give life to your mortal bodies through his Spirit who dwells in us* [Rom 8.11]. And the Lord is life itself and, as Peter said, *the author of life* [Acts 3.15]. The Lord himself said: *The water that I will give to him shall become in him a spring of water welling up to eternal life* [Jn 4.14]. **1.23.3.** *He said this about the Spirit whom those who believe in him were about to receive* [Jn 7.39]. As has been said, creatures are given life through him. But he who does not participate in life, but is himself participated in and gives life to creatures: what sort of affinity does he have with things which have come into existence? In sum, how is the Spirit one of the creatures to whom the Word gives life through him?

Creatures are anointed and sealed, whereas the Spirit is the anointing and seal

1.23.4. The Spirit is said to be an anointing and is a seal. John writes: *The anointing which you have received from him abides in you, and you have no need for anyone to teach you, since, rather, his anointing teaches you about everything* [1 Jn 2.27]. **1.23.5.** In the Prophet Isaiah it is written: *The Spirit of the Lord is upon me, because he has anointed me* [Is 61.1]. Paul says: *In whom you who believe have also been sealed by the promised Holy Spirit* [Eph 1.13]. And again a little further on he says: *And do not grieve the Holy Spirit of God, in whom you who believe have been sealed for the day of redemption* [Eph 4.30]. **1.23.6.** It is creatures who are sealed in him and anointed by him and taught about all things by him. But if the Spirit is the anointing and the seal by whom and in whom the Word anoints and seals all things, in what way can the anointer and sealer be like or proper to those who are anointed and sealed? Thus for this reason he cannot be one of the *all things* [Jn 1.3]. The seal cannot be one of the things sealed,

nor can the anointing be one of the things anointed, but he is proper
to the Word who anoints and seals. **1.23.7.** For the anointing has the
sweet fragrance and the good odor of the anointer, and those who
are anointed say, when they participate in him: *We are the good odor
of Christ* [2 Cor 2.15]. And the seal has the form of Christ who seals,
and those who are sealed participate in him, being formed into him,
as the Apostle says: *My children, with whom I am again in labor until
Christ be formed in you!* [Gal 4.19]. Thus sealed, it is proper that we
also *become*, as Peter said, *sharers of the divine nature* [2 Pet 1.4]. And
thus all creation partakes of the Word in the Spirit.

We participate in God through the Spirit

1.24.1. {1.24} And it is through the Spirit that all of us are said to
be partakers of God: *Do you not know that you are the temple of God
and that the Spirit of God dwells in you? If anyone destroys the temple
of God, God will destroy him. For the temple of God is holy, which
you are* [1 Cor 3.16–17]. **1.24.2.** If the Holy Spirit were a creature, we
would not have participation in God through him. But if we were
joined to a creature, we would become strangers to the divine nature,
inasmuch as we did not partake of it in any way. But as it is, when
we are said to be partakers of Christ and partakers of God, it shows
that the anointing and the seal which is in us does not belong to the
nature of things which have been brought into existence, but to the
Son, who joins us to the Father through the Spirit that is in him.
1.24.3. This is what John taught, as we said above, when he wrote:
*By this we know that we remain in him, and he in us, because he has
given to us of his Spirit* [1 Jn 4.13]. **1.24.4.** But if we become *sharers
of the divine nature* [2 Pet 1.4] by partaking of the Spirit, someone
would have to be insane to say that the Spirit has a created nature and
not the nature of God. For it is because of this that those in whom
the Spirit dwells are divinized. And if he divinizes, there can be no
doubt that his nature is of God.

The Father creates all things through the Word in the Spirit

1.24.5. And there is something even clearer for the destruction of this heresy sung in Psalm 103, as we said before: *You take away their spirit, and they die, and return to the dust from which they came. You send forth your Spirit, and they are created, and you renew the face of the earth* [Ps 103.29–30].[59] And Paul writes to Titus: *through the washing of regeneration and the renewal of the Holy Spirit whom he poured out upon us abundantly through Jesus Christ* [Titus 3.5–6]. **1.24.6.** But if the Father creates and renews all things through the Word in the Holy Spirit, what sort of likeness or kinship could the Creator have with creatures? How could the one in whom he creates all things possibly be a creature? Such an impious statement leads to blasphemy against the Son, in that those who claim that the Spirit is a creature would also have to claim that the Word through whom all things are created is a creature.

The Spirit is the Image of the Son

1.24.7. The Spirit is said to be and is the Image of the Son. For *those whom he foreknew he also predestined to be conformed to the Image of his Son* [Rom 8.29]. Therefore, if our opponents confess that the Son is not a creature, it is impossible for his Image to be a creature. For an image must be just like that of which it is an image. **1.24.8.** Hence the Word is suitably and appropriately confessed not to be a creature, since he is the Image of the Father. And so, the one who classifies the Spirit with creatures will undoubtedly also classify the Son with them, thereby also blaspheming the Father because of the blasphemy against his Image.

[59]See *Serap.* 1.9.6.

The Spirit is proper to the Son, and thereby
proper to the divinity of the Father

1.25.1. {1.25} And so, the Spirit is different from creatures and instead has been shown to be proper to the Son and not foreign to God. But let's return to that clever question of theirs: "If the Spirit is from God, why isn't he also called a son?"[60] In what precedes it was already shown how reckless and audacious this question is, and now it will be shown to be no less so. **1.25.2.** For if he is not called a son in the Scriptures, but Spirit of God, he is said to be in God himself and from God himself, as the Apostle wrote. And if the Son is proper to the Father's substance because he is from the Father, the Spirit who is said to be from God must be proper to the Son in substance. **1.25.3.** Indeed, the Son is Lord, and the Spirit himself is called *the Spirit of adopted sonship* [Rom 8.15]. And again, the Son is Wisdom and Truth, and it is written that the Spirit is *the Spirit of Wisdom* [Is 11.2; Eph 1.17] and *the Spirit of Truth* [Jn 14.17; 15.26; 16.13; 1 Jn 4.6]. And again, the Son is *the Power of God* [1 Cor 1.24] and *the Lord of Glory* [1 Cor 2.8], and the Spirit is called *the Spirit of Power* and *the Spirit of Glory* [1 Pet 4.14]. Scripture speaks in this manner with respect to each of them. Paul wrote to the Corinthians: *For if they had known, they would not have crucified the Lord of glory* [1 Cor 2.8]. And elsewhere: *You did not receive the spirit of slavery leading you back into fear, but you have received the Spirit of adopted sonship* [Rom 8.15]. **1.25.4.** And again: *God has sent the Spirit of his Son into your hearts, crying out, "Abba, Father!"* [Gal 4.6]. And Peter wrote: *If you are insulted in the name of Christ, you are blessed because the Spirit of Glory and of Power and of God rests upon you* [1 Pet 4.14]. And the Lord said that the Spirit was *the Spirit of Truth* [Jn 14.17; 15.26; 16.13; 1 Jn 4.6] and *the Paraclete* [Jn 14.16; 14.26; 15.26; 16.7]. By this he shows that the Trinity is complete in the Spirit.

1.25.5. So then, in the Spirit the Word glorifies creatures, and after he has divinized them and made them sons of God, he leads

---

[60]See *Serap.* 1.15.1–2.

them to the Father. But that which joins creatures to the Word cannot be a creature. And that which makes creatures sons cannot be foreign to the Son. Otherwise another spirit would be needed by which this Spirit could be joined to the Word. But this is absurd. And so, the Spirit is not one of the things that has come into existence, but is proper to the divinity of the Father. In him the Word divinizes all that has come into existence. And the one in whom creatures are divinized cannot himself be external to the divinity of the Father.

Creatures are mutable, whereas the Spirit is immutable

1.26.1. {1.26} That the Spirit is superior to creatures, being different than the nature of things that have come into existence and proper to the divinity, can also be recognized from the following considerations. The Holy Spirit is immutable and unchangeable. For it says: *For the Holy Spirit of discipline will flee from deceit, and will withdraw from foolish thoughts* [Wis 1.5]. **1.26.2.** And Peter says: *In the incorruptibility of the humble and quiet Spirit* [1 Pet 3.4]. And again in Wisdom: *For your incorruptible Spirit is in all things* [Wis 12.1]. And if *no one knows the things that belong to God except the Spirit of God that is in him* [1 Cor 2.11], and if there is in God, as James said, *no variation or shadow of change* [Jam 1.17], then, since the Holy Spirit is in God, it is reasonable to conclude that he must be immutable, unvarying, and incorruptible. **1.26.3.** But those who have come into existence and are creatures have a nature that is mutable, because it is external to the substance of God and comes into subsistence from nothing. For *every human being is a liar* [Ps 115.2], and *all have sinned and fall short of the glory of God* [Rom 3.23]. **1.26.4.** *Yet as for the angels who did not keep to their own dominion but abandoned their proper habitation, he has kept them in eternal chains under gloom until the judgment of the great day* [Jud 1.6]. And in Job: *See, he does not place his trust in his holy angels* [Job

4.18];[61] *the stars are not pure in his sight* [Job 25.5]. **1.26.5.** And Paul writes: *Do you not know that we shall judge angels? And even more so matters pertaining to this life?* [1 Cor 6.3]. And we have also heard that the devil, who was *between the cherubim* [Ezek 10.7] and was *a seal of resemblance* [Ezek 28.12], *fell like a flash of lightning from heaven* [Lk 10.18]. **1.26.6.** If creatures have a mutable nature and such things are written of the angels, but if the Spirit is the same and unchangeable, and possesses the immutability of the Son, remaining always with him immutably, what sort of likeness does the immutable have with the mutable? For it should be clear that the Spirit is neither a creature nor does he in any way possess the nature of the angels, since they are mutable, but he is the Image of the Word and proper to the Father.

Creatures are circumscribed, whereas the Spirit is omnipresent

1.26.7. Again, *the Spirit of the Lord fills the world* [Wis 1.7]. This is what David sings in the psalm: *Where can I go from your Spirit?* [Ps 138.7]. And again in Wisdom it is written: *For your incorruptible Spirit is in all things* [Wis 12.1]. But all things which have come into existence are in discrete places: the sun and the moon and the stars are in the firmament of heaven, while the clouds are in the air. **1.26.8.** As for human beings, the boundaries of the nations are fixed.[62] And the angels *are sent to minister* [Heb 1.14]. And as is written in Job: *the angels came to present themselves before the Lord* [Job 1.6]. And Jacob the patriarch *dreamed, and behold! there was a ladder set up on the earth whose top reached into heaven, and the angels of God were ascending and descending upon it* [Gen 28.12]. But if the Spirit fills all things and is present in the midst of all things through the Word, and if the angels are inferior to the Spirit and are only present where they are sent, there can be no doubt that the Spirit is neither one of

---

[61]Here some mss. continue the quotation: *but rather has perceived some perversity in his angels.*
[62]See Deut 32.8; Acts 17.26.

the things that have come into existence, nor in any way an angel, as you claim, but is superior to the nature of the angels.

Creatures participate in the Spirit, whereas the Spirit is participated in

1.27.1. {1.27} Again, from the following considerations anyone will be able to see that the Holy Spirit is participated in but does not participate—for one must not hesitate to affirm the same things.[63] For it says: *it is impossible for those who were once enlightened, who have tasted the heavenly gift, and who have become partakers of the Holy Spirit and have tasted the good word of God* [Heb 6.4]. The angels and the other creatures participate in the Holy Spirit himself. Thus they can fall away from the one in whom they participate. But the Spirit is always the same. For he is not one of those who participate, but all things participate in him. **1.27.2.** But if he is always the same and participated in,[64] and creatures participate in him, the Holy Spirit can be neither an angel nor a creature in any way, but must be proper to the Word. It is when he is given by the Word that creatures participate in him. For our opponents would have to say that the Son is also a creature, by whom all of us come to participate in the Spirit.

There is a multitude of creatures but just one Spirit

1.27.3. And again, there is one Holy Spirit, but there are many creatures. As for angels, there are *a thousand thousand* and *ten thousand times ten thousand* [Dan 7.10]. And there are many luminaries,[65] and many *thrones and dominions* [Col 1.16], and many heavens,

---

[63] See *Serap.* 1.19.3 and 3.4.1.
[64] Gk. μεθεκτόν. See Didymus, *Spir.* 265.
[65] See Gen 1.14.

cherubim, seraphim, and archangels. Simply put, there is not one creature, but there are many of them, all of them different. But if there is one Holy Spirit and many creatures and many angels, then what sort of likeness does the Spirit have with things that have come into existence? And so, it could not be any clearer that the Spirit is neither of the many nor even an angel, but he is the only one. Or rather, he is proper to the one Word and proper to and the same as the one God in substance.[66]

Conclusion to the section

1.27.4. So then, these arguments about the Holy Spirit demonstrate, of their own accord and on their own merits, that in terms of nature and substance the Spirit has nothing in common with or proper to creatures. Rather, he is different from things that have come into existence, and he is proper to and not foreign to the substance and divinity of the Son. And so, because of this he belongs to the Holy Trinity and their stupidity is put to shame.

THE SPIRIT IS UNLIKE CREATURES: TRINITARIAN ARGUMENTS [1.28–31]

The Church's confession of the Trinity

1.28.1. {1.28} Nonetheless, in addition to these arguments, let us also examine the tradition, teaching, and faith of the Catholic Church from the beginning, which is nothing other than what the Lord gave, and the Apostles preached, and the Fathers preserved. On this the Church is founded, and whoever falls away from it can no longer be nor be called a Christian.

---

[66]This is the only passage in *Serap.* where Athanasius applies the term *homoousios* to the Holy Spirit.

1.28.2. So, the Trinity is holy and perfect, confessed in Father and Son and Holy Spirit. It has nothing foreign or external mixed with it, nor is it composed of Creator and creature, but is entirely given to creating and making. It is self-consistent[67] and indivisible in nature, and it has one activity. **1.28.3.** The Father does all things through the Word in the Holy Spirit. In this way is the unity of the Holy Trinity preserved, and in this way is the one God preached in the Church, *who is above all and through all and in all* [Eph 4.6]— *above all* as Father, as beginning, as source; *through all*, through the Word; *in all*, in the Holy Spirit. It is not a Trinity in name alone and in linguistic expression, but in truth and actual existence. For just as the Father is *"He Who Is,"* [Ex 3.4] so too is his Word *"He Who Is"* and *God over all* [Rom 9.5]. And the Holy Spirit is not without existence, but exists and subsists truly.

1.28.4. And the Catholic Church does not entertain the thought of anything less than these [three] lest she fall to the level of Sabellius and today's Jews, who take after Caiaphas.[68] Nor does she conceive of anything more than these [three] lest she slip into Greek polytheism. And that this is the faith of the Church, let our opponents learn from when the Lord sent the Apostles, how he ordered them to lay this faith down as the foundation of the Church, saying: *Go, make disciples of all nations, baptizing them in the name of the Father, and of the Son, and of the Holy Spirit* [Mt 28.19]. When the Apostles departed, this is how they taught, and this is the proclamation for the whole Church under heaven.

If the Spirit is a creature, God is not a Trinity, but a dyad

1.29.1. {1.29} Therefore, since the Church has this foundation for its faith, let our opponents speak with us once again and respond to this question: Is there a Trinity or a dyad? If there is a dyad, then

---

[67] Gk. ὁμοία ἑαυτῇ, lit. "like itself." See *Serap.* 1.17.1.
[68] For Athanasius's view of Sabellius, see *Serap.* 3.5.3.

you should classify the Spirit with creatures. But if you hold such a thought, it has nothing to do with the one God *who is above all and through all and in all* [Eph 4.6]. For you do not have the *in all* when you separate and alienate the Spirit from the divinity.

1.29.2. And when you think in this way, the baptismal initiation that you believe you perform does not initiate completely into the divinity. For a creature is mixed with it, and like the Arians and the Greeks, you also believe that the created order is divine, just like the God who created it through his own Word. If this is your state of mind, what hope do you have? Who will join you to God if you do not have the Spirit of God himself but the spirit of the created order? What sort of audacity and recklessness do you have, that you bring the Father and his Word down to the level of creatures and yet equate a creature with God? For this is what you are doing when you imagine the Spirit to be a creature and rank him in the Trinity.

1.29.3. What sort of madness afflicts you, that you think unjust thoughts against God, namely, that not all angels nor all creatures but just one of them is classified with God and his Word? For if, as you say, the Spirit is simultaneously an angel and a creature and ranked in the Trinity, then not just one but all the created angels would also have to be ranked with it, and it would no longer be a Trinity but an uncountable throng of divinity, and your baptismal initiation, which once again only appears to initiate into this Trinity, is divided here and there, and due to this variety is rendered insecure. **1.29.4.** Such are your initiatory rites and those of the Arians. For both of you argue against the divinity and worship the created order instead of the God who created all things.[69]

If God is a dyad, Christian baptism is invalid

1.30.1. {1.30} So then, such are the absurdities that result when you say that there is a dyad. But if there is a Trinity—as there truly

[69]See Rom 1.15.

is—and it has been revealed that the Trinity is indivisible and not inconsistent with itself,[70] then the Trinity must have one holiness, and it must have one eternity and immutable nature. For just as there is one faith in the Trinity handed down to us and this is what joins us to God, and just as anyone who removes something from the Trinity and is baptized only in the name of the Father, or only in the name of the Son, or in the Father and the Son without the Spirit, receives nothing, but he and the person who only appears to give the Spirit remain empty and uninitiated (for baptism initiates into the Trinity), **1.30.2.** so too anyone who divides the Son from the Father, or brings the Spirit down to the level of creatures, has neither the Son nor the Father, but lacks God and is *worse than an unbeliever* [1 Tim 5.8] and is anything but a Christian—and rightly so. For just as there is one baptism given in Father and Son and Holy Spirit, and just as there is one faith in the Trinity (as the Apostle said),[71] so too the Holy Trinity, which is identical with itself and united in itself, has nothing in it that belongs to things which have come into existence. This is the indivisible unity of the Trinity, and there is one faith in it. **1.30.3.** But if the Trinity is not like this (now this is what you Tropikoi imagine), and instead you dreamed that the Holy Spirit is called a creature, then you no longer have only one faith, nor only one baptism, but two—one in the Father and Son, and another in an angel who is a creature—and you are bereft of all security and truth. For what sort of fellowship is there between a maker and what he has made? What sort of unity is there between inferior creatures and the Word who made them?

The Spirit's role in the common activity of the Trinity

1.30.4. Because he knew all this, the blessed Paul did not divide the Trinity as you do, but taught its unity when he wrote to the Cor-

---

[70]Gr. οὐκ ἀνόμοιος, lit. "not unlike [itself]."
[71]See Eph 4.5.

inthians about the spiritual gifts and traced them all back to the one God, the Father, saying: *Now there are distributions of gifts, but the same Spirit; and there are distributions of service, but the same Lord; and there are distributions of activity, but the same God who works all of them in all people* [1 Cor 12.4–6]. The gifts which the Spirit distributes to each are bestowed by the Father through the Word. For all that the Father has is the Son's.[72] Thus what is given by the Son in the Spirit is a gift of the Father. **1.30.5.** And when the Spirit is in us, the Word who gives the Spirit is in us, and the Father is in the Word. And so it is just as has been said: *I and the Father will come and make our home with him* [Jn 14.23]. For wherever there is Light, there is also Radiance; and wherever there is Radiance, there is also its activity and luminous grace.

1.30.6. Once again, this is what Paul taught when he wrote a second letter to the Corinthians, saying: *The grace of our Lord Jesus Christ, and the love of God, and the fellowship of the Holy Spirit be with you all* [2 Cor 13.13]. For this grace and gift given in the Trinity is given by the Father through the Son in the Holy Spirit. **1.30.7.** Just as the grace given through the Son is from the Father, so too we cannot have fellowship with the gift except in the Holy Spirit. For it is when we participate in the Spirit that we have the love of the Father and the grace of the Son and fellowship of the Spirit himself. **1.31.1.** {1.31} And so, it is also shown from these considerations that there is one activity of the Trinity. The Apostle does not mean that the gifts given by each are different and distinct, but that whatever gift is given is given in the Trinity, and that all the gifts are from the one God.

1.31.2. So, the Spirit who is not a creature but is united to the Son as the Son is united to the Father, who is glorified together with the Father and Son, who is acknowledged as God along with the Word, and who is active in what the Father accomplishes through the Son—how can anyone say that the Spirit is creature without being guilty of flagrant impiety against the Son himself? For there is nothing which is not brought into being and actualized through the

---

[72]See Jn 16.15.

Word in the Spirit. **1.31.3.** This is sung in the Psalms: *By the Word of the Lord the heavens were made, and by the Spirit of his mouth all their power* [Ps 32.6]. And in Psalm 147: *He will send forth his Word and melt them; he will blow his Spirit and the waters will flow* [Ps 147.18]. And we are justified, as the Apostle said, *in the name of our Lord Jesus Christ and in the Spirit of God* [1 Cor 6.11]. For the Spirit is not divided from the Word. **1.31.4.** Indeed, when the Lord said: *I and the Father will come* [Jn 14.23], the Spirit comes with them and dwells in us in a manner no different than the Son does, as Paul writes to the Ephesians: *that according to the riches of his glory he may grant you to be strengthened with power through his Spirit in the inner man, and that Christ may dwell . . .* [Eph 3.16–17]. And when the Son is in us, the Father is still there, as the Son said: *I am in the Father and the Father is in me* [Jn 14.10].

1.31.5. Hence it was when the Word came to the Prophets that they used to prophesy in the Holy Spirit himself. So when Scripture says, "And the Word of the Lord came,"[73] to such-and-such Prophet, it indicates that he prophesied in the Holy Spirit. **1.31.6.** For in Zechariah it is written: *Yet receive my words and my statutes which I commanded to my servants the prophets by my Spirit* [Zech 1.6]. A little further on, when he rebuked the people, he said: *And they made their heart disobedient, so as not to hearken to my law, and the words which the Lord Almighty sent forth by his Spirit by the hands of the prophets of old* [Zech 7.12]. **1.31.7.** Peter said in Acts: *Men, brothers, it was fitting for the scripture to be fulfilled which the Holy Spirit predicted* [Acts 1.16]. The Apostles cried aloud together: *Sovereign Lord, who made the heaven and the earth and the sea and everything in them, who by the mouth of our father David, your servant, said through the Holy Spirit . . .* [Acts 4.24–25]. **1.31.8.** When he was in Rome, Paul spoke with boldness to the Jews who came to him: *The Holy Spirit was right to have said to your fathers through Isaiah the prophet . . .* [Acts 28.25]. He wrote to Timothy: *The Spirit expressly says that in the last times some will depart from the sound faith, giving heed to a spirit*

[73]This is a frequent formula: e.g. Jer 1.4 and Ezek 16.1.

of error [1 Tim 4.1]. **1.31.9.** Thus whenever the Spirit is said to be in someone, it means that the Word is in him, giving the Spirit. When the prophecy was being fulfilled: *I will pour forth of my Spirit upon all flesh* [Joel 2.28], Paul said: *According as the Spirit of Jesus Christ is supplied to me* [Phil 1.19]. And to the Corinthians he wrote: *Do you seek proof that Christ is speaking in me?* [2 Cor 13.3]. **1.31.10.** If the one speaking in him was Christ, it is clear that the Spirit speaking in him was Christ's. For when Christ was speaking in him, he said once again in Acts: *And now, behold, bound in the Spirit I am going to Jerusalem, not knowing what shall happen to me there; except that the Holy Spirit testifies in every city, saying to me that imprisonment and afflictions await me* [Acts 20.22–23].

1.31.11. Hence, when saints say, "Thus says the Lord," they are not speaking otherwise than in the Holy Spirit, and when they speak in the Spirit, whatever it is that they say, they say it in Christ. When Agabus says in Acts: *Thus says the Holy Spirit* [Acts 21.11], it is not otherwise than by the Word coming to him that the Spirit granted the power to speak in him and to testify to the things that were awaiting Paul in Jerusalem. **1.31.12.** Indeed, when the Spirit again testified to Paul, it was Christ himself who spoke in him, so that the testimony which came from the Spirit was the Word's. Thus also when the Word visited the holy virgin Mary,[74] the Spirit came to her with him, and the Word in the Spirit formed the body[75] and accommodated it to himself, out of a desire to join and present[76] the created order to the Father through himself and *to reconcile all things in himself, making peace between the things that are in heaven and the things that are on earth* [Col 1.20].

---

[74]Athanasius understands the "Power of the Most High" in Lk 1.35 as a reference to the Son; see *Serap.* 1.11.1 and 2.15.2.

[75]I.e. of Jesus.

[76]See *Serap.* 2.9.2.

CONCLUSION [1.32–33]

1.32.1. {1.32} And so, the Divine Scriptures consistently show that the Holy Spirit is not a creature, but is proper to the Word and to the divinity of the Father. Thus the teaching of the saints[77] is in agreement on the holy and indivisible Trinity, and this is the one faith of the Catholic Church. But the irrational fictions of the Tropikoi diverge from the Scriptures and agree with the irrationality of the Ariomaniacs.[78] It is not surprising that they have put on such a pretense to deceive the simple.

1.32.2. But thanks be to the Lord! As you write, their attempt to conceal their true intentions by feigned opposition to the Arians has not gone undetected. Indeed, even the Arians hate them because they only call the Spirit a creature, not also the Word. But in fact everyone condemns them because they are in truth fighting against the Spirit,[79] and soon enough they will be dead, being as they are deprived and devoid of the Spirit. **1.32.3.** To use the words of the blessed Apostle,[80] since they are unspiritual men they cannot receive the gifts of the Spirit of God because these things are spiritually judged. But those whose mind gives thought to what pertains to the truth judge all things and yet are judged by no one. For within themselves they have the Lord revealing himself to them in the Spirit and the Father through himself.

1.33.1. {1.33} So then, even though I am living in the desert, nonetheless, because of the brazenness of those who have turned away from the truth, I have paid no attention to those who would be glad to laugh at the flimsiness and inadequacy of the arguments used in my logical demonstration, and so composed a brief letter. Now I send it to Your Piety. I strongly urge you, when you've read what

---

[77] That is, the Scriptures.

[78] See n. 36 above on the connotations of "irrationality."

[79] Gk. πνευματομαχοῦντες. Athanasius's description of the Tropikoi here will later evolve into a label for those who deny the divinity of the Holy Spirit: οἱ πνευματομάχοι, the "Pneumatomachians" or "Spirit-fighters."

[80] See 1 Cor 2.14–15.

I've written, and find things to be inadequately expressed, to correct some of it and to excuse the rest.

1.33.2. What I have handed on accords with the Apostolic faith that the Fathers handed down to us. I have not made anything up that falls outside of it, but have written only what I learned in harmony with the Holy Scriptures. For it also harmonizes with those passages of the Holy Scriptures cited as proof. **1.33.3.** It is not something made up on the basis of external sources, but it is what the Lord Jesus Christ himself taught the Samaritan woman and, through her, us: the perfection of the Holy Trinity, which is one indivisible divinity. The Truth himself bears witness when he says to the Samaritan woman: *Believe me, woman, the hour is coming and is now here when true worshippers will worship the Father in Spirit and Truth. For the Father seeks such to worship him. For God is Spirit, and those who worship him must worship him in Spirit and Truth* [Jn 4.21–24]. **1.33.4.** From this passage it is clear that the Son is the Truth, as he said: *I am the Truth* [Jn 14.6]. And the Prophet David petitioned for the Truth, saying: *Send forth your Light and your Truth* [Ps 42.3]. Therefore, true worshippers worship the Father but in Spirit and Truth, confessing the Son and the Spirit who is in him. For the Spirit is inseparable from the Son, just as the Son is inseparable from the Father. The Truth himself bears witness to this when he says: *I will send you the Paraclete, the Spirit of Truth, who proceeds from the Father, whom the world cannot receive* [Jn 15.26+14.17]—that is, those who deny that he is from the Father in the Son. Therefore, in imitation of true worshippers they must confess **1.33.5.** and side with the Truth.[81]

1.33.6. And if even after all this, our opponents are still unwilling to learn and still unable to understand, they should at least stop speaking evil. They should not divide the Trinity lest they be divided

---

[81]The ancient Armenian translation expands this sentence considerably: "Therefore, in imitation of true worshippers they must confess, and by the grace of the Lord and through meditation upon the Holy Scriptures you must become very capable of refuting the heretics and make the full and complete word of Truth clear to those who are willing, so that it may be fulfilled, and perhaps even at some point later on they themselves will realize this and turn away from falsehood and side with the Truth."

from life.[82] They should not classify the Holy Spirit with the creatures, lest, like the Pharisees of old who ascribed the works of the Spirit to Beelzebul,[83] they too, on account of equal audacity, incur along with them the punishment which is unpardonable both now and in the future.[84]

---

[82] I.e., eternal life.
[83] See Mk 3.22; Mt 12.24–27; Lk 11.15–19.
[84] See Mk 3.29; Mt 12.31; Lk 12.10.

Letter Two

{formerly known as Letter Two-Three}

INTRODUCTION [2.1.1]

2.1.1. {2.1} I thought what I wrote was ever so brief,[85] and I accused myself of great lethargy for not being able to write as much as is humanly possible against those who are impious toward the Holy Spirit. But some of the brothers, as you write, have requested an epitome of what I have written, so that they might have a brief and readily accessible arsenal from which they can both answer those who ask questions about our faith and refute the impious. On account of this request I have undertaken the present work, confident that if I have omitted something you will supply what is lacking in good conscience.

THE SON IS NOT A CREATURE [2.1.2–2.9.4]

The insolent speculation of the Arians

2.1.2. The Arians, being self-absorbed and thinking, like the Sadducees, that there is nothing greater than or external to themselves, understand the inspired Scriptures with human reasoning.[86] So, when they hear that the Son of the Father is Wisdom and Radiance

---

[85]See *Serap.* 1.1.4; 1.33.1. The first part of Letter Two (2.1.1–2.9.4) is transmitted in the mss. with the following title: "[Letter] of the same [Athanasius] to the same Bishop Serapion against those who claim the Son is a creature." The second part of Letter Two (2.10.1–2.16.4) is transmitted in the mss. with the following title: "Letter of the same [Athanasius] to the same Bishop Serapion on the Holy Spirit."

[86]The sense is not "mere human reasoning," but "reasoning rooted in human experiences." Athanasius holds that the Arians have misinterpreted the Father-Son relationship as described in Scripture because of their misapplication of the notions of human fatherhood and sonship to the divine order.

and Word, they are in the habit of saying, "How can this be?," as if what they cannot conceive cannot be. **2.1.3.** Indeed, they should also occupy their mind with the same sort of questions about the universe. How can creation come into existence when it did not exist? How can a rational human being be formed from the dust of the earth?[87] How can what is corruptible become incorruptible?[88] How was the earth *founded upon the sea*, and how did God *set it upon the rivers* [Ps 23.2]? There is nothing left for them to do except to say to themselves: *Let us eat and drink, for tomorrow we die* [1 Cor 15.32]. Let them do this, so that it may be clear that when they perish, the insanity of their heresy will perish along with them!

The scriptural account of the Son's relation to the Father

   2.2.1. {2.2} So then, this opinion of the Arians is mortal and corruptible. But the true account, which even they should ponder, goes like this: If God is Fountain and Light and Father, it is not right to say that the Fountain has been exhausted or that the Light is without its brilliance or that God is without the Word, lest God be deprived of his Wisdom, his Word, and his Splendor.[89]
   2.2.2. Therefore, if the Father is eternal, the Son must also be eternal. For there can be no doubt that whatever we conceive as being in the Father is also in the Son, as the Lord himself said: *All that the Father has is mine* [Jn 16.15] and "all that is mine is the Father's."[90] And so, the Father is eternal; the Son is also eternal. For the ages came to be through him.[91] As the Father is, so must the Son be, *who, as Paul said, is God over all blessed forever. Amen* [Rom 9.5]. **2.2.3.** In the case of the Father it is not right to say, "There was once when he

[87]See Gen 2.7.
[88]See 1 Cor 15.42, 53–54.
[89]At this point the ancient Armenian translation inserts the following words: "and lest God be Father by changing."
[90]See Jn 17.10.
[91]See Heb. 1.2.

was not."[92] In the case of the Son it is not right to say, "There was once when he was not." The Father is Almighty; the Son is also Almighty, as John said: *Thus he speaks: The one who is and who was and who is to come, the Almighty* [Rev 1.8]. The Father is Light; the Son is Radiance and true Light. The Father is true God; the Son is true God. For such is what John wrote: *We are in him who is true, in his Son Jesus Christ. He is the true God and eternal life* [1 Jn 5.20].

And in sum, there is nothing that the Father has which does not also belong to the Son. Thus the Son is in the Father and the Father in the Son.[93] For what the Father has is in the Son and furthermore is perceived in the Son. This is how one should understand the passage: *I and the Father are one* [Jn 10.30]. For there are not some things in the Father and other things in the Son, but that which is in the Father is in the Son. And what you see in the Son is what you see in the Father. This is the correct understanding of the passage: *He who sees me sees the Father* [Jn 14.9]. **2.3.1.** {2.3} Now that these points are thus demonstrated, whoever says that the Son is a creature is impious. For he will be also compelled to say that the abundant Fountain is a creature, that Wisdom is a creature, and that the Word, in whom all that is the Father's exists, is a creature.

Creatures are servants, whereas the Word is almighty like the Father

One can see particularly well how corrupt the heresy of the Ariomaniacs is from the following consideration. With those whom we are like and with whom we have identity we are the same in substance. For example, since we human beings are alike and have identity, we are the same as each other in substance. For everyone has the same mortality, corruptibility, mutability, and status of coming

---

[92] Athanasius attributed this slogan to Arius as a kind of encapsulation of his entire theology; see *Orationes contra Arianos* 1.11–13.

[93] See Jn 14.10.

from nothing. In a similar way, the angels too, and all other things, are among themselves the same in nature with each other. **2.3.2.** So let our curious opponents investigate whether there is some likeness between the Son and creatures, or whether what belongs to the Son can be found in those who have come into existence, so that they may dare to call God the Word a creature. But nothing of the sort will be found by these utterly reckless men who wander from the road of piety. Among creatures none is almighty and none is ruled by another. For each belongs to God himself. *The heavens proclaim the glory of God* [Ps 18.2]. And *the Lord's is the earth and its fullness* [Ps 23.1]. *The sea fled at his sight* [Ps 113.3]. And all things are the servants of the one who made them, *doing his word* [Ps 102.20] and obeying his command. But the Son is almighty, just as the Father is—this has been written and demonstrated.[94]

Creatures are mutable, whereas the Son is immutable like the Father

2.3.3. Again, among creatures, none is immutable by nature. For some angels did not keep to their own rank,[95] and *the stars are not pure in his sight* [Job 25.5]. And the devil fell from heaven,[96] Adam transgressed,[97] and *all things* [Jn 1.3] are changeable. But the Son is immutable and unchangeable, just as the Father is. Paul has reminded us of this, citing Psalm 101: *And in the beginning, O Lord, you founded the earth, and the heavens are the work of your hands. They will perish but you will remain; they will all grow old like a garment, like a mantle you will roll them up, and they will be changed. But you are the same, and your years will never end* [Heb 1.10–12; Ps 101.26–28]. And again he says: *Jesus Christ is the same yesterday and today and forever* [Heb 13.8].

[94]See *Serap.* 2.2.3.
[95]See Jude 1.6.
[96]See Lk 10.18.
[97]See Gen 3.

Creatures are made from nothing,
whereas the Son makes all things

2.4.1. {2.4} And again, all that has come into existence did not exist and then was brought into existence. For God *made the earth when it was nothing* [Is 40.23]. And he is *the one who calls into existence the things that do not exist* [Rom 4.17]. These are the things which have been made and the creatures. Thus there is a beginning to their coming into existence. For *in the beginning God made heaven and earth* and all that is in them [Gen 1.1]. And again: *My hand made all these things* [Is 66.2]. **2.4.2.** But the Son is *"He Who Is"* [Ex 3.4] and *God over all* [Rom 9.5], just as is the Father—this has been shown.[98] Just as the Son is not made but makes, so too he is not created but creates and does the works of the Father. For through him the ages came into existence,[99] and *all things came to be through him and without him not one thing came to be* [Jn 1.3]. And, as the Apostle showed, using the same psalm: *in the beginning you founded the earth, and the heavens are the work of his hands* [Heb 1.10; Ps 101.26].

2.4.3. And again, no creature is God by nature, but to each of those things that have been brought into being he gave a name that corresponds to what it has become. He named one the heaven and another the earth, some the heavenly lights and others the stars, others the sea, the deeps, the quadrupeds, and moreover, human beings and before them angels, archangels, cherubim, seraphim, powers, rulers, authorities, dominions, and paradise. And thus each of these remains. **2.4.4.** But if some have been called gods, they are not gods by nature but by participation in the Son. For so he spoke: *if he called them gods to whom the Word of God came* [Jn 10.35]. Hence, since they are not gods by nature, there comes a time when some of them change and hear him say: *I said: you are gods and all of you the sons of the Most High, but you will die like men* [Ps 81.6–7]. Such was the one who heard: *You are a human being, and not a god* [Ezek 28.2].

---

[98]See *Serap.* 2.2.2; also 1.28.3.
[99]See Heb 1.2.

2.4.5. But the Son is true God, just as the Father is. For the Son is in the Father and the Father in the Son—this is what John wrote this, as has been shown.[100] And David sings in the psalm: *Your throne, O God, will endure forever and ever; a scepter of justice is the scepter of your kingdom* [Ps 44.7]. And the Prophet Isaiah cries out: *Egypt has toiled, and the merchandise of the Ethiopians, and the Sabeans, men of stature, will pass over to you, and they shall follow after you bound in fetters, and make supplication to you, because God is in you. For you are the God of Israel, and we did not know it* [Is 45.14–15]. Who is the God in whom God is, if not the Son who says: *I am in the Father and the Father is in me* [Jn 14.10]?

The Son is the same as the Father in substance

2.5.1. {2.5} Since all of this is true and written in Scripture, who cannot see, inasmuch as the Son has no likeness to creatures but has all that belongs to the Father, that the Son must be the same as the Father in substance? For if he were to have any likeness to creatures or any kinship with them, then he would be the same as them in substance. Likewise, since he is foreign in substance to those who have come into existence and is the proper Word of the Father, and since he is different from them, and since all that is proper to the Father is his, it follows that he must be the same as the Father in substance. **2.5.2.** This is what the fathers thought, when at the Council of Nicaea they confessed that the Son is "the same as the Father in substance" and "from the substance of the Father."[101] For it was perfectly clear to them that no created substance would ever say: *All that the Father has is mine* [Jn 16.15]. Since a created substance has a beginning to its coming into existence, the phrases "he is" and "he was eternally"

---

[100]See Jn 14.10.

[101]The Nicene Creed reads: "We believe . . . in one Lord Jesus Christ, the Son of God, begotten from the Father as the Only-Begotten, that is, from the substance of the Father, God from God, Light from Light, True God from True God, begotten, not made, the same as the Father in substance . . . "

cannot be said of a created substance. But since these phrases can be said of the Son, and since all the things mentioned earlier that belong to the Father are the Son's, the substance of the Son must not be created, but he must be the same as the Father in substance. **2.5.3.** His substance cannot be created above all for this reason: it is capable of receiving the distinguishing marks[102] of God. Now his distinguishing marks are the characteristics by which God is recognized. For example, that he is almighty, that he is, that he is immutable, and the other things mentioned earlier. Therefore, God himself will not appear to be the same as creatures in substance, as these fools want him to be, as if he possessed what creatures can possess.

The fact that God is called "Father" ensures that the Son is the same as him in substance

2.6.1. {2.6} The impiety of those who call the Word of God a creature can also be refuted in the following manner. Our faith is in Father and Son and Holy Spirit, as the Son himself said to the Apostles: *Go, make disciples of all nations, baptizing them in the name of the Father, and of the Son, and of the Holy Spirit* [Mt 28.19]. He spoke in this way so that on the basis of what we already know we may understand the matters on which we just now spoke.[103] So then, just as we would not call our fathers 'makers' but 'begetters,' and just as no one would call us 'creatures' of our fathers but 'sons' by nature who are the same as our fathers in substance, so too, if God is Father, surely he is Father of one who is his Son by nature and who is the same as him in substance. **2.6.2.** Abraham certainly did not create Isaac, but begot him. Bezalel and Oholiab did not beget all the products in the tabernacle, but made them.[104] The shipbuilder and the housebuilder do not beget what they make, but each produces a

---

[102]Gk. τὰ ἴδια.

[103]I.e., the last section which discussed the Son's unlikeness to creatures and his possession of the distinguishing marks of God.

[104]See Ex 26.1–2.

work, the former a ship and the latter a house. Isaac does not make Jacob but begets him by nature, and Jacob is the same as him in substance. The same holds true for Jacob and Judah and his brothers. **2.6.3.** So then, just as it is insane for anyone to claim that the house is the same as the housebuilder in substance and the ship the same as the shipbuilder in substance, so too it is appropriate for someone to say that every son is the same as his own father in substance.

So if there is Father and Son, then the Son must be Son by nature and in truth. But this is what it means to be the same as the Father in substance, as has been shown by many passages.[105] Indeed, of the things which have been made it is said: *God spoke and they came to be; he commanded, and they were created* [Ps 148.5]. But of the Son it is said: *My heart overflowed with a good Word* [Ps 44.2]. **2.6.4.** Daniel knew the Son of God and knew the works of God. He saw the Son quench the furnace,[106] but he said of the works: *Bless the Lord, all you works of the Lord* [Dan 3.57 LXX]. He listed each of the creatures, but he did not classify the Son with them. For he knew that the Son was not a work, but that through him the works came into existence, and that he is praised and exalted in the Father. **2.6.5.** So then, just as through him God is revealed to those who know him, so too through him *blessing and honor and glory and might* [Rev 5.13] are confessed to the Father, through him and in him, so that such a confession may be, as the Scriptures say, *acceptable* [1 Pet 2.5]. So then, on the basis of many passages and these reasons, it has been demonstrated and is now demonstrated that only the impious would call the Word of God a creature.

---

[105]It is not clear what these "many passages" are: these are not scriptural passages since "same in substance" (ὁμοούσιος) is not used there. Presumably Athanasius is referring to the whole of *Serap.* 2.1.2–2.6.3.

[106]See Dan 3.25.

On the correct interpretation of Proverbs 8.22:
in what sense the Son is created

2.7.1. {2.7} But our opponents adduce that passage written in Proverbs: *The Lord created me as the beginning of his ways for his works* [Prov 8.22], and say: "Look, he created him, and so he is a creature." Therefore, we must also demonstrate on the basis of this passage the extent to which they have erred through their ignorance of the plot of the Divine Scripture. So then, if he is a son, let him not be called a creature. But if he is a creature, let him not be called a son. For in what precedes we have already shown how great a difference there is between a creature and a son. Furthermore, since the baptismal initiation is not valid if it is in the Creator and a creature, but only if it is in the Father and the Son, the Lord must not be called a creature, but Son.

2.7.2. "But," our opponents say, "isn't that what's written in the Scriptures?" Yes, that's what's written in the Scriptures! And it must be said. But what is well said is poorly understood by these heretics. For if they had understood and knew the character of Christianity, they would not have called the Lord of glory a creature, nor stumbled over what is well written. So then, these men *neither know nor understand* [Ps 81.5]. Thus, as it written, *they grope in the darkness* [Ps 81.5]. Nonetheless, we must speak, not only so that in this matter our opponents may be unmasked as the fools that they are, but also so that we do not neglect to refute their impiety and thereby perhaps spark their repentance.

2.7.3. So the character of faith in Christ is as follows: the Son of God, who is God the Word since *in the beginning was the Word, and the Word was God* [Jn 1.1], who is the Father's Wisdom and Power since *Christ is God's Power and God's Wisdom* [1 Cor 1.24], became human at the *end of the ages* [Heb 9.26] for our salvation. **2.7.4.** For John, after he said: *in the beginning was the Word* [Jn 1.1], a little further on added: *and the Word became flesh* [Jn 1.14], which is equivalent to saying: "he became human." And the Lord said of himself: *Why do you seek to kill me, a human being who has spoken the truth to you?* [Jn 7.19+8.40]. And Paul, having learned from him, said: *There is one God, and one Mediator between God and humanity, the human being Jesus Christ* [1 Tim 2.5]. Having become human, fulfilled his human economy, defeated and abolished our death,[107] now he is seated at the right hand of the Father,[108] being in the Father and the Father in him,[109] just as he always was and is forever.

2.8.1. {2.8} This is the character of the faith which we have received from the Apostles through the Fathers. Anyone who reads the Scripture must examine and judge where it speaks of the divinity of the Word and where it speaks of his human acts, so that we do not fall prey to the same delirium that has befallen the Arians[110] by understanding the one when the other is meant. **2.8.2.** So, we know that he is the Word, and so we know that *through him all things were made, and without him not one thing was made* [Jn 1.3], that *by the Word of the Lord the heavens were made* [Ps 32.6], and that *He sends forth his Word and healed all things* [Ps 106.20]. We know that he is Wisdom, and so we know that *God by Wisdom founded the earth* [Prov 3.19], and that the Father *made all things in Wisdom* [Ps 103.24]. We know that he is God, and so we have come to believe that he is the Anointed One, the Christ. For *your throne, O God,* sings David in the psalm, *shall endure forever. A scepter of justice is the scepter of your kingdom. Your love is for justice; your hatred for evil. Therefore, God, your God, has anointed you with the oil of gladness above other kings* [Ps 44.7–8]. And in Isaiah he himself says: *The Spirit of the Lord is upon me, because he has anointed me* [Is 61.1]. Peter too confessed this: *You are the Christ, the Son of the living God* [Mt 16.16].

2.8.3. So likewise, we know that he became human, and so we do not deny whatever is said about him that reflects his humanity,

[107] See 2 Tim 1.10.

[108] See Col 3.1.

[109] See Jn 14.10–11.

[110] At this point the ancient Armenian translation inserts the following words: "and all heretics."

for example, that he was hungry, that he was thirsty, that he was slapped, that he wept, that he slept, and finally, that he accepted death on a cross for our sake. For all of this was written about him. Similarly, the Scripture has not refrained from using the phrase, "he created," but has used it since it applies to human beings. For we human beings have been created and made. But just as, when we hear that he was hungry, slept, and was slapped, we do not deny his divinity, so too, when we hear the phrase, "he created," it would be consistent to remember that, though he is God, he was created a human being. For being created is proper to human beings, as is the case for the other characteristics mentioned above, such as being hungry, and the like.

On the correct interpretation of Mark 13.22: in what sense the Son is ignorant

2.9.1. {2.9} And there is another passage which is well said but poorly understood by our opponents, I mean: *Of that day or that hour no one knows, not even the angels, nor the Son* [Mk 13.32]. Now this passage has a correct interpretation. Yet on the basis of *nor the Son*, our opponents think that his ignorance proves that he is a creature. But such is not the case. God forbid! For just as, when he said: *He created me* [Prov 8.22], he meant it as a reference to his humanity, so too, when he said: *nor the Son*, he meant it as a reference to his humanity.[111] And there is a good reason why he spoke in this way. For he became human, as it is written, and being ignorant is proper to human beings, just like being hungry and all the rest, since they do not know something unless they hear and learn it. **2.9.2.** Therefore, when he became human, he indicated his human ignorance for two reasons: first, so that he could show that he really has a human body; second, since he had human ignorance in his body, so that he could

---

[111]In both cases, "he meant it as a reference to his humanity" translates ἀνθρωπίνως εἴρηκεν.

redeem his humanity from all and cleanse it and so offer it perfect and holy to the Father.

2.9.3. Will the Arians discover yet another pretext? What else will they concoct to murmur about? They have been convicted of misunderstanding the verse: *The Lord created me* [Prov 8.22]. And they have been shown to have no understanding of the verse: *Of that day or that hour no one knows, not even the angels, nor the Son* [Mk 13.32]. For when he says *he created*, he signifies his humanity, that he became human and was created. But when he says: *I and the Father are one* [Jn 10.30], and: *He who sees me sees the Father* [Jn 14.9], and: *I am in the Father and the Father in me* [Jn 14.10], he signifies his eternity and that he is the same as the Father in substance. Likewise, when he says: *No one knows, not even the Son* [Mk 13.32], he again speaks as a human being. For being ignorant is proper to human beings. But when he says: *No one knows the Father except the Son, and no one knows the Son except the Father* [Mt 11.27], so much more does he know the things which have come into existence! **2.9.4.** So then, in the Gospel according to John the disciples said to the Lord: *Now we know that you know all things* [Jn 16.30]. Thus it is clear that there is nothing of which he is ignorant, seeing that he is the Word *through whom all things were made* [Jn 1.3]. But since *that day* is one of the *all things*, it will certainly come to pass through him, even though the Arians in their ignorance burst ten thousand times![112]

---

[112]On several other occasions Athanasius attributes "bursting" to his enemies; see *De decretis* 17; *Orationes contra Arianos* 2.23 and 2.64; *De synodis* 34 and 54. In this, he may be subtly comparing his enemies to Judas Iscariot, who in Acts 1.18 is said to have "burst open in the middle" when he hanged himself.

THE HOLY SPIRIT IS NOT A CREATURE [2.10.1–2.13.3]

We must derive our knowledge about the Spirit
from our knowledge about the Son

2.10.1. {3.1} Perhaps you will wonder why, when I was asked for an epitome and a brief explanation of the letter I had written on the Holy Spirit, you see me, as it were, laying aside what I had said on that subject and writing against those who are impious toward the Son of God and claim that he is a creature. But I know for a fact that you will not blame me when you learn of the reason. On the contrary, Your Reverence will give your approval when you see that the reason I have is a good one. The Lord himself said that the Paraclete *will not speak on his own, but whatever he hears he will speak, for he will take from what is mine and declare it to you* [Jn 16.13–14]. And he gave the Spirit to his disciples from himself when *he breathed on them* [Jn 20.22], and in this way the Father *poured him out on all flesh* [Joel 3.1], as had been written. **2.10.2.** Thus it is with good reason that we speak and write about the Son of God first, so that from our knowledge of the Son we may be able to have true knowledge of the Spirit.

Because the Spirit is proper to the Son,
he is also proper to the Father

For we will find that the way in which we know the Son belongs to the Father corresponds to the way in which the Spirit belongs to the Son. Just as the Son says: *All that the Father has is mine* [Jn 16.15], so too we will find that all these things through the Son are in the Spirit. Just as the Father indicated the Son, saying: *This is my beloved Son, with whom I am well pleased* [Mt 3.17], so too is the Spirit the Son's. **2.10.3.** For the Apostle says: *He has sent the Spirit of his Son into our hearts, crying: "Abba, Father!"* [Gal 4.6]. And it is quite remarkable that, just as the Son says: *all that is mine is the Father's* [Jn 17.10], so too is the Holy Spirit, who is said to be the Son's, also the Father's. For on the one hand the Son himself says: *When the Paraclete comes, whom I will send you from the Father, the Spirit of Truth, who proceeds from the Father, he will bear witness about me* [Jn 15.26]. And on the other hand Paul writes: *No one knows the things that belong to a human being except the human spirit who is in him. Thus also no one knows the things that belong to God except the Spirit of God who is in him. Now we have not received the spirit of the world but the Spirit that is from God, so that we might understand the gifts bestowed on us by God* [1 Cor 2.11–12]. **2.10.4.** And you will find in every passage of Divine Scripture that the Holy Spirit, who is said to be the Son's, is also said to be God's: this is precisely what we wrote in our previous letter.[113] Hence, if the Son is not a creature because of the way in which he belongs to the Father and because he is the proper offspring of the Father's substance, but is the same as the Father in substance, then likewise the Holy Spirit is not a creature—indeed, whoever says such a thing is impious!—because of the way in which the Spirit belongs to the Son, and because he is given from the Son to all people and all that he has is the Son's.

If the Son is not a creature, then neither is the Spirit

2.11.1. {3.2} So then, these considerations are sufficient to dissuade anyone, however contentious he may be, from continuing to call *the Spirit of God* [1 Cor 2.11] a creature (who is in God[114] and *scrutinizes the depths of God* [1 Cor 2.10] and is given from the Father through the Son);[115] lest by extrapolating from such an idea he be compelled also to call the Son a creature (who is the Word, the Wisdom, the Character, and the Radiance;[116] when anyone sees him, he

---

[113]See *Serap.* 1.20, 1.30, etc.
[114]See the citation of 1 Cor 2.10–11 in *Serap.* 2.10.3.
[115]See 1 Cor 2.12.
[116]See Heb 1.3.

sees the Father),[117] and in the end hear these words: *Whoever denies the Son does not even have the Father* [1 Jn 2.23]. Indeed, not much time will pass before such a person will speak like the fool: *There is no God* [Ps 13.1]. Nonetheless, in order to demonstrate the refutation of our impious opponents in a more convincing manner, it is a good idea to demonstrate that the Spirit is not a creature on the basis of those passages which demonstrate that the Son is not a creature.

Creatures are from nothing, whereas the Son and the Spirit are from God

2.11.2. Creatures are from nothing and have a beginning to their existence.[118] For *in the beginning God made the heaven and the earth and all that is in them* [Gen 1.1]. But the Holy Spirit is and is said to be from God, as the Apostle said.[119] And if it is reasonable to conclude that the Son is not a creature because he is not from nothing but from God, then of necessity it must be concluded that the Holy Spirit is not a creature because he is confessed to be from God. For creatures are from nothing.

Creatures are anointed and sealed by the Son and the Spirit

2.12.1. {3.3} And again, the Spirit is said to be and is an anointing and a seal. John writes: *But the anointing which you received from him abides in you, and you have no need for anyone to teach you, since, rather, his anointing—his Spirit—teaches you about everything* [1 Jn 2.27]. In the Prophet Isaiah it is written: *The Spirit of the Lord is upon me, because he has anointed me* [Is 61.1]. **2.12.2.** Paul writes: *By believing you have been sealed in him* [Eph 1.13]. And again: *Do*

---

[117] See Jn 12.45.
[118] See *Serap.* 1.22.1–2.
[119] See 1 Cor 2.12

not sadden the Holy Spirit in whom you have been sealed for the day of redemption [Eph 4.30]. So it is creatures who are anointed by him and sealed in him. But if it is creatures who are anointed by him and sealed in him, then the Spirit cannot be a creature. For that which anoints is unlike that which is anointed. Indeed, this anointing is the breath of the Son, so that whoever has the Spirit can say: *We are the good odor of Christ* [2 Cor 2.15]. **2.12.3.** The seal makes an imprint of the Son, so that whoever has been sealed has the form of Christ, as the Apostle says: *My little children, with whom I am again in travail until Christ is formed in you!* [Gal 4.19]. But if the Spirit is the good odor and form of the Son, then it is perfectly clear that the Spirit cannot be a creature. For the Son too, *being in the form of God* [Phil 2.6], is not a creature.

Whoever has the Son has the Spirit, and thereby is the temple of God

2.12.4. And in fact, just as anyone who has seen the Son sees the Father,[120] so too anyone who has the Holy Spirit has the Son. When anyone has him, he is the temple of God, as Paul writes: *Do you not know that you are the temple of God and that the Spirit of God dwells in you?* [1 Cor 3.16]. John says: *By this we know that we remain in him, and he in us, because he has given to us of his Spirit* [1 Jn 4.13]. **2.12.5.** But if it has been confessed that the Son is not a creature because he is in the Father and the Father in him,[121] then there is every necessity that the Spirit is not a creature. For the Son is in him, and he is in the Son. Therefore, whoever receives the Spirit is called *the temple of God.*

---

[120]See Jn 14.9.
[121]See Jn 14.11.

There is a multitude of creatures but the Son
and the Spirit are each of them one

Once again, it is good to understand this issue in the light of the following consideration: if the Son is the Word of God, he is one as the Father is one. **2.12.6.** For *there is one God, from whom are all things, and one Lord Jesus Christ* [1 Cor 8.6]. Therefore, it is said and written that the Son is "only-begotten."[122] But there are many different creatures: angels, archangels, cherubim, principalities, powers, and the others, as has been said.[123] But if the Son is not a creature because he does not belong to the many, but is one as the Father is one, then the Spirit too—for we must derive our knowledge of the Spirit from the Son—cannot in any way be a creature. For he does not belong to the many but is himself one. **2.13.1.** {3.4} The Apostle knows this, saying: *All these things are worked by the one and the same Spirit, who distributes to each individual as he wills* [1 Cor 12.11]. And a little further on: *In the one Spirit all of you have been baptized into one body, and all were made to drink of the one Spirit* [1 Cor 12.13].

Creatures are circumscribed, whereas the Spirit is omnipresent

And again, since we must derive our knowledge about the Spirit from the Son, it will be fitting to provide logical demonstrations based on him. **2.13.2.** So, the Son is everywhere. Because he is in the Father and the Father in him,[124] he rules and holds all things together. And it is written: *In him all things hold together*, both the visible and the invisible, *and he is before all things* [Col 1.17]. But creatures are in the places assigned to them: sun and moon and the other luminaries are in the firmament,[125] angels in heaven, and

---

[122]See Jn 1.14, 1.18, 3.16, and 3.18.
[123]See *Serap.* 1.27.3; 2.4.3.
[124]See Jn 14.11.
[125]See Gen 1.14.

human beings upon the earth. **2.13.3.** But if the Son is everywhere because he is not in places assigned to him but in the Father, and if he is not a creature because he is outside of all things, then it cannot follow that the Spirit is a creature, because he is not in places assigned to him but fills all things and is outside of all things. For thus it is written: *The Spirit of the Lord has filled the world* [Wis 1.7]. And David sings in the psalm: *Where can I go from your Spirit?* [Ps 138.7]. For he is not in a place but outside all things and in the Son, as the Son is in the Father.[126] For this reason then he is not a creature, as has been shown.[127]

The Spirit's Role in the Common Activity of the Trinity [2.13.4–2.16.3]

The Father creates all things through the Word in the Spirit

2.13.4. In addition to all these things, the following consideration will confirm the condemnation of the Arian heresy and once again show that our knowledge of the Spirit is derived from the Son. So, the Son is Creator like the Father;[128] he says: *For whatever I see the Father doing, this is what I also do* [Jn 5.19]. Indeed, *all things came to be through him, and without him not one thing came to be* [Jn 1.3]. But if the Son is Creator like the Father, then he is not a creature. And if he is not one of the created things because all things are created through him, it is clear that the Spirit is also not creature. For it is written about him in Psalm 103: *You take back your Spirit, they die and they return to their dust; you send forth your Spirit, they are created, and you renew the face of the earth* [Ps 103.29–30]. **2.14.1.** {3.5} Seeing that this has been written, it is clear that the Spirit is not a creature but is involved in the act of creating. The Father creates all

---

[126]See Jn 14.11.

[127]See *Serap.* 1.22–31 (esp. 26.1–27.4); 2.11.1–13.3.

[128]See *Serap.* 1.24.5–6.

things through the Word in the Spirit. For where the Word is, there also is the Spirit, and the things created through the Word have their strength to exist through the Spirit from the Word. Thus it is written in Psalm 32: *By the Word of the Lord the heavens were made, and by the Spirit of his mouth all their power* [Ps 32.6].

The Father gives prophetic inspiration through the Word in the Spirit

2.14.2. It is so certain that the Spirit cannot be divided from the Son that there is no need for us to have any doubts about what is now being said. When the Word came to the Prophet, the Prophet said what he said through the Word in the Spirit. This is what is written in Acts, when Peter says: *Men, brothers, it was fitting for the scripture to be fulfilled which the Holy Spirit predicted* [Acts 1.16]. And in Zechariah, when the Word came to him,[129] it is written: *Yet receive my words and my statutes which I commanded to the prophets by my Spirit* [Zech 1.6]. And a little further on, when he rebuked the people, he said: *And they made their heart disobedient, so as not to hearken to my law, and the words which the Lord Almighty sent forth by his Spirit by the hands of the prophets of old* [Zech 7.12]. **2.14.3.** Moreover, when Christ spoke in Paul—as Paul himself said: *Do you seek proof that Christ is speaking in me?* [2 Cor 13.3]—nonetheless, it was the Spirit who administered to him what he should say. For Paul himself writes as follows: *According to the administration of the Spirit of Jesus Christ with respect to me* [Phil 1.19]. Again, when Christ was speaking in him, he said: *Except that the Holy Spirit testifies to me in every city, saying that imprisonment and afflictions await me* [Acts 20.23]. **2.14.4.** For the Spirit is not external to the Word, but is in the Word, and through the Word is in God. Hence the spiritual gifts are given in the Trinity. For as Paul writes to the Corinthians, in their distribution there is the same Spirit and the same Lord and the same

---

[129]See Zech 1.1.

God, *who works them all in every one* [1 Cor 12.6]. The Father himself through the Word in the Spirit works and gives all things.

The unity and indivisibility of the Trinity is the faith of the Catholic Church

2.15.1. {3.6} Indeed, when Paul prayed for the Corinthians, he prayed in the Trinity, saying: *The grace of the Lord Jesus Christ, and the love of God, and the fellowship of the Holy Spirit be with you all* [2 Cor 13.13]. When we participate in the Spirit, we have the grace of the Word and, in the Word, the love of the Father. Just as there is one grace of the Trinity, so too is the Trinity indivisible. **2.15.2.** One can see this in the case of holy Mary herself. For when the angel Gabriel was sent to announce that the Word would descend upon her, he said: *The Holy Spirit shall come upon you* [Lk 1.35]. He was very much aware that the Spirit was in the Word. Then he immediately added: *And the Power of the Most High will overshadow you* [Lk 1.35]. **2.15.3.** For Christ is *the Power and the Wisdom of God* [1 Cor 1.24]. Since the Spirit was in the Word, it should be clear that through the Word the Spirit was also in God. In addition, when the Spirit comes to us, the Son and the Father will also come and make their home in us.[130] **2.15.4.** For the Trinity is indivisible, and there is one divinity of the Trinity, and *there is one God over all, and through all, and in all* [Eph 4.6].

This is the faith of the Catholic Church. For it was in the Trinity that the Lord established and founded the Church, as he said to his disciples: *Go, make disciples of all nations, baptizing them in the name of the Father, and of the Son, and of the Holy Spirit* [Mt 28.19]. If the Spirit were a creature, he would not have ranked him together with the Father, lest the Trinity be inconsistent with itself[131] by being ranked together with something that is foreign and alien to it.

---

[130]See Jn 14.23.
[131]Gk. ἀνόμοιος ἑαυτῇ, lit. "unlike itself."

2.15.5. For what could God have lacked such that he needed to add something alien and be glorified along with it? God forbid! Such is not the case. He himself said: *I am full* [Is 1.11]. Therefore the Lord himself ranked the Spirit together with the name of the Father in order to show that the Holy Trinity is not compounded of two different things, that is, Creator and creature, but that there is one divinity in the Trinity. **2.15.6.** Because Paul learned this, he taught that there is one grace bestowed in the Trinity, saying: *One Lord, one faith, one baptism* [Eph 4.5]. Just as there is one baptism, so too is there one faith. For whoever believes in the Father knows the Son in the Father and knows the Spirit inseparably from the Son. And therefore he believes in both the Son and the Holy Spirit. For there is one divinity of the Trinity, and it is manifested by the one Father.

If the Spirit is a creature, a dyad became
a Trinity when the Spirit was created

2.16.1. {3.7} So then, this is the character of the Catholic faith. But as for those who blaspheme the Spirit and claim that he is a creature, if they do not repent on the basis of what we've said, let them be overcome with shame on the basis of what we're about to say. If there is a Trinity, and if the faith is faith in the Trinity, let them tell us whether the Trinity is always a Trinity or whether there was a point when the Trinity was not a Trinity. So then, if the Trinity is eternal, the Spirit is not a creature since he exists eternally with the Word and is in him. For there was a point when creatures did not exist.[132] But if the Spirit is a creature, and if creatures are from nothing, it is clear that there was a point when the Trinity was not a Trinity but a dyad. **2.16.2.** But could anyone utter something more impious than this? Our opponents are claiming that the Trinity has been established by a process of change and progress, that when it was a dyad it waited for the generation of a creature so that this creature could

---

[132] An allusion to the slogan attributed by Athanasius to Arius; see n. 92 above.

be ranked together with the Father and the Son, and thereby become the Trinity. God forbid that such an idea should ever enter the mind of Christians! **2.16.3.** For just as the Son is not a creature because he is always a son, so too there is no creature in the Trinity because it is always a Trinity. Hence the Spirit is not a creature. For as the Trinity always was, so it is even now; and as it is now, so it always was: it is the Trinity, and in it are the Father and the Son and the Holy Spirit. And *there is one God, the Father who is over all and through all and in all, who is blessed forever. Amen* [Eph 4.6+Rom 9.5].

CONCLUSION [2.16.4]

2.16.4. So then, now that I have written this brief summary as you requested, I am sending it. If I have omitted something, please supply what is lacking, as you are a man of good conscience. Read it *to those who are of the household of faith* [Gal 6.10] and refute those who love contention and utter blasphemies. Perhaps, repenting ever so late, they will purify their own souls of the malice that used to be in them. Indeed, it would be a good idea for them, as it written, *to turn aside and not delay* [Prov 9.18a], lest by delaying they hear what was said by the Lord: *Whoever blasphemes against the Holy Spirit has no forgiveness either in this age or in the age to come* [Mt 12.32].

Letter Three

{formerly known as Letter Four}

Introduction [3.1.1–3.1.3]

3.1.1. {4.1} I have read the letter recently written by Your Reverence.[133] I am so flabbergasted at the shamelessness of the heretics that I have come to realize that nothing can be adequately said about them except what the Apostle enjoined: *After a first and a second admonition, you should avoid someone who is a heretic, knowing that such a person is corrupt and sinful, being self-condemned* [Titus 3.10–11].[134] Because the mind of a heretic is perverse,[135] he inquires, not so that he may hear and be persuaded, not so that he many learn and repent, but simply on behalf of those he has deceived, so that they won't condemn him for his silence.

3.1.2. So then, what has already been said should have been sufficient. It would have been sufficient if after receiving such proofs our opponents had stopped blaspheming the Holy Spirit. But it was not sufficient for them. Once again, by their shamelessness they show that, having formerly trained themselves to fight against the Word,[136] they are now fighting against the Spirit.[137] Soon they will be dead in their irrationality.[138] **3.1.3.** Indeed, even if someone were to answer their most recent questions, they will nonetheless be *fabricators of evil things* [Rom 1.30]. For they seek but have no interest in finding, and they hear but have no interest in understanding.

---

[133]Letter Three is transmitted in the mss. with the following title: "Letter of the same [Athanasius] to the same Serapion likewise on the Holy Spirit."

[134]See *Serap.* 1.15.3 and 3.6.7.

[135]See Mt 17.17.

[136]Gk. Λογομαχεῖν. See *De synodis* 54. Athanasius may be adapting 1 Tim 6.4 and 2 Tim 2.14.

[137]Gk. πνευματομαχοῦντες. See n. 79 above.

[138]On "irrationality," see n. 36 above.

On the Correct Understanding of Father-Son Language [3.1.3–3.6.7]

The insolent questions of the Tropikoi

What sort of clever questions do they ask? "If the Holy Spirit is not a creature," they say, "then is he a son? Aren't he and the Word two brothers?" Then, as you write, they add: "If the Spirit *shall receive from* [Jn 16.14] the Son, and is given from him (for so it is written)," they immediately draw the conclusion: "then is the Father a grandfather, and the Spirit his grandson?" **3.2.1.** {4.2} Who can hear such things and still think that they are Christians and not Greeks? For the Greeks say such things against us in conversation among themselves. Who would want to respond to such foolishness on their part?

The fitting response to such questions

As for myself, after conducting an extensive search for a response that would be appropriate for our opponents, I have found none except the one made to the Pharisees long ago.[139] **3.2.2.** For when the Pharisees asked a question out of malice, the Savior asked them a question in return so that they might realize their own malice. Likewise, when these men ask such questions, let them tell us, or rather, let them answer questions asked of them which are just like the questions they ask us. For if, when they speak, they do not understand their own fabrications, perhaps, when they listen, they will realize their own foolishness.[140] **3.2.3.** If the Holy Spirit is not a creature (as has been shown in our previous letters) but is in God and is given from God, then is he a son, and are there two brothers, the Spirit and the Word? And if the Spirit belongs to the Son, and if the Spirit receives all things from the Son (as he himself said), and

[139]See Mk 11.27–33.
[140]See *Serap.* 1.15.4.

if the Son gave the Spirit to his disciples *after he breathed on them* [Jn 20.22] (for you yourselves even confess such things), then is the Father a grandfather and the Spirit his grandson?

Now it is only fair that you be asked, based on the same Scriptures, the same questions as you asked us. **3.2.4.** So then, if you deny what is said in the Scriptures, you can no longer be called Christians, and it is only fair that you ask us questions since we are Christians. But if you read the same Scriptures as we do, we must ask you questions about these same Scriptures. **3.2.5.** So tell us, and do not hesitate: is the Spirit a son and the Father a grandfather? Now if, like the Pharisees long ago,[141] you ponder the matter and say to each other: "If we say, 'He is a son,' then we will hear the question, 'Where is that written?' But if we say, 'He is not a son,' then we are afraid they will say to us, 'How then can it be written: *We have not received the spirit of the world, but the Spirit that comes from God* [1 Cor 2.12].'" **3.2.6.** But if, when you debate such matters among yourselves, you say, "*We don't know* [Mt 25.27]," then the person whom you have asked the questions must keep silent, in obedience to the one who says: *Give no answer to a fool according to his foolishness lest you become like him; rather, give an answer to a fool according to his foolishness lest he seem wise in his own estimation* [Prov 26.4–5]. Silence is the answer that is especially appropriate for you, so that you may realize your ignorance.

Similar insolent questions reveal the
absurdity of the Tropikoi's questions

3.3.1. {4.3} So then, again, it is only fair that you be asked questions based on the questions you have asked us. If the Prophets speak in the Spirit of God, and if the Holy Spirit prophesies in Isaiah (as has been shown in our previous letters),[142] then is the Spirit a Word

---

[141]See Mt 21.25–27.
[142]See *Serap.* 1.31.5–12; 2.14.2–4.

of God, and are there two Words, the Spirit and the Son? **3.3.2.** For it was when the Word of God came to them that the Prophets used to prophesy.[143] And in addition to these points, if *all things came to be through the Word and without him not one thing came to be* [Jn 1.3], and *God by his Wisdom founded the earth* [Prov 3.19] and *made all things by his Wisdom* [Ps 103.24], and if it is written (as has been shown in our previous letters):[144] *You send forth your Spirit, and they are created* [Ps 103.30], then is the Spirit the Word, or did God make all things by two agents,[145] that is, by his Wisdom and by his Spirit? And why does Paul say: *There is one God, from whom are all things, and one Lord, through whom are all things* [1 Cor 8.6]? **3.3.3.** And again, if *the Son is the Image of the invisible Father* [Col 1.15], and if the Spirit is the Image of the Son[146] (for it is written: *Those whom he foreknew he also predestined to be conformed to the Image of his Son* [Rom 8.29]), then in light of these facts is the Father a grandfather? And if the Son comes in the name of the Father, and if, as the Son says, *the Holy Spirit whom the Father will send in my name* [Jn 14.26], then even in this way is the Father a grandfather?

3.3.4. What is your response to these questions, even though every word you speak is cavalier? What are you thinking among yourselves? Or is it the case that you find fault with such questions, now that you realize you are at a loss? But here's what you need to do: Blame yourselves first, since it is you who used to ask such questions. Be obedient to the Scriptures, and when you are at a loss for words, become their disciples at long last.

What the Scriptures say about the Son and the Spirit

In the Scriptures the Spirit is not called son but Holy Spirit and Spirit of God. Just as the Spirit is not called son, so too it is not writ-

---

[143]See e.g. Jer 1.1; Jon 1.1.
[144]See *Serap.* 1.22.5.
[145]Gk. ἐν δυσί, lit. "by two."
[146]See *Serap.* 1.24.7–8.

ten that the Son is the Holy Spirit. **3.3.5.** So then, if the Spirit is not called son, nor is it said that the Son is the Spirit,[147] does the faith diverge from the truth? God forbid! On the contrary, each of the above mentioned names has its own distinct meaning. The Son is the offspring proper to the substance and the nature of the Father: this is what the name signifies. The Spirit, who is said to be of God and is in God, is foreign neither to the nature of the Son nor to the divinity of the Father. Thus there is in the Trinity—in the Father, and in the Son, and in the Spirit himself—one divinity, and in the same Trinity there is one baptism and one faith.[148] **3.3.6.** Indeed, when the Father sends the Spirit,[149] it is the Son who breathes upon his disciples and gives the Spirit to them.[150] For *all that the Father has is the Son's* [Jn 16.15]. It was when the Word came to the Prophets that they used to prophesy in the Spirit, as is written and has been shown.[151] And: *By the Word of the Lord the heavens were made, and by the Spirit of his mouth all their power* [Ps 32.6].

3.4.1. {4.4} Thus the Spirit is not a creature but is said to be proper to the substance of the Word and proper to God and in God. I'll say it again: one must not hesitate to affirm the same things.[152] Even if the Holy Spirit is not called son, yet he is not external to the Son. For he is called *the Spirit of adopted sonship* [Rom 8.15]. And since Christ is *the Power of God and the Wisdom of God* [1 Cor 1.24], it is logical to say that the Spirit is *the Spirit of Wisdom* [Is 11.2] and *the Spirit of Power* [Wis 5.23 and 11.20]. **3.4.2.** When we participate in the Spirit, we possess the Son, and when we possess the Son, we possess the Spirit, as Paul said, crying out in our hearts: *Abba, Father* [Gal 4.6]. But if the Spirit is of God, and if it is written that he is in God (*No one knows the things that belong to God except the Spirit of*

---

[147]Here we prefer to read ὁ υἱός instead of υἱός (PG 26.641; AW I/1.570), following Shapland (183 n. 3[13]).

[148]See Eph 4.5.

[149]See Jn 14.26.

[150]Jn 20.22.

[151]See *Serap.* 1.31.5–12; 2.14.2–4; 3.3.1–2.

[152]See *Serap.* 1.19.3 and 1.27.1.

God who is in him [1 Cor 2.11]), and if the Son said: *I am in the Father and the Father in me* [Jn 14.10], why isn't the same name given to the one and the other, but the one is called Son and the other Spirit? **3.4.3.** If anyone were to ask this question, he would have to be crazy. For such a person is scrutinizing the inscrutable and disregarding the Apostle when he says: *For who has known the mind of the Lord? Who has been his counselor?* [Rom 11.34]. In addition, who would dare to rename what God has named? Let him name what belongs to the created order! Let our opponents tell us, when the created order came into existence by one and the same command, why one thing is the sun, and another thing the heaven, the earth, the sea, and air? **3.4.4.** But if the fools cannot do this since each thing remains as it was brought into being, then so much more does what transcends the created order have eternal permanence. It is not otherwise than that the Father is Father and not grandfather, and the Son is the Son of God and not the father of the Spirit, and the Holy Spirit is Holy Spirit and not grandson of the Father nor the brother of the Son.

*One should believe the Scriptures, not speculate
about them or alter what they say*

3.5.1. {4.5} With these points thus demonstrated, a person would have to be crazy to ask: "Is the Spirit also a son?" Let no one, simply because this is not written in the Scriptures, remove the Spirit from the nature of God and annul the way in which he belongs to God. Rather, as it is written, so should one believe[153] and not say, "Why are things this way and not that way?" If someone were to mull over such questions, he may begin to get the idea to ask, "Where is God? How does God exist?" And thus in the end he may hear the words: *The fool has said in his heart: "There is no God"* [Ps 13.1]. **3.5.2.** The traditions handed down by faith cannot be known by futile investigations.

---

[153]This is possibly an allusion to Heb 11.6.

Indeed, when the disciples heard the words: *Baptize them in the name of the Father, and of the Son, and of the Holy Spirit* [Mt 28.19], they did not futilely investigate why the Son comes second and the Spirit third, or why the whole is a Trinity. Rather, as they heard, so they believed. And they did not ask questions like you: "Is the Spirit a son?" Nor, when the Lord mentioned the Spirit after the Son, did they ask: "Is the Father a grandfather?" For they did not hear the words "in the name of the grandfather," but *in the name of the Father*. And this is the faith which they preached everywhere, having drawn the correct conclusions about it. **3.5.3.** For the faith was not to be stated otherwise than as the Savior stated it, that he is the Son and the other is the Spirit, nor was it right to change the manner in which they have been ranked together. And as for the Father, just as it is not permitted to speak of him otherwise than that he is Father, so too it is impious to ask whether the Spirit is a son or the Son is the Spirit. Sabellius was judged to be a stranger to the Church because he dared to apply the name 'Son' to the Father and the name 'Father' to the Son.[154]

3.5.4. So then, after all this, will anyone still dare to say, when he hears Son and Spirit, "Is the Father a grandfather? Is the Spirit a son?" Yes, some will dare, the Eunomiuses, and the Eudoxiuses, and the Eusebiuses.[155] For having once professed the Arian heresy, they can-

---

[154]See also *Serap.* 1.28.4. Sabellius was thought to have taught that the Father and the Son were merely different modes of the single divine reality known as the υἱοπάτωρ, "the Son-Father." Here Athanasius attempts to score debating points by comparing his opponents' view that the Son becomes the father of the Spirit with the Sabellian view. Note that Athanasius's polemical strategy here differs from that which represents orthodoxy as the middle ground between the extremes of Arianism and Sabellianism.

[155]Gk. Εὐνόμιοι καὶ Εὐδόξιοι καὶ Εὐσέβιοι. Note that Athanasius does not say "Eunomians, Eudoxians, and Eusebians." Eudoxius, formerly bishop of Germanica, became bishop of Antioch in late 357 or early 358. He soon emerged as a staunch advocate of the Sirmium Confession of 357, which had condemned the use of all *ousia* language when speaking about God, and publicly supported the Heteroousian teaching of Aetius. Though soon deposed through the machinations of the emergent Homoiousians, Eudoxius managed to be re-instated by the Council of Seleucia in the fall of 359, and shortly after the Council of Constantinople in January, 360, he became

not keep their tongue from impiety. Who indeed has handed on such things to them? Who taught it? Rest assured, no one taught them this from the Divine Scriptures! It was *from the surfeit of their own heart* [Mt 12.34; Lk 6.45] that they belched up such nonsense.[156]

3.6.1. {4.6} Now if you ask, "Is the Spirit a son?" because we have shown that the Spirit is not a creature, is it time to ask, "Is the Son a father?" because you have learned that the Son is not a creature? For it is through him that the creatures come into existence.[157] Or you may put it this way: "Is the Spirit the Son, and the Son himself the Holy Spirit?" **3.6.2.** But those who think such things will be external to the Holy Trinity and considered godless.[158] For they change the names of Father, Son, and Holy Spirit, transposing them at will on the analogy of human generation, calling them grandsons and grandfathers, and refashioning for themselves the cosmogony of the Greeks. **3.6.3.** Yet this is not the faith of the Church. On the contrary, as the Savior himself said, our faith is in the Father and the Son and the Holy Spirit: the Father who cannot be called grandfather, the Son who cannot be called father, and the Holy Spirit who is given no other name than the one he has. **3.6.4.** It is not permitted to exchange the names of this faith: the Father is always Father, and the Son always Son, and the Holy Spirit is and is said to be always Holy Spirit.

On the correct understanding of the analogy of human begetting

Now in the case of human relations,[159] this is not so, even if the Arians delude themselves that it is. For just as it is written: *God is*

bishop of Constantinople. At this same council Eunomius, a disciple of Aetius, emerged as an eloquent spokesman for the Heteroousians, and was made bishop of Cyzicus. Athanasius, by polemically linking his present opponents, the Eudoxians and the Eunomians, with his purported opponents from the 330s and 340s, the Eusebians, implies a continuity between them that is hard to demonstrate.

[156] See *Serap.* 1.15.1.

[157] See *Serap.* 1.24.5–6.

[158] See *Serap.* 1.30.1–3.

[159] Gk. ἐπὶ μὲν γὰρ τῶν ἀνθρωπίνων, lit. "with regard to human things."

not like a human being [Num 23.19], so too one might say, "human beings are not like God." **3.6.5.** In the case of human relations, a father is not always a father nor a son always a son. The same man becomes the father of a son while being the son of another; and a son, while being the son of a father, can himself become the father of another. For example, Abraham, while being the son of Nahor,[160] became the father of Isaac; and Isaac, while being the son of Abraham, became the father of Jacob. Even though each was a part of his parent and is begotten as a son, each in his turn became the father of another.

But in the case of the divinity, this is not so, since *God is not like a human being* [Num 23.19]. **3.6.6.** For example, the Father is not from a father; accordingly, he does not beget someone who will become the father of another. Nor is the Son a part of the Father; accordingly, he is not something begotten in order to beget a son. Hence in the case of the divinity alone, the Father is and was and always is Father because he is Father in the proper sense[161] and only Father. And the Son is Son in the proper sense and only Son. In these cases, it is certain that the Father is and is said to be always Father and that the Son is and is said to be always Son. And the Holy Spirit is always Holy Spirit. And we have come to believe that he is of God and that he is given from the Father through the Son. **3.6.7.** For thus the Holy Trinity remains immutable, known in the one divinity. Therefore, whoever asks, "Is the Spirit a son?" as if the name could be changed, is self-deluded and beset with insanity. And whoever invents a name for the Father and asks, "Is the Father a grandfather?" *goes astray in his heart* [Ps 94.10; Heb 3.10]. So then, it is not safe to continue to respond to the shamelessness of the heretics. For this would be to fight against the Apostle's exhortation.[162] Rather, we would do well to offer advice, as he himself commanded.

[160]Athanasius is mistaken here: Nahor was Abraham's grandfather; Terah the son of Nahor was Abraham's father (see Gen 11.24–28). He makes the same mistake in *Serap.* 1.16.4.

[161]Gk. κυρίως.

[162]See Titus 3.10; see also *Serap.* 1.15.3; 3.1.1.

CONCLUSION [3.7]

3.7.1. {4.7} These considerations are sufficient for the refutation of your foolish talk. No longer ridicule the divinity. For it is a trait of those who ridicule to ask questions about what is not written in the Scripture and say, "Isn't the Spirit a son? Isn't the Father a grandfather?" Such are the mockeries of the bishop of Caesarea and the bishop of Scythopolis.[163] **3.7.2.** It is sufficient for you to believe that the Spirit is not a creature, but rather that the Spirit is of God and in him there is a Trinity, Father, Son, and Holy Spirit. And there is no need to call the Son by the name Father, nor is it permitted to say that the Spirit is the Son, or that the Son is the Holy Spirit. On the contrary, they are precisely what they are said to be. And in the Trinity there is one divinity, and there is one faith and one baptism, which is given in the Trinity, and one baptismal initiation into our Lord Jesus Christ, through whom and with whom *be glory and might* to the Father along with the Spirit *for ever and ever. Amen.* [1 Pet 4.11].

---

[163]That is, Acacius of Caesarea in Palestine and Patrophilus of Scythopolis, both of whom at the time when Athanasius wrote his letters to Serapion were among the most prominent Homoians.

Jerome's Prologue to the Book of Didymus on the Holy Spirit

When I was staying in Babylon[1] as a tenant of the harlot draped in purple,[2] living according to the law of the Quirites,[3] I got it in my mind to spout some nonsense about the Holy Spirit and dedicated a small work I had started to the Pontiff[4] of the same city. Imagine my surprise when the pot facing away from the north that is seen in Jeremiah after the rod began to boil[5] and the senate of the Pharisees[6] shouted out together. Not a scribe nor even someone pretending to be one but rather everyone in that coalition of ignorance, as if a battle over doctrines had been declared, conspired against me.[7] I returned to Jerusalem at once just as if I were going home after exile,[8] and after having seen the hut of Romulus[9] and the festive rite

[1] That is, Rome, according to Rev 14.8, 16.9, 17.5, 18.2, 10, and 21.

[2] Another designation for Rome, according to Rev 17.1, 4.

[3] Originally designating the inhabitants of the Sabine town Cures, the term "Quirites," after the full integration of Sabines into the Roman community around 268 B.C.E., came to be used of Romans in their capacity as citizens.

[4] From around 382 to 384, Jerome was secretary to Damasus, bishop of Rome from 366 to 384.

[5] Cf. Jer 1.11–13.

[6] The Roman clergy had criticized his relationship with certain aristocratic women in Rome.

[7] Interestingly, Jerome compares the vehemence of the attack on him with that of the doctrinal controversies of his day, as if the ferocity of these debates had already become a commonplace.

[8] Jerome fled Rome in August 385; see his *Ep.* 45.

[9] Lat. *casa Romuli.* One of the "tourist sights" in ancient Rome was a straw hut with a thatched roof on the southwestern corner of the Palatine Hill. It was thought to be the hut of Romulus. The most detailed report can be found in Dionysius of Halicarnassus, *Roman Antiquities*, 2.79.11. Jerome's mention of the *casa Romuli* here is the last eye-witness report from antiquity.

at the Lupercal,[10] I gazed upon the inn where Mary stayed[11] and the cave of the Savior.[12] And so, Paulinian my brother,[13] since the above-mentioned Pontiff Damasus who first urged me to undertake this work has already fallen asleep in the Lord, now at your insistence and with the help of your prayers as much as those of my dear Paula and Eustochium,[14] those venerable handmaidens of Christ, here in Judaea I mumble the song I could not sing *in a foreign land* [Ps 136.4]. For I judge the place which gave birth to *the Savior of the world* [1 Jn 4.14] to be far more glorious than the place which spawned the one who murdered his brother.[15]

By acknowledging the author of this book in the title, I confess that I have preferred to be the translator of another's work rather than to do what certain men do, that is, to adorn a hideous little crow with colors from another.[16] Not long ago I read a certain man's little books on the Holy Spirit[17] and I saw that what the Comic said

---

[10]Lat. *ludicrum Lupercal.* The Lupercal was a cave at the foot of the Palatine Hill where the she-wolf supposedly reared Romulus and Remus. Each year on February 15 odd rites were conducted whose meaning was disputed in antiquity as much as now.

[11]Lat. *diversorium Mariae.* Cf. Lk 2.7. This was one of the "tourist sites" in fourth-century Palestine. See Jerome, *Ep.* 46.11.

[12]Lat. *speluncam Salvatoris.* This cave, not mentioned in the New Testament, was identified as the place of the birth of Jesus. See Jerome, *Ep.* 46.11, where he praises the cave and contrasts it with the Tarpeian rock in Rome. In these lines Jerome is signaling his rejection of Rome by stating his preference for the sites associated with the birth of Jesus rather than with the birth of Rome.

[13]Paulinian was in fact the blood-brother of Jerome.

[14]Jerome provided spiritual direction to the aristocrats Paula (+404) and her daughter Eustochium (+419) while in Rome from 382 to 385. It was the criticism of his association with them that precipitated his departure in 385. Both accompanied Jerome when he fled Rome, and eventually settled with him in Bethlehem where they founded a monastery.

[15]In the story of the foundation of Rome, Romulus kills his brother Remus.

[16]See Horace, *Ep.* 1.3, 14–20, where he compares the writer Celsus, who tends to borrow mostly from others when he writes, to a little crow (*cornicula*) that steals its colors from other birds.

[17]Here Jerome refers to the three books *On the Holy Spirit* hastily written by Ambrose of Milan in 381 at the request of Emperor Gratian. Ambrose based his work closely on that of Didymus.

was true: good Latin does not come from good Greek.[18] The work was utterly devoid of logical structure, completely lacking the force and rigor that would draw the reader even unwillingly to agreement. Rather, everything was languid, weak, elegant, and refined, and adorned here and there with artificial colors.[19]

But my dear Didymus, who has the eye of the bride in the Song of Songs[20] and those lights which Jesus commanded be lifted up to the white harvests,[21] gazed even higher and restored for us the ancient custom of calling a Prophet a "seer."[22] Whoever reads this will certainly recognize how the Latins have robbed him[23] and will scorn the trickling stream once he begins to drink from the gushing spring. However unskilled in speaking he may be, he is not lacking in knowledge,[24] for his very style shows that he is an apostolic man as much as by the authority of his thoughts as by the simplicity of his words.

[18]Lat. *ex graecis bonis latina vidi non bona.* Cf. Terence, *Eunuchus* prol. vv. 7–8: *qui bene vortendo et easdem scribendo male / ex Graecis bonis Latinas fecit non bonas.*

[19]Here Jerome borrows Horace's characterization of Celsus to characterize Ambrose in relation to Didymus.

[20]Cf. Song 1.14, 4.1, 9; 6.4.

[21]Cf. Jn 4.35.

[22]Cf. 1 Sam 9.9.

[23]A reference to Ambrose acting like the little crow that steals its colors from other birds.

[24]Cf. 2 Cor 11.6.

ON THE HOLY SPIRIT

PART I: INTRODUCTION [1–9]

Speaking about the Holy Spirit is a fearsome endeavor [1–2]

1. It is important to investigate all divine matters with reverence and zealous attention, but especially what is said about the divinity of the Holy Spirit, particularly since blasphemy against him is without forgiveness, so much so that the punishment of the blasphemer extends not only throughout the entirety of this present age, but also into the age to come. It was the Savior himself who said that there would be no pardon for whoever blasphemes against the Holy Spirit, *either in this age or in the age to come* [Mt 12.31–32; Mk 3.29]. Hence it is all the more important to investigate what the Scriptures report about him lest any error of blasphemy creep up, at least any error that comes through ignorance.

2. It is normally expedient for a faithful and reverent man in control of his capacities to pass over the enormity of the present question in silence and not to subject a matter so full of danger to his own judgment. Nonetheless, some have raised themselves up to investigate heavenly matters by a kind of recklessness rather than by living rightly, and they brandish certain things concerning the Holy Spirit which are neither read in the Scriptures nor taken from any one of the old ecclesiastical writers. And so, we are compelled to acquiesce to the oft-repeated exhortation of the brothers that we set forth our opinion on the Holy Spirit by means of proof-texts from the Scriptures, lest those who hold contrary opinions deceive people through their lack of familiarity with so great a doctrine and instantly drag them away into the opinion of their enemies without careful reflection.

Evidence for the Holy Spirit is found in both Old and New Testaments [3–9]

3. The designation "Holy Spirit" and the substance[1] which is indicated by this designation are altogether unknown to those who do philosophy outside of Sacred Scripture. For only in our writings, as much in the new as in the old, is reference made to both the idea and name of the Holy Spirit. For David, a man of the Old Testament who was made a sharer in him, used to pray that he would remain in him, saying: *Do not take your Holy Spirit from me!* [Ps 50.13]. And it is said that God stirred up the Holy Spirit in Daniel while he was still a boy, as if the Holy Spirit were already dwelling in him.[2]

4. Similarly, in the New Testament, those men described as pleasing to God were filled with the Holy Spirit. For John leapt upon being sanctified while he was still in his mother's womb.[3] And after Jesus had risen from the dead, he breathed into the face of his disciples, saying: *Receive the Holy Spirit* [Jn 20.22].

5. The books of the Divine Scriptures are filled with such statements. But for the moment I have refrained from enumerating the bulk of them in the present work because it is easy for each reader to discover similar statements for himself on the basis of those we have cited here.

6. But no one ought to consider that the Holy Spirit was one thing in the saints before the coming of the Lord and another thing

---

[1] Lat. *substantia*. In what follows, "substance" is our normal translation of this word; instances in which it is not translated thus will be footnoted.
[2] Cf. Dan 13.45.
[3] Cf. Lk 1.44.

in the Apostles and the other disciples, as if the same name[4] indi-cated different realities. For we are able to produce evidence from the Divine Writings that the same Spirit was both in the Prophets and in the Apostles.

7. In the letter which he wrote to the Hebrews, Paul cited a text from the book of Psalms and signaled that it was said by the Holy Spirit: *And as the Holy Spirit said: "Today if you should hear his voice, harden not your hearts,"* and so forth [Heb 3.7; cf. Ps 94.7–8]. And at the end of the Acts of the Apostles when he was arguing with the Jews, he said: *As the Holy Spirit spoke through the prophet Isaiah to your fathers: "You will hear what is said but will not understand"* [Acts 28.25; cf. Is 6.9–10]. Paul did not write about one Holy Spirit who was in the Prophets before the coming of the Lord as though he himself had another Holy Spirit, but wrote about the Holy Spirit in whom he himself shared, as did all those who were brought to a faith perfect in power.[5]

8. This is why Paul also speaks of him using the definite article, attesting that he is unique and one. Paul says: *And as the Holy Spirit said* [Heb 3.7], not with an unmodified[6] Πνεῦμα ἅγιον (that is, "a holy spirit"), but he adds the definite article, τὸ Πνεῦμα τὸ ἅγιον (that is, *the Holy Spirit*). Paul also signals that Isaiah prophesied using the definite article: Διὰ τοῦ ἁγίου Πνεύματος (that is, *Through the Holy Spirit*) [Acts 28.25], and not with an unmodified Διὰ ἁγίου Πνεύματος (that is, "Through a holy spirit").[7] Furthermore, in that speech in which Peter won over his audience, he said: *It was*

---

[4]Lat. *homonymum.*

[5]Cf. Origen, *De principiis* 1.4: "It is, however, certainly taught with the utmost clearness in the Church, that this Spirit inspired each one of the saints, both the Prophets and the Apostles, and that there was not one Spirit in the men of old and another in those who were inspired at the coming of Christ." Translation by G. W. Butterworth, *Origen: On First Principles* (Gloucester: Peter Smith, 1973), 3–4.

[6]Lat. *non simpliciter.* Here and a few lines down Didymus is employing technical grammatical terminology.

[7]The text of Acts 28.25 in modern critical editions differs from that of Didymus: τὸ πνεῦμα τὸ ἅγιον ἐλάλησεν διὰ Ἡσαίου τοῦ προφήτου. Nonetheless, the point about the use of the definite article remains valid.

appropriate for that Scripture to be fulfilled which the Holy Spirit—τὸ Πνεῦμα τὸ ἅγιον—*spoke beforehand through the mouth of David concerning Judas* [Acts 1.16], demonstrating that the very same Spirit was working in the Prophets and in the Apostles.[8]

9. We will deal with this more fully in what follows when we begin to discuss not only how the Lord came as Word to the Prophets, but also how the Holy Spirit came to them, since he too is possessed inseparably with the only-begotten Son of God.[9]

PART II: THE NATURE OF THE SPIRIT [10–73]

The Holy Spirit is the incorporeal producer of wisdom and sanctification [10–15]

10. Therefore, the very expression "Holy Spirit" is not a meaningless designation but indicates the underlying essence that is associated with the Father and the Son and altogether foreign to creatures. Now creatures are divided into invisible and visible ones, that is, into incorporeal and corporeal ones. The Holy Spirit is not placed among corporeal substances, but indwells the soul and the mind as the producer of speech, wisdom and knowledge. Nor is he placed among invisible creatures, for all such realities are capable of participating in wisdom, the other virtues, and sanctification. **11.** On the contrary, this substance we are now discussing produces wisdom and sanctification. Nor is it possible to find in the Holy Spirit any strength which he receives from some external activity of sanctification and virtue, for a nature such as this would have to be mutable. Rather, the Holy Spirit, as all acknowledge, is the immutable sanctifier, the bestower of divine knowledge and all goods. To put it simply, he exists in those goods[10] which are conferred by the Lord.

---

[8]For similar comments on the definite article, see *Spir.* 73, and Athanasius, *Serap.* 1.4.

[9]See *Spir.* 125.

[10]Lat. *ipse subsistens in his bonis.*

12. Matthew and Luke record the same text in the Gospel. The one said: *How much more will the heavenly Father give good things to those who ask him!* [Mt 7.11], while the other said: *How much more will your heavenly Father give his Holy Spirit to those who ask him!* [Lk 11.13]. From these lines it is apparent that the Holy Spirit is the fullness of the gifts of God and that the goods bestowed by God are nothing other than the subsistent Holy Spirit. For it is this fountain that pours forth all benefits received by the grace of God's gifts.[11]

13. Moreover, that which is essentially good cannot be capable of participating in an external goodness, since it is what bestows goodness on other things. Therefore, it is clear that the Holy Spirit is distinct from not only corporeal but also incorporeal creatures because other substances receive this substance for their sanctification. Indeed, it is not only incapable of participating in a foreign sanctification, but, above all, it is the Bestower and Creator of sanctification.

14. Next, those who enjoy communion with him are called "sharers" in the Holy Spirit, since they have surely been sanctified by him, as is clearly written: *And he insulted the Spirit of grace in whom he was sanctified* [Heb 10.29].[12] This *he* clearly refers to someone who has sinned after receiving the Holy Spirit. But if he had been sanctified through communion with the Holy Spirit, it has been shown that he himself must have been a sharer in him and that the Holy Spirit bestows sanctification.

15. Furthermore, when the Apostle wrote to the Corinthians and listed those who would not attain the kingdom of heaven, he added:

[11]Cf. Didymus, *Trin.* 2.8 (PG 39.532a).

[12]Lat. *Et Spiritu gratiae contumeliam faciens in quo sanctificatus est.* Didymus's citation of Heb 10.29 deviates from the modern critical editions of the Greek text, which is the same as the source of the Vulgate: *et sanguinem testamenti pollutum duxerit in quo sanctificatus est et Spiritui gratiae contumeliam fecerit,* "he has profaned the blood of the covenant in which he was sanctified, and insulted the Spirit of grace." Didymus has therefore not only altered the word order, but also construed the relative clause *in quo sancificatus* as modifying *Spiritus gratiae,* not *sanguis testamenti.* He does the same in *Zacc.* 247, commenting on the πνεῦμα χάριτος of Zech 12.10 and making the same point as in the present passage, that the Spirit of grace is identical with the Holy Spirit.

And you were indeed such things. But now you have been washed, you have been sanctified, you have been justified in the name of our Lord Jesus Christ and in the Spirit of our God [1 Cor 6.11]. He asserts that the Spirit of God is none other than the Holy Spirit. And indeed in what follows he demonstrates this very same point when he says: *No one speaking in the Spirit of God says, "Cursed be Jesus!" and no one says "Jesus is Lord!" except in the Holy Spirit* [1 Cor 12.3]. In this way the Apostle confirms that the Spirit of God is the Holy Spirit.

Why the Holy Spirit is placed with the Father and the Son, not creatures [16–20]

16. Therefore, if the Holy Spirit is the sanctifier, then it is evident that his substance is not mutable but rather immutable. Now the Divine Discourses report in the clearest possible way that immutable substance belongs to God alone and to his only-begotten Son, even as they proclaim that every creaturely substance is changeable and mutable. Therefore, since it has been shown that the substance of the Holy Spirit is not changeable but unchangeable, he will not be ὁμοούσιος [the same in substance] with a creature. To be sure, even a creature would be immutable if he were placed with the Father and the Son, possessing the same unchangeability. For everything which is capable of participating in the good of another is separated from this substance. All such realities are creatures.

17. Now because he is good, God is the source and principle of all goods. Therefore he makes good those to whom he imparts himself; he is not made good by another, but is good. Hence it is possible to participate in him but not for him to participate.[13] Furthermore, his only-begotten Son is *Wisdom* [1 Cor 1.24] and sanctification; he does not become wise but makes wise, and he is not sanctified but sanctifies. For this reason too it is possible to participate in him but not for him to participate.

---

[13] Lat. *capabilis non capax.*

18. Therefore, since an invisible creature (which we customarily call a rational and incorporeal substance) cannot be participated in but is capable of participating (for if it could be participated in, it would not be capable of participating in any good), although it is simple in itself and receives another's good, it must have its good by participation and must not be thought to be placed among those possessed by others but rather among those possessing other things. For the Father and the Son are possessed rather than possessors, but the creature possesses while not being possessed.

19. Let us once more consider the Holy Spirit: if he too is actually holy through participation in another's sanctity, then he should be classified with the rest of creatures. But if he sanctifies those who are capable of participating in him, then he should be placed with the Father and the Son. Both here and in our book *On the Sects*,[14] we have stated to the best of our abilities that the Holy Spirit may be participated in by others and may not participate in other realities. And it is very easy to confirm this statement of ours from the whole of Scripture.

20. The blessed Apostle wrote to the Ephesians and said: *Believing in him, you have been sealed with the promised Holy Spirit, who is the guarantee of our inheritance* [Eph 1.13–14]. For if some are sealed with the Holy Spirit and take on his form and likeness, the Spirit is among those which are possessed and do not possess, seeing that those who possess him are imprinted with his seal. And to the Corinthians the same Apostle writes: *Do not sadden the Holy Spirit in whom you have been sealed* [Eph 4.30],[15] testifying that they are sealed who have accepted communion with the Holy Spirit. For just as someone, who takes up a practice and a virtue, receives into his mind, as it were, a seal and an image of the knowledge which he takes up, so too the one who is made a sharer in the Holy Spirit becomes, through communion in him, simultaneously spiritual and holy.

[14]Nothing is known about this book; it is also mentioned in *Spir.* 93.
[15]Didymus has mistaken the source of this text.

The Holy Spirit is uncircumscribed [21–23]

21. If the Holy Spirit were one of the creatures, he would indeed have a circumscribed substance just like all things which are made. For even if invisible creatures are not circumscribed by place and limits, they are nonetheless limited by the distinctive feature of their substance.[16] But the Holy Spirit, even though he is in many, does not have a circumscribed substance.

22. For when Jesus sent forth those who were to preach what he taught, he filled them with the Holy Spirit, and breathing into their face, he said: *Receive the Holy Spirit* [Jn 20.22], and: *Go, teach all nations* [Mt 28.19], as if he were sending all of them to all nations. For all the Apostles did not travel in equal numbers to all nations, but some went to Asia, some to Scythia, and others were dispersed among the other nations, in accordance with the dispensation of the Holy Spirit whom they possessed among themselves, as the Lord said: *I am with you all days even unto the consummation of the age* [Mt 28.20]. This agrees with the following text: *You will receive power when the Holy Spirit comes upon you, and you will be witnesses to me in Jerusalem and in all Judaea and Samaria and even unto the end of the earth* [Acts 1.8].

23. Therefore, if those stationed at the farthest ends of the earth in order to bear witness to the Lord were separated from each other by the greatest possible distances, and yet the Holy Spirit was present to and indwelt them, then it is clear that the substance of the indweller is uncircumscribed. Being able to do such a thing would be completely foreign to an angelic power; for example, the angel who came to the Apostle in Asia as he was praying could not at the same time be present to others stationed in the other parts of the world.[17]

---

[16]Lat. *proprietate substantiae*.
[17]This is possibly a reference to Acts 20.36. Cf. Didymus, *Trin.* 2.4 (PG 39.488a).

The Holy Spirit and the angels [24–29]

24. But the Holy Spirit is not only present to human beings who are separated from each other, but also he is present to and indwells each single one of the angels, principalities, thrones, and dominions.[18] Just as he sanctifies human beings and has a nature different from that of human beings, so too he sanctifies other creatures and he is different from them in substance. For every creature is sanctified not from his own substance but by communion with another's sanctity.

25. It is true that the angels were called holy in the Gospel when the Savior said that the Son of man would come *in his glory and that of the Father and the holy angels* [Lk 9.26]. And it is written in the Acts of the Apostles that Cornelius *was directed by a holy angel* to invite Peter, the disciple of Christ, to his house [Acts 10.22]. But the angels are holy through participation in the Holy Spirit and through the indwelling of the only-begotten Son of God, who is holy and the communion[19] of the Father, about whom the Savior said: *Holy Father!* [Jn 17.11].

26. Therefore if angels are not holy by their own nature[20] but by participation in the Holy Trinity, it is clear that the substance of the angels is different from the Trinity.[21] For just as the Father sanctifies and is different from those who are sanctified and the Son is different from those whom he sanctifies, so too the Holy Spirit's substance is different from those whom he sanctifies by the bestowal of himself.

27. But if the heretics should propose that the angels are holy due to their natural condition, it follows that they would be forced to say that the angels are ὁμοουσίους [the same in substance] with the Trinity and thus are immutably holy by nature.[22] But if they reject

---

[18]Cf. Col 1.16.

[19]Lat. *communicatio*. This is Jerome's translation of κοινωνία, translated throughout as "communion."

[20]Lat. *substantia*.

[21]See Athanasius, *Serap.* 1.26–27, for similar comments on the angels.

[22]Lat. *iuxta substantiam*.

this and actually say that the angels share a single nature with the rest of the creatures but nevertheless do not have the same sanctity that human beings have, then they are by necessity reduced to saying that the substance of human beings is much better than that of angels. For if this were the case, human beings would have sanctity through communion with the Trinity, whereas the angels, being holy in their own nature, would nonetheless be foreign to the Trinity.

28. But perfect human beings approaching the consummation of sanctity pray to become *equal to angels* [Lk 20.36]. For it is angels who give help to human beings, not human beings to angels, being servants of their salvation[23] and announcing the one who bestows it. This clearly shows that angels are more honorable than and much superior to human beings because they participate in the Trinity with greater affinity (if I may use such an expression) and more completely.

29. Therefore, since the Holy Spirit is different from those whom he sanctifies, he does not share a single nature with the other creatures who receive him. But if his nature is different from those other creatures and he subsists in his own essence, it is clear that he is not created and not made.[24] There are many passages of Scripture which unambiguously prove that his nature is different from all created beings.

The Holy Spirit fills creatures [30–34]

30. It is also said that certain people are filled with the Holy Spirit, but it is never said, either in the Scriptures or in our habitual way of speaking, that anyone is filled with a creature. For neither Scripture nor ordinary language sanctions saying that someone is filled with an angel, with a throne, with a dominion.[25] For this way

---

[23]Cf. Heb 1:14.
[24]Lat. *increatus et ineffectus*.
[25]Cf. Col 1.16.

of speaking is only appropriate for the divine nature. But we do say that certain people are filled with power and teaching, such as, "He is filled with the Holy Spirit," which indicates nothing other than that "they are filled completely and perfectly."

31. It is written about John: *And he will be filled with the Holy Spirit even from his mother's womb* [Lk 1.15]. And again: *Elizabeth was filled with the Holy Spirit* [Lk 1.41]. And then a little further on: *And Zechariah his father*—meaning John's father—*was filled with the Holy Spirit and he prophesied* [Lk 1.67]. And also in the Acts of the Apostles it is said of the many believers who were gathered together that *they were filled with the Holy Spirit* [Acts 2.4].

32. Yet even though the Holy Spirit can be participated in as one can participate in wisdom and teaching, he does not possess the reality[26] of knowledge in name alone. Rather, he is goodness itself because his nature sanctifies and fills the universe with good things. In connection with this, some are also said to be filled with the Holy Spirit, as is written in the Acts of the Apostles: *And all were filled with the Holy Spirit and spoke the word of God with confidence* [Acts 4.31]. For just as the one who is filled with another's knowledge can deliver a speech based on it in a learned and subtle manner because he perfectly grasps it, so too do they speak the word of God with confidence who perfectly receive the Holy Spirit to such an extent that they are filled with him, because the Holy Spirit is present furnishing a word worthy of God.

33. This is also why someone boldly said: *Thus says the Holy Spirit* [Acts 21.11] and the Apostle: *Be filled with the Spirit* [Eph 5.18]. In many passages of the Acts of the Apostles the disciples of the Lord were described as filled with the Holy Spirit: *Carefully choose from among you, brothers, seven men of good reputation filled with the Spirit and wisdom* [Acts 6.3]. Furthermore, it is said concerning Stephen: *But since he was filled with the Holy Spirit, he looked up to heaven and saw the glory of God and Jesus standing at the right hand of God* [Acts 7.55]. And it is said concerning the chosen vessel: *But*

[26]Lat. *substantia*.

Saul, who is also Paul, filled with the Holy Spirit and looking at him, said [Acts 13.9]. In addition, it is noted concerning all believers in common: *The disciples too were filled with joy and the Holy Spirit* [Acts 13.52].

34. But the presence of an angel or some other lofty nature that was made fills neither the mind nor the understanding since it too is filled up from elsewhere. For just as someone who participates in the fullness of the Savior is made full of wisdom, truth, justice, and the word of God, so too whoever is filled with the Holy Spirit is at once filled with all the gifts of God, wisdom, knowledge, faith, and the rest of the virtues.[27] Therefore, whoever fills all creatures, at least those which are able to participate in power and wisdom, is not one of those whom he himself fills. It must be concluded from this that his nature[28] is different from that of all creatures. We have also said elsewhere that the fullness of the divine gifts is implied in the substance of the Holy Spirit.[29]

The Holy Spirit is the substance of the gifts of God [35–53]

35. Next, it is impossible for anyone to receive the grace of God unless he has the Holy Spirit, in whom we confess that all the gifts of God consist. But now the Word demonstrates as clearly as possible that he who has the Holy Spirit acquires perfectly the word of wisdom and the other goods. We said a little before that the Holy Spirit is the substance of the goods of God, when we offered the example: *The Father will give the Holy Spirit to those who ask him* [Lk 11.13], and: *The Father will give good things to those who ask him* [Mt 7.11].[30]

36. Nor ought we to think that the Holy Spirit is divided in substance because it is said that he is *a multitude of goods* [Is 63.7]. For

[27]Note the difference and similarities regarding what virtues one is filled with respectively by the Savior and Holy Spirit: wisdom alone appears in both lists.

[28]Lat. *substantia.*

[29]See *Spir.* 12.

[30]See *Spir.* 12.

he is impassible and indivisible and immutable. But according to the diversity of actions and notions, he is called by multiple titles of good things because he does not give one and the same power equally to those who participate in him through communion in him. For he is suitable for the benefit of each individual and fills with goods those in whom he judges that he ought to be present.

37. After all, Stephen, that first witness to the truth and a man worthy of his name,[31] was said to be *filled with wisdom and the Holy Spirit* [Acts 6.3]—consequently, wisdom is implied when the Holy Spirit abides in him—as the Scripture says: *And the Apostles chose Stephen, a man filled with faith and the Holy Spirit* [Acts 6.5]. And after some other passages: *But Stephen, a man filled with grace and power, was doing great signs and wonders among the people* [Acts 6.8]. And still concerning the same: *And they were not able to withstand the wisdom and Spirit that was speaking in him* [Acts 6.10].[32]

38. For the blessed man was filled with the Holy Spirit, and was made a participant in the faith which comes from the Holy Spirit, in accordance with the passage: *But to another, faith by the same Spirit* [1 Cor 12.9]. Having grace and power according to the same Spirit, he did great signs and wonders among the people. Indeed, he also abounded in those gifts according to the same Spirit which are called the graces of healing and power. For in the first epistle of the Apostle Paul to the Corinthians these are numbered among the gifts of God in the Spirit and according to the Spirit.[33]

39. But Stephen overflowed with divine grace to such an extent that none of his opponents and those disputing with him were able to withstand the wisdom and Spirit who spoke in him. For he was wise according to the Lord and the Holy Spirit. This is why Jesus clearly proclaimed to his disciples: Whenever you are brought to authorities and powers and councils and synagogues, do not be

---

[31] The name "Stephen," from the Greek στέφανος, means "crown." Hence even his name indicates that he was worthy of the "crown of martyrdom."

[32] Or, "in which he spoke." Lat. *et non valebant resistere sapientiae et Spirtui qui loquebatur in illo.*

[33] Cf. 1 Cor 12.8–10.

anxious regarding what you ought to say or how you should speak at that time. For words of wisdom shall be given to you by the Holy Spirit, which not even those very experienced in disputation will be able to oppose.[34]

40. But let us cite the testimony itself, which goes thus: *But when they bring you in to synagogues and authorities and powers, do not be anxious regarding how and what you should respond, for the Holy Spirit will teach you the appropriate response at that hour* [Lk 12.11–12]. And in another [passage of the] Gospel: *Therefore keep it in your hearts not to prepare beforehand how you will respond since I myself will give you a mouth and wisdom which no one will be able to oppose and refute* [Lk 21.14–15].

41. Therefore, since the Holy Spirit grants words to the Apostles against those who go against the Gospel, it is quite clear that the speech of wisdom and knowledge is understood to be in his substance. But it is not the time to examine how the Savior bestows at that hour a mouth and knowledge on his disciples, whom not even those among men considered to be the most eloquent are able to oppose. For our present purpose is to demonstrate that the gifts of the virtues always imply the Holy Spirit, in such a way that he who has him is considered to be filled with the gifts of God.

42. For this reason, in Isaiah God himself says to someone: *I will place my Spirit upon your seed, and my blessings upon your sons* [Is 44.3], seeing that no one ever receives the spiritual blessings of God unless the Holy Spirit precedes. For he who receives the Spirit will consequently have blessings, that is, wisdom, understanding, and so forth. The Apostle wrote as follows about them: *For this reason, from the day we heard we also have not ceased praying for you and begging that you be filled with the knowledge of his will in all wisdom and spiritual understanding, leading a life worthy of God* [Col 1.9–10]. He is saying that those who worthily advance in good deeds through works and speech and prudence are filled with the will of God, who places his Spirit upon them so that they may be filled with wisdom,

---

[34]Cf. Mt 10.17–20; Mk 13.9–11; Lk 21.12–15.

understanding, and the rest of the spiritual goods. But wisdom and understanding, which are in the Holy Spirit, are given by God: *The Lord will give wisdom, and from his face knowledge and understanding* [Prov 2.6], since that wisdom which comes from human beings is not spiritual, but carnal and human.

43. Concerning this, the Apostle wrote: *Not by carnal wisdom, but by the grace of God we have lived our lives in the world* [2 Cor 1.12]. By *carnal wisdom* he means that which arises from human reflections upon corporeal realities. Spiritual and intellectual wisdom, however, concerns itself with invisible and intellectual things and gives its own presence to those who receive it through the activity of the Holy Spirit.

In many other passages the Apostle reminds us that the gifts of God reside in the substance of the Holy Spirit, as in this one: *May the God of hope fill you with all joy and peace in your believing so that you may abound in hope and in the power of the Holy Spirit* [Rom 15.13]. **44.** God, the bestower of goods, in the power of the Spirit grants the hope he promised to those who have the Spirit. With joy and peace he fills those who possess undisturbed, peaceful thoughts, and have minds joyful and calmed from every storm of the passions. Now whoever obtains the aforementioned goods in the power of the Holy Spirit also obtains the correct faith in the mystery of the Trinity.

45. In another passage of the same epistle, Paul says: *The kingdom of God is not food and drink, but justice and peace and joy in the Holy Spirit* [Rom 14.17]. By affirming, for those who were able to hear it, that justice in the Holy Spirit (that is, the entirety of virtue and the peace mentioned above) is united to the joy of God, he most clearly demonstrates that these goods are nothing other than the substance of the Holy Spirit.

46. Therefore, since these goods come to human beings from the bounty of the Holy Spirit, the very calling of the nations ushered in by the teaching of the Gospel is rendered acceptable and holy in the Holy Spirit. Since in this calling it is the Holy Spirit who makes holy and acceptable, he is the substance of the goods of God. And whoever is filled with him acts entirely according to reason, teaching correctly, living irreprehensibly, doing signs and wonders in a true and perfect manner. For he has the strength of the Holy Spirit manifesting to himself the treasure and cause of the fullness of all goods.

47. Now Peter, the disciple of Jesus, knew that the nature of the gifts of God was the bounty of the Holy Spirit. For he said to those who rebuked him for entering the house of Cornelius: *And so, if God gave to them an equal grace when he bestowed the Holy Spirit as he gave to us in the beginning, who was I that I could withstand the Lord?* [Acts 11.17]. In addition, he said to his own: *And God the knower of hearts bore witness to them, giving the Holy Spirit as he gave him to us; and he made no distinction between us and them, by faith cleansing their hearts* [Acts 15.8–9].

48. This also agrees with the point made in many passages, that the Holy Spirit is given by God: *Jacob my son, him I will help; Israel my chosen, him my soul will help; I have put my Spirit in him* [Is 42.1]. And again: *He who gives breath to the people established upon it*—without a doubt this *it* refers to the earth—*and the Spirit to those who tread upon it* [Is 42.5]. Now we have demonstrated above that the Spirit of God is not one thing and the Holy Spirit another.[35]

49. Paul too has said: *The love of God has been poured out into our hearts through the Holy Spirit who has been given to us* [Rom 5.5]. And this: *How much more will your heavenly Father give the Holy Spirit to those who ask him* [Lk 11.13]. Now this Spirit is said to be poured forth by God upon all flesh, so that whoever receives him prophesies and sees visions, according to Joel who speaks in the person of God: *I will pour forth of my Spirit upon all flesh, and your sons will prophesize and your daughters will see visions* [Joel 2.28]. For the Spirit is poured forth for the sake of prophesying and seeing the beauty of truth in the mind.

50. The very expression *pouring forth* also indicates that the substance of the Spirit is uncreated. For when God sends an angel

[35]See *Spir.* 15.

or another creature, he does not say, "I will pour forth of my angel or power or throne or dominion." For this manner of speaking is employed only in the case of those who are participated in by others, as we are now saying and as we said a little before when we spoke of the love of God which is poured forth in the hearts of those who have received the Holy Spirit.[36] *The love of God*, says Paul, *is poured out into our hearts through the Holy Spirit who has been given to us* [Rom 5.5].

51. Since the Savior himself can be participated in, he is also said to be poured forth like perfume: *Your name is perfume poured forth* [Song 1.2]. For just as perfume contained in a bottle has a certain odor which is prevented from being spread outside because it is enclosed within the bottle, yet sends forth its fragrance far and wide when it is poured forth outside the bottle, so too the fragrant name of Christ, before his coming, dwelt in the people of Israel alone, as if the Jews were a closed bottle: *For God is known in Judah, in Israel his name is great* [Ps 75.2]. But when he was refulgent in the flesh, the Savior extended his own name through all the earth, or rather, through all creation, thereby fulfilling what is written: *How great is your name through all the earth!* [Ps 8.2]. In agreement with this, the Apostle said: *For there is no other name given under heaven by which we must be saved* [Acts 4.12]. In addition, in the Psalms it is said to the Lord: *Above everything you have exalted your holy name* [Ps 137.2]. It was only at this point that the following was accomplished: *Your name is perfume poured forth* [Song 1.2].

52. Now the expression *pouring forth* indicates a lavish gift of great bounty and abundance. **53.** And so, whenever one or two receive the Holy Spirit anywhere,[37] "I will pour forth of my Spirit" is not said. For this is only said when the gift of the Holy Spirit is given in abundance to all nations. The Apostle reminded Titus that salvation was given to the nations *not because of works of righteousness done by us, but through the washing of the second regeneration*

---

[36]See *Spir.* 49.
[37]I.e., anywhere in the Scriptures.

and the renewal of the Holy Spirit, whom he has poured forth upon us
abundantly [Titus 3.5–6]. For this too demonstrates that the expression *pouring forth* indicates a bountiful distribution of the Spirit.

Because the Holy Spirit can be participated in and is immutable, he is uncreated [54–60]

54. From all of this we learn that the substance of the Holy Spirit
can be participated in (*capabilis*), and because of this, that he is
uncreated.[38]

55. [Didymus] calls a substance "capable of being participated
in" (*capabilis*) when it is participated in (*capiatur*) by many and
bestows on them a share in itself. But a substance is "capable of
participating" (*capax*) when it is filled through communion with
another substance and participates in (*capiens*) something else,
while not being participated in (*capiatur*) by another.[39]

56. After all, immutability follows upon the capacity to be participated in, and eternity follows upon immutability. Conversely, mutability follows upon the capacity to participate, and being creatable
follows upon mutability. Therefore, no created thing is immutable;
for this reason, no created thing is eternal. **57.** Accordingly, not only
is rationality in human beings subject to mutability and being created, but this same mutability is also found in all creatures.

58. The Divine Utterances demonstrate that the angels changed
and fell. While the multitude of angels and the other pre-eminent
powers persevered in blessedness and holiness, it was nonetheless
those who were similar in nature to them that changed. This most
clearly shows that the former remained in their original state not
because their substance was immutable, but because they were
attentively devoted to God. **59.** For it is impossible for co-equals
to be diverse in nature. Just as individual human beings are mortal

---

[38]See *Spir.* 17.
[39]*Spir.* 55 is an addition by Jerome.

because the entire genus of human beings is mortal, so too, conversely, if some of the superior beings are immortal, all those beings in the same genus and species must surely also be immortal. **60.** Under conditions such as these, if but one angel is revealed to be mutable, then all must be mutable, although they need not change if they persevere in blessedness. Such too is the case for all human bodies: all are divisible, but not all are divided. Even if some of them undergo division, we realize that the rest of them are similar in nature to them.

An objection based on John 1.3, and its refutation [61–64]

61. These explanations show that the Holy Spirit has a nature[40] that is different from visible and invisible creatures. Now if this is true, it is the pinnacle of impiety for some people to classify the Holy Spirit with *all things*, claiming that the passage which states that *all things* have been made by God through the Word[41] indicates that the Holy Spirit has been made.[42] Regarding both of these points, we have shown that the Holy Spirit is not one of the *all things*, but another thing beyond *all things* in nature.[43] As we have shown above,[44] if creatures are divided into corporeal and incorporeal ones, and the Holy Spirit is created, then it is certain that he will be either a visible or an invisible creature, that is, either a corporeal or an incorporeal creature. As we explained earlier,[45] it is utterly impossible for him to be a body, since he teaches and bestows knowledge, and can be participated in by mind and soul.

62. Neither is the Holy Spirit an invisible creature, a point we discussed a little before.[46] This is why Paul proves in the epistle

[40]Lat. *substantia*.
[41]Cf. Jn 1.3.
[42]Cf. Didymus, *Trin.* 3.3 (PG 39.805c) and 3.32 (PG 39.957c).
[43]Lat. *per substantiam*.
[44]See *Spir.* 10 and 16.
[45]See *Spir.* 10.
[46]See *Spir.* 10.

he wrote to the Hebrews that he is different from all angels.[47] He begins by saying: *For to what angel has he ever said: Sit at my right until I shall place your enemies as a stool for your feet? Are they not all ministering spirits sent to minister to those who will receive salvation?* [Heb 1.13–14]. And after some other passages: *How shall we escape if we neglect such a great salvation? This salvation took its beginning when it was declared by the Lord, and it has been confirmed for us by those who heard him. All the while God has borne witness by signs and wonders and various acts of power, and by the distributions of the Holy Spirit according to his will* [Heb 2.3–4].

63. Now the passage that says *to what angel* can be taken as equivalent to saying "to none," since the noun *angel* indicates the nature[48] of all invisible creatures. For neither to any angel nor to another rational creature has God said: *Sit at my right*. And so, the text declares in general terms that *Sit at my right* is not said to any creature. And this holds true in general terms for creation. After he made a declaration about all invisible creatures, he said that they are ministering spirits, for which reason he added: *Are they not all ministering spirits sent to minister?* Not all invisible creatures are sent individually. Nonetheless, since others of the same kind and rank are sent, the rest are themselves somehow sent potentially, sharing in being sent and being of equal substance.

64. Therefore, the Lord is different from all creatures. The Apostle did not want us to neglect the great salvation initiated by the Lord, saying: *How shall we escape if we neglect such a great salvation?* This great salvation began when the Lord declared it and it was confirmed for us by those who heard him. Moreover, God bore witness to this salvation by signs and wonders, and he is different from all the ministering spirits. Likewise, the Holy Spirit. God bore witness to the distributions of the Holy Spirit according to his will, distributing him not by cutting him into parts, but by his communion

---

[47]The "he" here is Christ. What follows in *Spir.* 62–64 is an argument based on the exegesis of Heb 1.13–14 and 2.3–4 that the Holy Spirit's substance, on the parallel of Christ's substance, is different from that of all creatures.

[48]Lat. *substantia*.

with those on whom God decided to bestow him. The Holy Spirit is himself of a nature[49] different from those in which he is dispersed when poured forth.

An objection based on Amos 4.13, and its refutation [65–73]

65. Since we have proved that, according to the sense of the Scriptures, the Holy Spirit is different from all creatures, it is therefore to no avail, or rather, it is with impiety that those who want to show that he is created use the testimony which says that all things were made through the Word[50] so that even the eternal substance may be included among all things. Since as proof that this is his condition they also appropriate the prophetic utterance in which God says: *I am the one who creates spirit* [Am 4.13],[51] we ought to show that even in this they are utterly estranged from understanding the truth.[52]

66. For the subject of the Prophet's utterance was not even the Holy Spirit, as is understood from the very flow and context of the speech, for indeed Amos speaks in the person of God: *Prepare to call upon your God, O Israel, since I am the one who gives strength to thunder and who creates spirit and who proclaims his Christ to humanity, who makes the dawn and foggy mist, and who mounts upon the high places of the earth: Almighty Lord is his name* [Am 4.12–13].

67. Note that God, who had already said he *creates spirit*, at the same time says he *gives strength to thunder* and *makes the dawn and foggy mist*. Therefore, if we closely follow the narrative just cited, namely, *thunder* and *dawn and foggy mist*, we also ought to place

[49]Lat. *substantia*.

[50]Cf. Jn 1.3.

[51]Lat. *Ego creo spiritum*. Gk. ἐγὼ ... κτίζων πνεῦμα. In Greek the word πνεῦμα can mean either "spirit" or "wind," just as in Latin *spiritus* can mean "breath" or "spririt." In the exegesis that follows, Didymus attempts to show that in Am 4.13 it means "wind" rather than being a reference to the "Spirit." In the Vulgate Jerome removes the ambiguity of the Greek with the translation: *creans ventum*.

[52]Cf. Didymus, *Trin.* 3.31 (PG 39.949–58).

spirit in the same narrative order, so that what God says is as follows: "When you call upon me, who am God, who administer the universe, who am the Creator of all things, who give strength to thunder and create spirit, who make the dawn and foggy mist useful for humanity, prepare to call upon me, O Israel, in such a way that, when you have prepared to call upon me and you have prayed to me who have established what I mentioned earlier, you may enjoy happy times and the lavish bestowal of other goods, as I guide all things to you year after year according to the order of nature, with the result that the year flows fruitfully, that the seasons unfold at the right intervals, that thunders rumble at the right time, and that a salutary dawn blows with favorable breezes."[53]

68. Now if *thunder* and *the dawn and the foggy mist* and the creation of *spirit* are understood through the cloud of allegory, they will not indicate the thing itself but a figurative interpretation. **69.** But if, on the contrary, they argue that these things are said about the Holy Spirit in a literal manner[54] on the grounds that mention is made of the creation of the Spirit in the passage which follows: *And who proclaims his Christ to humanity*, then it is also necessary to respond to this.

70. The Hebrew has *he proclaims what he is thinking to humanity*,[55] meaning that he who is the Creator of all things is also the one who inspires the Prophets and through them reveals his will to humanity.[56]

71. Now it is necessary to respond to this claim because certain heretics falsely allege that the Creator is different than the God and Father of the Savior.[57] Declaring this with great impiety, they do not

---

[53]Here Didymus practices a standard exegetical technique in which a passage is explained by paraphrasing it expansively in the style of someone else. The style here is bucolic.

[54]Lat. *manifeste*, i.e. not allegorically, as mentioned in *Spir.* 68.

[55]The reading of the Masoretic Text is: מַה־שֵּׂחוֹ (*mahsēkhō*), "what he is thinking." Apparently, this word was misconstrued as מְשִׁיחוֹ (*māshiakhō*), "his Messiah" or "his Christ."

[56]*Spir.* 70 is an addition by Jerome.

[57]This teaching was typically associated with Marcion and the Manichees.

foresee that their profane conjecture is stricken down by God who says: "I am the one who gives strength to thunder and who creates spirit and who makes and governs the other parts of the world, who proclaims my Christ to humanity. In fact, this latter providential work of mine stands above all my other works, such that I am the cause not only of externals, but also of those things which pertain to the advantage of the soul and the benefit of the mind."

72. Therefore this expression *who creates spirit* I judge to be the same as saying *who creates wind*. Indeed, by his providence God directs those winds produced by the motion of air, according to that passage we read elsewhere: *Who brings forth winds from his treasuries* [Ps. 134.7]. But it is a good thing that in this text he did not say "who created" but *who creates wind*. For if the passage were about the existence of the Holy Spirit, he would have certainly said "who created." For he does not create the same thing continually. Thus it follows that *who creates* is said about wind because winds were not made just once, but inasmuch as they exist, they come into existence daily.

73. But it is not without purpose that in the present case *spirit* is said to be created without the use of the definite article (which in Greek indicates uniqueness).[58] For in this case *spirit* is not holy. In almost every case, the Holy Spirit is named with the use of the definite article, such as: *The Spirit himself*—Αὐτὸ τὸ Πνεῦμα—*bears witness with our spirit* [Rom 8.16]. And elsewhere: *It is the Spirit who gives life*—Τὸ Πνεῦμά ἐστιν τὸ ζωοποιοῦν [Jn 6.64]. And again: *So too no one knows the things of God except the Spirit of God*—τὸ Πνεῦμα Θεοῦ—*for the Spirit*—τὸ Πνεῦμα γάρ—*scrutinizes all things, even the depths of God* [1 Cor 2.10–11]. It is possible to excerpt many such passages from the Sacred Writings. On those rare occasions when the Holy Spirit is named without the use of the definite article, one ought to realize that he is named with some additional indication of his magnificence. It is true that he is sometimes also

---

[58]This parenthetical remark is probably Jerome's. Didymus made similar comments in *Spir.* 8.

mentioned without the use of the definite article when the focus is not on him *per se* but on participation in him, as for example *Elijah's Spirit* [2 Kg 2.15],[59] *Walk by Spirit* [Gal 5.16],[60] and other passages similar to these.

PART III: THE SPIRIT'S ACTIVITY [74–110a]

74. On the basis of the passages I have brought to our attention (as well as many others), we have shown that the Holy Spirit is not a creature and is never classified with created things but is rather always placed together with the Father and the Son. And so, let us now investigate in what way he is not different from either of them.[61]

The Spirit bestows the same grace and love as the Father and Son [75–80]

75. At the end of the second epistle he wrote to the Corinthians, Paul said: *The grace of our Lord Jesus Christ and the love of God and the communion of the Holy Spirit be with you all* [2 Cor 13.13]. This passage clearly shows that there is a single reception of the Trinity, since whoever receives the grace of Christ has it as much by the Father's administering as by the Holy Spirit's bestowing. Now God the Father and the Lord Jesus Christ give grace in the way described in the passage: *Grace be with you and peace from God the Father and the Lord Christ* [Rom 1.7]. It is not the case that the Father gives one

---

[59] But the LXX has the article at 2 Kg 2.15. Perhaps Didymus was thinking of Elisha's words to Elijah in 2 Kg 2.9: "Let a double-share of your Spirit (διπλᾶ ἐν πνεύματι σου) come upon me."

[60] Gk. πνεύματι περιατεῖτε.

[61] Lat. *nunc videamus quam cum utroque habeat indifferentiam.* The word *indifferentia* is unusual in Latin, probably representing the Gk. τὸ ἀδιάφορον or ἀδιαφορία. It appears also in *Spir.* 87 and 100.

grace and the Savior another, inasmuch as Paul writes that the grace given by both the Father and the Lord Jesus Christ is perfected by the communion of the Holy Spirit.

76. Indeed the Spirit himself is also called grace, according to the passage: *And he insulted the Spirit of grace in whom he was sanctified* [Heb 10.29].[62] In Zechariah too God promised that he would pour himself out: that is, he would be most lavish in granting to Jerusalem the Spirit of grace and compassion.[63] For whenever anyone receives the grace of the Holy Spirit, he has it as a gift from God the Father and our Lord Jesus Christ. Therefore, the fact that there is a single grace of the Father and the Son perfected by the activity[64] of the Holy Spirit demonstrates that the Trinity is of one substance.[65]

77. In yet another passage: *The love of God be with all of you* [2 Cor 13.13], it is the Trinity who both grants and sustains the love. In fact the Savior says: *Whoever keeps my commandments and obeys them loves me, but whoever loves me will be loved by my Father, and I will love him* [Jn 14.21]. After all, the Savior's love for those who are loved is not different from the Father's love. For God loves in order to save, since *God so loved the world that he gave his only-begotten Son, so that all who believe in the Son may not perish, but have eternal life* [Jn 3.16]. The same holds true also for the Son, who is life: in order to grant life and salvation, he loves those whom he wants to become better. This is why he says that he loves whoever is loved by the Father. The same point is made in the Prophet: *And he himself will save them because he loved them* [Is 33.22; 35.4].

78. The Apostle bears witness that this love is the fruit of the Holy Spirit, just like the joy and the peace granted by the Father and Son, when he says: *But the fruit of the Spirit is love, joy, and peace* [Gal 5.22]. This love is poured into the hearts of believers by the Holy Spirit: *Indeed, the love of God is poured into our hearts by*

---

[62]See the comments at *Spir.* 14 on Didymus's reading of Heb 10.29.

[63]Cf. Zech 12:10.

[64]Lat. *operatio*, probably representing Gr. ἐνεργεία.

[65]The argument here is that the Holy Spirit is not an activity but a substance that has an activity, and that activity demonstrates substance.

the Holy Spirit [Rom 5.5]. In fact, according to the passages: *And the communion of the Holy Spirit be with all of you* [2 Cor 13.13], and: *If there is any communion with the Spirit* [Phil 2.1], since everyone who has communion with the Holy Spirit through participation in him possesses God's Wisdom and Word and Truth in every way, he will also possess a share[66] of holiness with the Father and the Son and the Holy Spirit. *For God is faithful, through whom you have been called to communion with his Son* [1 Cor 1.9]. **79.** John too writes concerning the Father: *If we walk in the light, just as he himself is in the light, we have communion with him* [1 Jn 1.7]. And again: *But our communion is with the Father and his Son Jesus Christ* [1 Jn 1.3].

80. Therefore, since whoever has communion with the Holy Spirit immediately has communion with both the Father and Son, whenever anyone has the love of the Father, he has it as a gift from the Son through the Holy Spirit. In addition, whenever anyone is a participant of the grace of Jesus Christ, he has the same grace as a gift from the Father through the Holy Spirit.

The Father, Son, and Spirit have a single activity,
indicating a single substance [81–86]

81. On the basis of all these passages it is proved that the activity of the Father and the Son and the Holy Spirit is the same. But those who have a single activity also have a single substance. For things of the same substance—ὁμοούσια—have the same activities, and things of a different substance—ἑτεροούσια—have discordant and distinct activities.[67]

82. Beside these passages just mentioned, countless others teach the unity of the Trinity. We will now cite a few of these one by one.

---

[66]Lat. *consortium.*

[67]Elsewhere Jerome prefers to leave the ὁμοούσιον untranslated (see *Spir.* 16, 27, and 145), but here he supplies the translation *euisdem substantiae*, avoiding *consubstantialis.*

83. When Peter publicly exposed Ananias as a fraud in the passage where Ananias claimed he was offering all the proceeds from the sale of his field, Peter proved the Holy Spirit's unity with God not according to number but according to substance, when he said: *Ananias, why has Satan so filled your heart that you lied to the Holy Spirit and hid away part of the proceeds of the field? Isn't it true that while it remained unsold it remained yours and that when it was sold it was at your disposal? Why have you contrived such a thing in your heart? You have not lied to men, but to God* [Acts 5.3–4].[68] Now if whoever lies to God lies to the Holy Spirit, and whoever lies to the Holy Spirit lies to God, there can be no doubt that the Spirit has partnership[69] with God. And it is understood that in whatever way holiness subsists in God, in the same way deity subsists in the Holy Spirit.

84. Now it is also true that this Holy Spirit, whom we have said is of the same nature as the Father, does not differ from the divinity of the Son. The Savior said to his disciples: *When they bring you in to synagogues and authorities and powers, do not be anxious regarding how and what you should respond, for the Holy Spirit will teach you at that hour what it is fitting to say* [Lk 12.11–12]; *therefore keep it in your hearts not to prepare beforehand how you will respond since I myself will give you a mouth and wisdom which no one will be able to oppose and refute* [Lk 21.14–15].[70] After saying in these passages that "they ought not be anxious regarding what they should respond to opponents because at that hour they will be taught the appropriate response by the Holy Spirit,"[71] he immediately adduces the grounds for this confidence: *Keep it in your hearts not to prepare beforehand how you will respond since I myself will give you a mouth* (that is, a word)[72] *and wisdom which no one will be able to oppose and refute* [Lk 21.14–15]. For after he said that when it is time to respond they will be taught the appropriate response by the Holy Spirit, he says in

---

[68]The example of Ananias also appears in *Spir.* 131 and 259.

[69]Lat. *consortium*.

[70]These are the same two verses cited in *Spir.* 39–40.

[71]Didymus here paraphrases Lk 12.11–12.

[72]This parenthetical remark may be another insertion of Jerome.

what follows: *since I myself will give you a wisdom which no one will be able to oppose and refute* [Lk 21.14–15].

85. These passages show that the wisdom given to the disciples by the Son is the wisdom of the Holy Spirit, and that the teaching of the Holy Spirit is the teaching of the Lord, and that the partnership[73] which the Spirit has with the Son is one in both nature and will. And since it was demonstrated above[74] that the Spirit is associated by nature with the Only-Begotten of God and God the Father—and certainly the Son and Father are one according to the passage: *I and the Father are one* [Jn 10.30]—it is shown that the Trinity is undivided and inseparable according to nature.

86. Also, in another Gospel it is said: *For it is not you who speak but it is the Spirit of your Father who is speaking in you* [Mt 10.20]. Therefore, if the Spirit of the Father speaks in the Apostles, teaching them the appropriate response, and if what they are taught by the Spirit is wisdom, which we cannot understand as anything other than the Son, then it is clear that the Spirit is of the same nature as the Son and as the Father whose Spirit he is. Furthermore, Father and Son are one. Therefore, the Trinity is associated in a unity of substance.

The Spirit is the same nature and power as the Father and Son [87–90]

87. Another scriptural example shows that Trinity has a single nature and power. The Son is called the Hand, the Arm, and the Right-hand of the Father. Just as we have often taught[75] that these terms demonstrate that the one nature lacks difference,[76] so too is the Holy Spirit named the Finger of God because he is conjoined in nature to the Father and the Son.

---

[73]Lat. *consortium*.

[74]See *Spir.* 10–73.

[75]Here Didymus probably refers to his oral teaching. See p. 43 above.

[76]Lat. *unius naturae indifferentiam demonstrari*. See n. 61 above on *indifferentia*.

88. In one of the Gospels, when some were disparaging the miracles of the Lord by saying: *He casts out demons by Beelzebub, the prince of demons* [Lk 11.15], the Savior, asking why they said this, replied: *If it is by Beelzebub that I cast out demons, by whom do your sons cast out demons? But if it is by the Finger of God that I cast out demons, then the reign of God has come upon you* [Lk 11.19–20]. When writing about this same event, another evangelist has the Son say: *But if it is by the Spirit of God that I cast out demons* [Mt 12.28]. These passages show that the Finger of God is the Holy Spirit. Therefore, if a finger is joined to a hand and a hand to him whose hand it is, then without a doubt the finger is ascribed to the substance of him whose finger it is.

89. But be careful not to descend to lowly things, forget what we are now discussing, and thereby depict in your mind a variety of bodily limbs and begin to imagine for yourself their sizes, their inequalities, and other body parts larger or smaller than they, saying "a finger differs in size from a hand by quite a bit and a hand differs likewise from him whose hand it is." For Scripture is speaking here of incorporeal realities, and wishes only to demonstrate the unity of a substance, not also its dimensions.

90. For just as the hand, through which everything is accomplished and worked, is not divided from the body, and just as the hand belongs to him whose hand it is, so also is the finger not separated from the hand of which it is the finger. And so, spurn inequalities and dimensions when you think about God, and understand the unity that obtains among the finger and the hand and the entire body.[77] Now it is by this Finger that the Law was written on tablets of stone [cf. Ex 31.18].

---

[77]The unity of the various parts of the body is recognized by Aristotle as an example of things which are one in themselves (καθ' αὐτό), i.e. essentially or by nature (*Phys.* Δ.6.1016a3).

The Spirit gives the same wisdom and truth
as the Father and Son [91–95]

91. But it is easy enough to prove our faith also through another Scripture. **92.** God is called *Only-Wise* [Rom 16.27] not by receiving wisdom from another. Nor is he named wise through participation in someone else's wisdom. If in fact many are called wise, it is due not to their own nature but to their communion with wisdom. But God is called *Only-Wise* not because he is made wise by participation in another's wisdom or from some other source, but because he generates wisdom and makes others wise. This wisdom is our Lord Jesus Christ. For Christ is *the Power of God and the Wisdom of God* [1 Cor 1.24]. The Holy Spirit is also called the Spirit of Wisdom, since in the old books it is recorded that *Joshua the son of Nun was filled* by the Lord *with the Spirit of Wisdom* [Deut 34.9].

93. Therefore, since God is the *Only-Wise* not by receiving wisdom from any source, but by making others wise and generating wisdom, out of all who are called wise based on his name,[78] he alone is wise. *A multitude of the wise is the salvation of the world* [Wis 6.24]. And: *Those who know themselves are wise.*[79] And again: *When you have been with the wise, you will be wise* [Prov 13.20]. In the same way the Holy Spirit is called the Spirit of Wisdom not by receiving wisdom from some other source. For his very being is the Spirit of Wisdom, and his nature is nothing other than the Spirit of Truth and the Spirit of God. Now we discussed these matters at length in the book *On the Sects.*[80] Hence in order to avoid needlessly repeating the same points, let the previous discussion suffice for us.

94. Therefore, since the Spirit of Wisdom and Truth is inseparable from the Son, he too is Wisdom and Truth. If he were to

[78]Lat. *per nuncupationem.* The thought here is that God alone is properly called wise; all others who are called wise are thus designated because God has made them wise and share in the designation that belongs properly to God.

[79]Lat. *Qui semetipsos cognoscunt, hi sunt sapientes.* This passage cannot be traced to a known scriptural source.

[80]See n. 14 above.

participate in wisdom and truth, at some point he could descend into a state of ceasing to possess what he received from somewhere, namely, wisdom and truth. And the Son, who is himself Wisdom and Truth, is not separated from the Father, whom the words of the Scriptures proclaim as the *Only-Wise* and Truth. We will see that the Holy Spirit, because he is the Spirit of Wisdom and Truth, possesses the same circle of unity and substance[81] as the Son, and, moreover, that the Son is not divided from the substance of the Father.

95. Since *the Son is the Image of the invisible God* [Col 1.15] and *the Form of his substance* [Heb 1.3], whoever is fashioned and formed according to this Image or Form[82] is led into likeness to God (though attaining such a form and image only insofar as the capacity of humans to advance allows). In a similar way, since the Holy Spirit is the seal of God, he seals those who receive the form and image of God and leads them to the seal of Christ, filling them with wisdom, knowledge, and above all faith.

The Spirit is "distributing" like the Father and the Son [96–97]

96. *Now there are varieties of gifts, but the same Spirit; and there are varieties of service, but the same Lord; and there are varieties of activity, but it is the same God who works them all in everyone* [1 Cor 12.4–7]. This manifold fullness of gifts is produced by the Father, multiplied by the Son, and exists through the Holy Spirit. *For to one is given a word of wisdom through the Spirit; to another a word of knowledge according to the same Spirit; to another faith by the same Spirit* [1 Cor 12.8–9]. After the Apostle lists the rest of the gifts, he adds: *But one and the same Spirit works all these, apportioning to each as he wills* [1 Cor 12.11].

---

[81]Lat. *circulum unitatis atque substantiae.*
[82]Lat. *quicumque ad hanc imaginem vel formam imaginantur atque formantur.* The translation cannot capture the parallelism of the Latin.

97. From this we learn that the nature of Holy Spirit is active and "distributing" (if I may speak thus). Accordingly, let us not be taken in by those who say that the Holy Spirit is an activity and not the substance of God.[83] Many other passages also show that the nature of the Holy Spirit is subsistent, as in the passage that the Apostles write: *For it seemed good to the Holy Spirit and to us* [Acts 15.28]. For the expression *it seemed good* does not indicate an activity but a nature, especially since we also find something similar said about the Lord: *as it seemed good to the Lord, so it was done* [Job 1.21].

The Spirit calls to ministry like the Father and Son [98–99a]

98. Next, there are the Spirit's own words that we read very frequently, as in the following passage: *While they were fasting and worshipping*—that is, the disciples of Christ—*the Holy Spirit said: "Set apart for me Barnabas and Paul for the work to which I have called them"* [Acts 13.2]. This voice of divinity and sign of authority indicates that his substance is not created but uncreated. For the Holy Spirit did not call Barnabas and Paul to some other work which is not that of the Father and of the Son, since the ministry which the Spirit entrusted and handed over to them is the ministry of the Father and the Son. Paul said to the Galatians: *For he who has worked in Peter for the apostolate to the circumcised, has worked in me and Barnabas for the gentiles* [Gal 2.9]; they are sent to the nations in the same way by the authority of the Holy Spirit. **99.** Similarly, when Christ works in the Apostles, the ministry of the Spirit is perfected. Because of this, the Apostles confessed that they *spoke in Christ* [2 Cor 2.17], that they *saw him with their own eyes* [1 Jn 1.1], that they were made *ministers of the Word* [Acts 6.4], that is, Christ, and that they were *stewards of the mysteries of God* [1 Cor 4.1].

[83]On this argument, see Andrew Radde-Gallwitz, "The Holy Spirit as Agent, not Activity: Origen's Argument with Modalism and its Afterlife in Didymus, Eunomius, and Gregory of Nazianzus," *Vigiliae Christianae* 65 (2011): 227–248.

The Spirit baptizes like the Father and Son [99b–103]

Next, since the Apostles possessed primacy in priesthood, Christ indicated that they were initiators of the faith by saying: *Go, go and teach all nations, baptizing them in the name of the Father, and of the Son, and of the Holy Spirit* [Mt 28.19]. **100.** And Paul was very correct to write: *There is one Lord, one faith, one baptism* [2 Cor 2.17]. Who, then, is not compelled by the truth itself to admit the absence of difference[84] in the Holy Trinity? For there is one faith in the Father and Son and Holy Spirit, and the baptismal washing is conferred and confirmed in the name of the Father, and of the Son, and of the Holy Spirit.[85]

101. Nor do I think that anyone would be so foolish and insane as to consider a baptism given in the name of the Father and the Son complete without also adding the Holy Spirit. Or think one given in the name of the Father and the Holy Spirit complete if the name of the Son is omitted. Or think one given in the name of the Son and the Holy Spirit complete without the name of Father placed at the beginning. **102.** For even if there could be someone with a stony heart[86] (if I may speak thus) and a very disturbed mind who tries to baptize in such a way that he omits one of the prescribed names—such a man would clearly legislate against the law of Christ![87]—he would still baptize incompletely,[88] or rather, he would be altogether unable to liberate those, whom he thinks he has baptized, from their sins.

103. From these texts we conclude that the substance of the Trinity is indivisible, and that the Father is truly the Father of the Son, and that the Son is truly the Son of the Father, and that the Holy Spirit is truly the Spirit of the Father and God, and especially the

---

[84] Lat. *indifferentia*. See *Spir.* 74.

[85] Cf. Didymus, *Trin.* 2.15 (PG 39.720a); also see Athanasius, *Serap.* 1.29.3 and 2.15.6.

[86] Cf. Ezek 11.19.

[87] Such a baptizer would legislate against the law laid down in Mt 28.19. Didymus here possibly also alludes to Jam 4.12.

[88] See Athanasius, *Serap.* 1.30.

Spirit of Wisdom and Truth, that is, of the Son of God. So then, this is salvation for those who believe.

The Spirit establishes ecclesiastical discipline like the Father and the Son [104–105]

104. Furthermore, the administration of ecclesiastical discipline[89] is made complete in this Trinity. For when the Savior sent his disciples to preach the Gospel and to teach the doctrines of truth, the Father is said to have established in the Church *first Apostles, second prophets, third teachers* [1 Cor 12.28]. On this same topic, the Apostle offers a similar opinion: *And just as we have been approved by God to believe the Gospel, so too we speak, not in order to be pleasing to men, but to God who has approved our hearts* [1 Thess 2.4]. Those whom Christ commanded to be teachers, these same the Father approved, and it is rightfully said that the Holy Spirit established the same as administrators and leaders in the Church.

105. When the Apostle Paul gathered presbyters from various places and many churches at Miletus, he said: *Watch over yourselves and the entire flock over whom the Holy Spirit has set you as bishops to direct the church of the Lord, which he has acquired through his own blood* [Acts 20.28]. If those whom Christ sent to evangelize and baptize the nations are those whom the Holy Spirit placed in charge of the Church and the Father appointed by his decree, there can be no doubt that the Father, Son, and Holy Spirit have a single activity and approval. It follows from this that the Trinity has the same substance.

---

[89]Lat. *disciplina.* By "discipline" here, Didymus means Church order and practice.

The Spirit indwells like the Father and the Son [106–110a]

106. We still need to consider the fact that it is impossible for any creature to dwell in a heart and mind, but that it is possible for God and his Word in the Holy Spirit. For instance, the Father said to a certain group of people: *I will dwell in them and I will walk among them* [2 Cor 6.16; cf. Lev 26.12 and Ezek 37.27]. In addition, someone directed his voice to him: *You dwell in a holy place, O praise of Israel!* [Ps 21.4]. For the *exalted* Creator of all creation *dwells in exalted places* [Ps 112.4–5].

107. The only-begotten Son also dwells in the pure minds and hearts of believers. For the Apostle said that Christ dwells through faith in the inner person in the Spirit when he wrote: *In the Spirit in the inner person Christ dwells through faith in your hearts* [Eph 3.16–17]. He also spoke of himself: *Christ lives in me* [Gal 2.20]. And again: *It is Christ who speaks in me* [2 Cor 13.3]. And our Savior said: *I and my Father will come*—no doubt *to the one who keeps his commands* [Jn 14.21]—*and we will make our dwelling-place with him* [Jn 14.23].[90] Then the following text is added: *If anyone loves me he will keep my word, and I will love him, and to him we will come and make our dwelling-place with him* [Jn 14.23].

108. In another passage, it is said that the entire nature of the rational creatures is the house of the Savior and that Christ is *over his house, whose house we are* [Heb 3.6]. This house of Christ is the temple of God in whom the Spirit of the same God dwells, for when he wrote to the Corinthians, Paul said: *Do you not know that you are the temple of God and that the Spirit of God dwells in you?* [1 Cor 3.16]. Now if the Holy Spirit is also found in the very house and temple where the Savior and Father dwells, this demonstrates that the substance of the Trinity is indivisible. Just a little further on in the same epistle, Paul writes: *Do you not know that your bodies are the temple of the Holy Spirit whom you have from God?* [1 Cor 6.19].

[90]Neither Vulgate nor the Greek contains the words *Ego et Pater*, which may be borrowed from Jn 10.30.

109. Therefore, since we have learned that the Holy Spirit dwells in the mind and the inner person in the same way as the Father and the Son, I will not say that it is silly but that it is impious to claim that he is a creature. After all, it is possible for that which we have learned (I mean the virtues and arts), and for the disturbances, ignorance and passions contrary to these, to dwell in souls, yet not as substances but as accidents. But it is impossible for a created nature to dwell in the mind. Now if it is true that the Holy Spirit unambiguously indwells the soul and heart, surely we ought to believe that, together with the Father and the Son, he is uncreated. **110.** Therefore, everything discussed in the preceding paragraphs has demonstrated that, in accordance with the nature of the Father and the Son, the Holy Spirit is incorruptible and everlasting.

PART IV: THE SPIRIT'S PROCESSION, SENDING, AND PROPER NAMES [110b–131]

The Spirit's "coming forth" from the Father [110b–116]

And so, the Holy Spirit removes all doubt and conjecture regarding himself so that he will not be classified as one of the created substances. He is the Spirit of God, and the words of the Savior in the Gospel declare that he has gone out from the Father: *When the Consoler whom I will send to you comes, the Spirit of Truth who comes forth from the Father, he himself will give testimony about me* [Jn 15.26]. Now the Holy Spirit is called *the Consoler who comes*, being given a name derived from his activity. He is thus named not only because he consoles those whom he has found worthy of himself and renders them free from all sadness and disturbance, but also because he bestows on them incredible joy and gladness, to such an extent that anyone who gives thanks to God for being considered worthy of such an important guest can say: *You have put joy into my heart* [Ps 4.8]. For there is abiding, everlasting joy in the heart of those indwelt by the Holy Spirit.

111. The Spirit, who is the Consoler, is sent from the Son, not in the way that the angels or the Prophets and Apostles are sent to minister, but as is appropriate for the Spirit of God to be sent from Wisdom and Truth.[91] For the Spirit has an undivided nature together with the same Wisdom and Truth. After all, when the Son is sent from the Father, he is not separated and sundered from him, as he remains in him and has him in himself.

112. Furthermore, the Spirit of Truth who is sent by the Son in the way mentioned above comes forth from the Father without moving from one place to another. After all, this is as impossible as it is blasphemous. For if the Spirit comes forth from one place and goes to another, then the Father himself resides in a place, and the Spirit of Truth is circumscribed by a particular location as befits a corporeal nature, and abandoning one place he migrates to another. But just as the Father is not in a place since he is beyond every corporeal nature, so too the Spirit of Truth is in no way confined by any spatial boundary, since he is incorporeal and, to tell the truth, he surpasses every essence of rational creatures.

113. And so, since it is impossible and impious to believe such things about incorporeal beings, we ought to understand that the Holy Spirit goes out from the Father as the Savior himself goes out from God, to which he bears witness when he says: *I have gone out from God and have come* [Jn 8.42]. And just as we separate places and changes of place from incorporeal realities, so too do we distinguish emissions[92] (whether internal or external) from the nature of intellectual realities, since they belong to bodies which can be touched and have extension.

114. And so, we ought to believe the following statements that used ineffable words known by faith alone: the Savior *has gone out from God* [Jn 8.42],[93] and *the Spirit of Truth comes forth from the*

---

[91] Cf. 2 Cor 3.8.

[92] Lat. *prolationes*, undoubtedly representing προβολαί. The term had corporeal overtones, implying a kind of generation in which the offspring was actually a divided-off portion of the parent.

[93] Cf. Jn 16.28 and 17.8.

Father [Jn 15.26]—the same Father who said: *The Spirit who comes forth from me* [Is 57.16]. Indeed, well-said is the passage: *he who comes forth from the Father* [Jn 15.26]. For even though it is possible to say "from God" or "from the Lord" or "from the Almighty," none of these is used. Instead, *from the Father* is used, but not because the Father is different from God Almighty—for it would be criminal to think this! Rather, the Spirit of Truth is said to *come forth from the Father* [Jn 15.26] according to the distinctive feature of the Father[94] and the concept of fatherhood.[95]

115. Although on many occasions the Savior says that he has gone out from God,[96] he nevertheless claims for himself the distinctive feature and, as it were, that kinship (to which we have already devoted much discussion) when he speaks of himself using the term "Father," as when he says: *I am in the Father and the Father is in me* [Jn 14.10], and elsewhere: *I and the Father are one* [Jn 10.30]. An observant reader will find in the Gospel many other passages that are similar to these.

116. And so, regarding this Holy Spirit who comes forth from the Father, the Lord said: *he will testify about me* [Jn 15.26]. In this, he bears testimony similar to the testimony of the Father, about whom the Lord says: *The Father who sent me has borne testimony about me* [Jn 5.37].

The sending of the Spirit by the Father and the Son [117–120]

117. Now when the Son *sends the Spirit of Truth*, whom he called *the Consoler* [Jn 15.26], at the same time the Father also sends him. The Father does not send the Spirit without the Son sending him since he comes through the identical will of the Father and Son, seeing that the Savior speaks through the Prophets (as will be clear

---

[94]Lat. *proprietatem Patris*, probably representing ἰδίωμα, ἰδιότης, or χαρακτὴρ πατέρος.
[95]Lat. *intellectum parentis*, probably representing ἐπίνοια or ἔννοια.
[96]E.g. Jn 8.42.

to anyone who reads through this entire passage): *And now the Lord has sent me and his Spirit* [Is 48.16]. Without a doubt, God sends not only the Son but also the Spirit. **118.** In addition, the Apostle says: *These things have now been announced to you through those who preached the Gospel to you by the Holy Spirit who is sent from heaven* [1 Pet 1.12].

Furthermore, in the Book of Wisdom (which is named Πανά-ρετος, or *All-Perfect*,[97] by those who have obtained from God the gifts of grace), the voice there is understood to be giving thanks to God: *Who has searched out what is in the heavens? Who has come to know your will, unless you have given Wisdom and sent your Holy Spirit from on high? And thus the paths of those on earth were made straight and people were taught what is pleasing to you* [Wis 9.16–18]. **119.** In this text the Father not only gives the Wisdom of God (that is, his Only-Begotten Son), but also sends the Holy Spirit.

120. The Gospel itself also declares that the Father gives and sends the Holy Spirit, when the Savior says: *And I will ask my Father, and he will give to you another Paraclete to be with you forever, the Spirit of Truth* [Jn 14.16–17]. And again: *But the Paraclete, the Holy Spirit, whom the Father will send in my name, he will teach you all things* [Jn 14.26]. These passages are saying that the Father gives another Paraclete [i.e. the Son], another apart from the one who is sent by the Son [i.e. the Spirit][98] according to the passage: *But when he comes, the Paraclete whom I will send you from the Father, the Spirit of Truth* [Jn 15.26]. The Son has not called him *another Paraclete* because they are different in nature, but because they have separate activities.

[97] Jerome keeps this in the Greek; this was a common name for the book among Greek speakers.
[98] Lat. *Nam et in his sermonibus alium Paracletum dare dicitur Pater alium absque eo qui a Filio mittitur.* The confusing thought in this passage has led to several unnecessary conjectural emendations both in the mss. and by Migne and Doutreleau. We follow the reading of A Θ. We have inserted words (in square brackets) to clarify the sense.

The Spirit as the Consoler [121–124]

121. Since the Savior has the role of mediator[99] and ambassador, in virtue of which he prays for our sins as high-priest, *forever saving those who draw near to God through him since he always lives to intercede for them with the Father* [Heb 7.25], the Holy Spirit has been named "Paraclete" in another sense: because he is the consolation for the sorrowing. **122.** But do not think that the natures of the Son and Holy Spirit are different because they have separate activities. After all, we find in other passages that the Spirit Paraclete fulfills the role of ambassador to the Father, as in this one: *For we do not know how we ought to pray as is fitting, but the Spirit himself intercedes for us with inexpressible groanings, and he who searches hearts knows what the Spirit desires since he makes requests for the saints according to God* [Rom 8.26–27].

123. The consolation for which the Holy Spirit is named "Paraclete" is also effected in the hearts of those in need by the Savior. For it is written: *And he has consoled the downcast* of his people [2 Cor 7.6].[100] It is for this reason that he who attained this benefit gave him praise, saying: *Lord, when there was a multitude of cares in my heart, your consolations gave joy to my heart*—or *have shown love to my soul* [Ps 93.19]. For even today we find both readings in different copies.

124. The Father himself is also called *the God of all consolation* [1 Cor 1.3]. He consoles those who are in affliction so that they may attain first salvation and then the crown of glory through patience in their distresses. And so, the Father gives the Spirit, who is the Consoler and Holy and the Spirit of Truth, so that he may always abide with the disciples of Christ. With them the Savior also abides, saying: *Behold! I am with you to the consummation of the age* [Mt 28.20].

[99]Cf. Heb 8.6, 9.15, 12.24.
[100]Lat. *Et humiles populi sui consolatus est*. Didymus has conflated 2 Cor 7.6 with either Is 49.13 or 52.9 to make the subject of the verse be the Lord.

The Spirit as the inspirer of the Prophets [125–131]

125. Since both the Holy Spirit and the Son are always present in the Apostles, it follows from this that the Father is also with them. For he who receives the Son receives the Father, and the Son with the Father makes his home in those who are worthy of his presence.[101] In addition, one instantly finds the Son wherever the Holy Spirit is. Thus, when the Holy Spirit is in the Prophets, causing them to predict future events and do the other things which pertain to the activity of prophets, it is said that the Word of God has come to them. For that phrase which customarily indicates prophetic activity, *Thus says the Lord* [Is 38.5] is preceded by the phrase, *the Word which came to Isaiah* [Is 38.4], or to one of the other Prophets.

126. We know that the Prophets have the Holy Spirit because this is what God clearly says: *Whatever I commanded to my servants the prophets by my Spirit* [Zech 1.6]. In addition, the Savior indicates in the Gospel that the just men and those who prophesied future events to the people before his coming were filled with the breath of the Holy Spirit. For when the Savior asked the Pharisees what they thought about the Christ and heard [their reply] that he would be the son of David, he said: *How is it then that David says about him: "The Lord said to my Lord: Sit at my right hand"? Therefore, if David by the Holy Spirit called him "Lord," how is he his son?* [Mt 22.43–45]. **127.** Furthermore, Peter says to his companions in faith: *It was fitting for the scripture to be fulfilled which the Holy Spirit predicted through the mouth of David of Judah*, and so forth [Acts 1.16]. Again, in the same book: *You who spoke through the Holy Spirit by the mouth of David your servant: "Why is there tumult among the nations, and among the peoples useless murmuring?"* [Acts 4.25].

128. It is reported at the end of the same Acts that the Word of God impelled Isaiah to prophesy, and Isaiah did so at the command of the Holy Spirit: *The Holy Spirit was right when he spoke to your fathers through Isaiah the prophet, saying: "Go to this people and say:*

---

[101]Cf. Jn 14.23.

'You will hear with your ears . . . '" and the rest [Acts 28.25–26]. **129.**
But the Prophet's own book relates that the prophecy Paul claimed
to be pronounced by the Holy Spirit was said by the Lord: *And I
heard,* said Isaiah, *the voice of the Lord saying: "Whom shall I send,
and who shall go to this people?" And I said: "Here I am! Send me."
And he said: "Go, and say to this people: "You will hear with your ears
. . .* Then after a few words, the Lord himself says: *and they turn and
I should heal them.* Then at once the Prophet replied: *How long, Lord?*
[Is 6.8–11]. Although the Lord told the Prophet to say what is written,
and although the Prophet replied to the Lord when commanded by
him, saying: *How long, Lord?*, Paul nevertheless claims that what
the Lord said through the Prophet was actually pronounced by the
Holy Spirit.[102]

130. This clearly shows (as we have often said) that the Lord and
the Holy Spirit have the same will and nature, and that the name of
Lord is also to be understood when the Spirit is mentioned. **131.** For
in [the epistle to the] Corinthians, attributing the name "God" to the
Father and the name "Lord" to Son[103] deprives neither the Father
of his lordship nor the Son of his deity. Likewise, the Holy Spirit is
named Lord by the same rationale by which the Father is Lord and
the Son is God. But if he is Lord, it follows from this that he is also
God (as we said a little earlier when we cited the saying of the Apostle
Peter to Ananias who withheld money).[104] For deity is also to be
understood when we say "Holy Spirit."[105]

---

[102]Thus the witness of Paul helps interpret the Book of Isaiah regarding who
speaks in the Prophets.

[103]Cf. 1 Cor 8.6.

[104]See *Spir.* 83.

[105]This is one of Didymus's three explicit expressions of the divinity of the Holy
Spirit; see also *Spir.* 83 and 224.

Part V: Scriptural Testimonies [132–230]

1. John the Evangelist: John 14.26 [132–145]

The Spirit sent in the name of the Son is the Spirit of the Son [132–139]

132. This line of inquiry finds its point of departure in the passage: *But when the Paraclete, the Holy Spirit, whom the Father will send in my name, comes, he will teach you all things* [Jn 14.26]. And so, come, let us now seek from this text points of agreement with our earlier discussion. **133.** The Savior affirms that the Father sends the Holy Spirit *in his name*. Now, properly speaking, the name of the Savior is "Son," because this name indicates the sharing of nature[106] and (so to speak) what is proper to the persons.[107] Since the Father sends the Holy Spirit in the name of the Son, one should not understand him as a servant, as foreign to, or as cut off from the Son.

134. In addition, just as the Son comes in the name of the Father, saying: *I have come in the name of my Father* [Jn 5.43]—after all, it belongs only to the Son to come in the name of the Father without violating what is proper to Son vis-à-vis the Father and what is proper to the Father vis-à-vis the Son[108]—so too, inversely, no one else comes in the name of the Father, but rather, for example, in the name of the Lord and in the name of Almighty God. You will be able to see this point more clearly by re-reading the Prophets.

135. For instance, Moses, the great minister and servant of God, came in the name of "He Who Is" and in the name of the God of Abraham, Isaac, and Jacob. For God said to him: *Say this to the sons of Israel: "He Who Is" sent me to you* [Ex 3.4]. And again: *Say to them:*

---

[106]Lat. *naturae consortium*.

[107]Lat. *proprietas personarum*. This is the sole appearance of the word *persona* in a Trinitarian context in the treatise. Doutreleau suggests that the underlying Greek is ἰδιότης τῶν προσώπων. Didymus's hesitancy in using the expression (*ut ita dicam*, "so to speak") may indicate that it was a new concept.

[108]Lat. *salua proprietate Filii ad Patrem et Patris ad Filium*.

the God of Abraham, Isaac, and Jacob sent me to you [Ex 3.15]. **136.**
Another example: when he said the following passage about his
righteous servants: *I will command to my servants the prophets by my
Spirit* [Zech 1.6], this sending was given in the name of God. Since
they proved themselves worthy of God, they are said to have come in
the name of God. Again, since they progressed to better things and
stood under the authority of the one God, they came in the name
of Almighty God. **137.** In addition, when the sons of Israel were
sojourning in Egypt, they learned to worship as gods those who are
not and to venerate the fathers of this world[109] with divine honors.
Accordingly, Moses was sent to them under the name of "He Who
Is." He liberated them from false gods and brought them over to true
deity, to the God of their fathers Abraham, Isaac, and Jacob.

138. And so, just as servants who have come in the name of
the Lord point toward the Lord and communicate what is proper
to him[110] because they are subject to and serve him—for they are
servants, after all, of the Lord—so too, the Son who comes in the
name of the Father communicates what is proper to the Father and
his name.[111] These supply the proof that he is the only-begotten Son
of God. **139.** Therefore, the Holy Spirit is sent by the Father in the
name of the Son, and has what is proper to the Son insofar as he[112]
is God, but does not have sonship such that he[113] is God's son. This
shows that he is joined to the Son in unity. For this reason, he is also
called the Spirit of the Son, and by adoption makes sons of those who
wanted to receive him: *For since you are sons of God, the Father has
sent the Spirit of his Son into your hearts, crying out, "Abba, Father!"*
[Gal 4.6; cf. Rom 8.14–16].

---

[109]This is possibly an allusion to Eph 6.12.
[110]Lat. *proprietatem eius.*
[111]Lat. *proprietatem Patris et nomen.*
[112]I.e. the Son.
[113]I.e. the Holy Spirit.

The Spirit teaches all things [140–143]

140. The Holy Spirit himself, who has been sent by the Father and comes in the name of the Son, will teach all things to those who are perfect in the faith of Christ,[114] (that is, all things which are spiritual and intelligible)[115]—in sum, the mysteries of truth and wisdom. **141.** But he will not teach as an instructor or teacher of a discipline which has been learned from another. For this method pertains to those who learn wisdom and the other arts by means of study and diligence. Rather, as he himself is the art, the teaching, the wisdom, and the Spirit of Truth, he invisibly imparts knowledge of divine things to the mind.

In fact, the Father also teaches his disciples in this way, as one of those taught by him says: *God, you have taught me wisdom* [Dan 2.23]. And another boldly cries out: *You have taught me, God, from my youth* [Ps 70.17]. In this way all of them have been taught. **142.** In addition, the Son of God, who is the Truth and the Wisdom of God, teaches those who participate in him in such a way that his instruction is imparted, not by some method, but in virtue of who he is by nature.[116] It is for this reason that his disciples[117] are taught to call him alone "teacher."[118]

And so, those same teachings that the Father and the Son give to the hearts of believers, the Spirit provides to those who have stopped living like animals. *For the one living like an animal does not receive what belongs to the Spirit*, thinking that what the Spirit says *is foolishness* [1 Cor 2.14]. But whoever cleanses his mind of disturbance is filled with the teachings of the Holy Spirit (that is, with words of wisdom and knowledge), to such an extent that he who has received them says: *But God has revealed these things to us through the Holy Spirit* [1 Cor 2.10].

[114]Cf. Jn 14.26.

[115]I.e. non sense-perceptible.

[116]Lat. *ut disciplinam non arte doceat, sed natura.*

[117]His "disciples" (*discipuli*) are those to whom the Son has imparted his "instruction" (*disciplinam*).

[118]Cf. Mt 23.10.

143. God bestows the Spirit of Wisdom and revelation on those who have prepared themselves in this way in order that they may know him.[119] Those who receive the Spirit of Wisdom are made wise not from another but from the Holy Spirit, and because of him they come to understand the Lord and what pertains to the will of God. When he reveals himself, they also recognize this same Spirit such that they know what the Lord has given them. Just as the one who has obtained the Spirit of revelation and wisdom is able to preach the doctrines of truth by relying not upon human skill but upon the skill of God,[120] so too we can hear one of them, the Apostle, saying: *And my word and my preaching are not with persuasive words of human wisdom but with the demonstration of the Spirit and the power of God* [1 Cor 2.4].

The Holy Spirit creates like the Father and the Son [144–145]

144. It is true that we cannot interpret the *power* which is equal to the Spirit as another besides Christ the Lord. For he himself said to his disciples: *For you will receive the power of the Holy Spirit when he comes upon you* [Act 1.8].[121] And the archangel said to Mary: *The Holy Spirit will come upon you, and the power of the Most High will overshadow you* [Luke 1.35]. Therefore, when the Holy Spirit came upon the virgin Mary, the creating power of the Most High fashioned the body of Christ: using it as a temple, he was born without the seed of a man.

145. All this shows that the Holy Spirit is the Creator, as we have already shown briefly in our volume *On Doctrines.*[122] And in the

---

[119]Lat. *semetipsum.* That is, God.

[120]Lat. *non humana sed Dei arte.*

[121]Lat. *accipietis enim virtutem Spiritus Sancti venientem super vos.* There is significant difference between Didymus's citation and the standard Greek text, which is the same as the source of the Vulgate: *sed accipietis virtutem supervenientis Spiritus Sancti in vos.* In the standard text it is "the Holy Spirit" who comes upon the disciples. Here, it is "the power of the Holy Spirit" which does.

[122]This work is no longer extant, but is also mentioned by Jerome in *De viribus illustribus* 109.

psalm it is said to the Lord: *You take back from them your Spirit, and they die and they return to the earth. You send forth your Spirit, and they are created, and you renew the face of the earth* [Ps 103.29–30]. Nor it is particularly astonishing if the Holy Spirit is the maker of the Lord's body, since along with the Father and the Son he creates all things which the Father and the Son create: *Send forth your Spirit, and they are created* [Ps 130.30]. Furthermore, we have already demonstrated at length that the Holy Spirit's activity is the same as that of the Father and the Son, and that a single substance is implied by the same activity, and, vice versa, that those who are ὁμοούσια [the same in substance] do not have an activity that is diverse.[123]

2. JOHN THE EVANGELIST: JOHN 16.12–15 [146–174]

146. Let us now cite yet another passage which can aid our faith in the Holy Spirit. Here is a text written in the Gospel:

> [12]*I still have many things to say to you, but you cannot bear them now.* [13]*But when the Spirit of Truth comes, he will guide you into the whole Truth. For he will not speak on his own accord, but whatever he hears he will speak, and the things that are to come he will announce to you.* [14]*He will glorify me since he will receive from what is mine and announce it to you.* [15]*All that the Father has is mine. It is for this reason that I have said to you that he will receive from what is mine and announce it to you* [Jn 16.12–15].

[123]See *Spir.* 81.

Interpretation of John 16.12–13a:
the Spirit guides to the Truth [147–152]

147. These words of mystery teach us that, after Jesus had taught his disciples many things, he said: *I still have many things to say to you* [Jn 16.12a]. The phrase *I still have many things to say to you* is not directed to novices or those totally ignorant of the wisdom of God, but to hearers of his words who have not yet attained *all things.* **148.** For he handed on to them whatever they could bear and deferred for a future time the rest which they would not be able to understand without the teaching of the Holy Spirit.

Now the Holy Spirit was not given to humanity before the Lord's passion took place, as the Evangelist says: *For the Spirit had not been given because Jesus was not yet glorified* [Jn 7.39]; being "glorified" here means that Jesus *tastes death for all* [Heb 2.9]. And so, after the resurrection he appeared to his disciples, breathed on their face, and said: *Receive the Holy Spirit* [Jn 20.22]. And again: *You will receive the power of the Holy Spirit when he comes upon you* [Acts 1.8].[124] **149.** When the Holy Spirit comes into the hearts of believers, they are filled with words of wisdom and knowledge. When they are made spiritual in this way, they receive the teaching of the Holy Spirit which can guide them toward the whole Truth.

150. Therefore, since it was still not appropriate for them to be filled with the Holy Spirit at the time when he said to them: *I still have many things to say to you* [Jn 16.12a], accordingly he added: *but you cannot bear them now* [Jn 16.12b]. Because they were still *serving a shadow and copies* [Heb 8.5] and a type of the law, they were not able to look upon the truth, *whose shadow the law conveyed* [Heb 10.1]. It is for this reason that they were unable to bear the weight of spiritual things. *When he comes*—that is, the Paraclete—*the Spirit of Truth will guide you into the whole Truth* [Jn 16.13a], through his own teaching and instruction conveying you from the death of the

---

[124]The citation of Acts 1.8 reflects the standard version. See *Spir.* 144 for an alternative.

letter to the Spirit that gives life [cf. 2 Cor 3.6]. In him alone resides all the truth of Scripture.

151. And so, when the Spirit of Truth himself enters into a pure and simple mind, he will impress upon you the knowledge of truth; since he always joins the new to the old,[125] he will guide you into all truth. **152.** Moreover, someone praying to God the Father said: *Guide me in your Truth* [Ps 25.5], meaning "in your Only-Begotten." He bears witness to this with his own voice: *I am the Truth* [Jn 14.6]. God grants this perfection by sending the Spirit of Truth who guides believers into the whole Truth.

Jn 16.13b: Divine speech [153–162]

153. Next, in what follows, the Savior, who is also the Truth, speaks about the Spirit of Truth who is sent by the Father and is the Paraclete: *For he will not speak on his own accord* [Jn 16.13b]. By this he means "not without me and not without my and the Father's authority, seeing that he is inseparable from my and the Father's will because he is not from himself but from the Father and me. For his very being and speaking belongs to him from the Father and from me. As for me, I speak the truth, by which I mean that I inspire what he speaks, for he is the Spirit, after all, of Truth."

154. Now when we say that there is "saying and speaking" within the Trinity, we should not understand this as taking place in the manner to which we are accustomed when we converse and speak among ourselves in turn, but in the way that conforms with incorporeal natures and especially with the Trinity, who instills his will in the heart of believers and those worthy of hearing it. This is what "saying and speaking" means.

---

[125]Cf. Mt 13.52. The scriptural allusion is here most apt: just like every scribe who has been trained for the kingdom of heaven is like a householder who brings out of his treasure what is new and what is old, the Holy Spirit brings new meaning to the old Scriptures.

155. When we human beings speak to one another about something, we first conceive what we want to say in our mind without speech. Then when we want to convey it into the mind of another, we set the tongue in motion as an instrument, and by striking it like a kind of plectrum on the strings of the teeth, we emit an articulate sound. So then, just as we control how we strike our tongue on the palate and the teeth and modulate how we force our air into various utterances in order to communicate to others what we have in mind, so too it is necessary for the listener to offer open ears uninhibited by any impediment and to turn them[126] to what is being said in order for him to be able to know what is being expressed just as the one who is speaking knows them.

156. But, God, who is simple and of a nature that is incomposite and unique, possesses neither ears nor organs with which he emits a voice. Rather, his solitary and incomprehensible substance is not composed of any members or parts. The very same point should be understood likewise with regard to the Son and the Holy Spirit. **157.** Therefore, when we read in Scripture: *The Lord said to my Lord* [Ps 109.2], and elsewhere: *God said: "Let there be light!"* [Gen 1.3], and things similar to these, we ought to understand them in a way worthy of God.

158. Nor does the Father announce his will to the Son, who is Wisdom and Truth, as if he does not already know it. For the Son, who is wise and true, has in wisdom and in substance everything that the Father speaks. Therefore, when Father speaks and the Son hears, or vice versa, when the Son speaks and the Father hears, it indicates that in the Father and the Son there is the same nature and agreement.[127] **159.** Nor is it possible for the Holy Spirit, who is the Spirit of Truth and the Spirit of Wisdom, to hear what he does not know when the Son speaks, since he is the very thing expressed by the Son.[128]

---

[126]Lit. "to prick them up."

[127]Lat. *consensus.*

[128]Several important mss. and Migne insert the following at this point: "that is, God proceeds from God, the Spirit of Truth proceeds from Truth, Consoler emanates from Consoler." Doutreleau does not attribute this insertion to Jerome, but judges it to be an interpolation by a later copyist.

160. Next, so that no one separates the Holy Spirit from the will and fellowship of the Father and the Son, it is written: *For he will not speak on his own accord, but he will speak as he hears* [Jn 16.13].[129] The Savior said something similar to this about himself: *As I hear, so I judge* [Jn 5.30]. And elsewhere: *The Son is not able to do anything on his own accord, but only what he sees the Father doing* [Jn 5.19]. **161.** For if the Son of the Father is one, not according to the error of Sabellius who confuses the Father and the Son, but according to their inseparability of essence or substance, then he is unable to do anything without the Father. The works of separate individuals are distinct, but when the Son sees the Father working, he is himself also working, yet working not in a second rank and after him. After all, the works of the Son would begin to diverge from those of the Father if they were not performed by equals.

162. In addition, it is written: *For whatever he does*—no doubt meaning the Father—*the Son does these same things likewise* [Jn 5.19]. When the Father and the Son work, if they do not work in order as a second after a first but simultaneously, then all the things which they do are the same and not dissimilar, and the Son is unable to do anything on his own accord since he cannot be separated from the Father. Likewise, the Holy Spirit, who is in no way separated from the Son on account of their sharing[130] of will and nature, is not believed to speak on his own accord, but speaks all that he speaks according to the Word and Truth of God.

Interpretation of John 16.14: how the Spirit "receives" the Son [163–169]

163. The following words of the Lord confirm this opinion: *He will glorify me*—that is, the Paraclete—*because he will receive from*

---

[129]Didymus's citation differs slightly from that found in Spir. 146, which reads: *but whatever he hears he will speak.*

[130]Lat. *consortium.*

what is mine [Jn 16.14]. Again, "receive" here ought to be understood in a way that is appropriate to divine nature. **164.** For just as, when the Son gives, he is not deprived of those things which he gives and does not share with others to his own detriment, so too the Spirit does not receive what he did not have before. If he receives what he did not have earlier, then when the gift is transferred to another, its bestower is left empty-handed, ceasing to have what he gave.[131]

165. Therefore, just as we understood the natures of incorporeals in our discussion above, so too we now ought to acknowledge that the Holy Spirit receives from the Son that which belongs to his own nature. This does not signify that there is a giver and a receiver, but one substance, since the Son is said to receive the same things from the Father which belong to his very being.[132] For the Son is nothing other than those things which are given to him by the Father, and the substance of the Holy Spirit is nothing other than that which is given to him by the Son. **166.** These statements are made for this reason: so that we may believe that in the Trinity the nature of the Holy Spirit is the same as that of the Father and the Son.[133]

167. Now every human term can indicate nothing other than corporeal things, and the Trinity (the subject of our present discussion) is beyond all material substances. For these reasons, no word can be applied to him in the proper sense and thereby signify his substance. Rather, when we speak about incorporeals in general and especially about the Trinity, every thing we say is said καταχρηστικῶς, that is, in an improper sense.

168. And so, the Holy Spirit glorifies the Son by showing him and manifesting him to the pure in heart who are worthy of understanding him, seeing him,[134] and knowing the Splendor of his

---

[131]The paragraph expresses the so-called doctrine of undiminished giving. The unexpressed assumption of the last sentence seems to be that in order to be an undiminished giver one must be what one gives rather than receiving it from another. See Didymus, *Trin.* 3.40 (PG 39.981b) for similar comments.

[132]I.e. wisdom, truth, etc.

[133]Several important mss. (BCΔ) omit: "of the Holy Spirit" and "as that of the Father and the Son."

[134]Cf. Mt 5.8.

substance[135] and *the Image of the invisible God* [Col 1.15]. The Image himself glorifies the Father in turn, by showing himself to pure minds, thereby introducing him to those who do not know him: *He who sees me sees the Father* [Jn 14.9]. **169.** In addition, the Father glorifies his Only-Begotten by revealing the Son to those who have merited to attain the summit of knowledge, showing his magnificence and power. Furthermore, the Son himself glorifies the Holy Spirit by bestowing him on those who have prepared themselves to be worthy of his gift and by distributing to them the sublimity of his glorification and greatness.

Interpretation of John 16.15: the mutual possessions of Father, Son, and Holy Spirit [170–173]

170. Next he explains the manner in which he said: *he will receive from what is mine,* by immediately adding: *all things which the Father has are mine; for this reason I said, "from what is mine he will receive and will announce to you."* [Jn 16.15]. It is as if he said: "Although *the Spirit of Truth proceeds*[136] *from the Father* [Jn 15.26] *and God gives the Holy Spirit to those who ask him* [Lk 11.13], nonetheless since all things which the Father has are mine, even the very Spirit of the Father is mine and he will receive from what is mine."

171. Now when such things are said be careful not to slip into the error of a depraved understanding and think that the Father and the Son hold some object or possession. Rather, that which the Father has substantially, that is, eternity, immutability, incorruptibility, immutable goodness subsisting of and in itself—these same things the Son has as well. In addition, whatever the Son himself is and whatever belongs to the Son, these same things the Father has as well.

---

[135]Cf. Heb 1.3.

[136]Lat. *procedat*. Jerome elsewhere translates ἐκπορεύεται by *egreditur* (*Spir.* 110 and 114).

172. Let the snares of the dialecticians be far from here! Banish from the truth those sophisms of theirs that seize an opportunity for impiety from pious preaching and say: "Therefore, the Father is the Son and the Son is the Father." For if he had said: "All things whatsoever God has are mine," then impiety would have an opportunity for fabrication and such a lie would seem to be plausible. But since he said: *All that the Father has is mine* [Jn 16.15], by using the name of "Father" he declared himself to be the Son. He who is his Son does not usurp his paternity, even if the Son himself is also the father of many saints through the grace of adoption, according to that passage in the psalms where it is read: *If your sons keep . . .* [Ps 131.12], and again: *If his sons forsake my law . . .* [Ps 88.31].

173. From this text and in the sense already established, it follows that the Son also possesses what belongs to the Father (we mentioned above what those things are), and that the Holy Spirit also possesses what belongs to the Son. For he said: *From what is mine he will receive, for this reason he will announce to you what is to come* [Jn 16.13]. Indeed, certain knowledge of future events is granted to holy men through the Spirit of Truth. This is why the Prophets, filled with this same Spirit, used to foretell in oracles events to come and gazed upon them as if they were already present.

Conclusion to the interpretation of John 16.12–15 [174]

174. This discussion of the present chapter of the Gospel should suffice and more than suffice, given the poverty of our talent. But if the Lord has accorded a revelation to certain others, drawing them close to the Truth and making them more capable of discerning the Truth, then we concede that their account is better since he who is the Spirit of Truth gives it support. Furthermore, we ask those who will read this to forgive our lack of expertise and pardon the eagerness of someone who desires to offer all that he can to God, even if he was unable to accomplish his plan.

3. THE APOSTLE PAUL: ROMANS 8.4–17 [175–196]

175. Now it is time to present the testimony of the Apostle Paul's epistle to the Romans and indicate how we think it pertains to our present subject:

176. *⁴So that the requirement of the law may be fulfilled in you, who do not walk according to the flesh but according to the Spirit. ⁵For those who are according to the flesh are wise about the things of the flesh, but those who are according to the Spirit are wise about the things of the Spirit. ⁶After all, the wisdom of the flesh is death, but the wisdom of the Spirit is life and peace. ⁷For the wisdom of the flesh is hostile to God; after all, it does not submit to God's law, nor can it. ⁸But those who are in the flesh cannot be pleasing to God.* **177.** *⁹However, you are not in the flesh but in the Spirit, if in fact the Spirit of God dwells in you. But if anyone does not have the Spirit of Christ, he does not belong to Christ. ¹⁰But if Christ is in you, although your body is dead because of sin, the Spirit is alive because of righteousness. ¹¹But if the Spirit of him who raised Jesus from the dead dwells in you, he who raised Jesus Christ from the dead will give life even to your mortal bodies through his Spirit who dwells in you. ¹²Therefore, brothers, we are not in debt to the flesh such that we have to live according to the flesh. ¹³For if you live according to the flesh, then you will die, but if you mortify the deeds of the body by the Spirit, then you will live.* **178.** *¹⁴For all who are led by the Spirit of God are children of God. ¹⁵For you have not received a spirit of slavery leading you back into fear, but you have received the Spirit of adopted sonship through whom we cry out, "Abba! Father!" ¹⁶For the Spirit himself bears witness with our spirit that we are children of God. ¹⁷And if children, then heirs, indeed heirs of God and fellow heirs with Christ, if we suffer with him in order that we may also be glorified together with him* [Rom 8.4–17].

179. This chapter of the Apostle has much to say about the fellowship that the Spirit has with the Father and the Son.

Interpretation of Romans 8.4–8:
Living according to the Spirit [180–183]

180. The Apostle says that the *requirement of the* divine and spiritual *law*[137] *is fulfilled by those who do not walk according to the flesh but according to the Spirit* [Rom 8.4]. The Apostle's text describes the person who walks according to the flesh: it is someone who is united to the body through the pleasures and the vices of the flesh and therefore does all the deeds that belong to the flesh and to the body. But the person who walks according to the Spirit is someone who advances in the precepts of the Gospel and therefore follows the prescriptions of the spiritual commandments. As a matter of fact, just as it is the vice of fleshly people to be wise in the matters of the flesh and to think about the concerns of the body, so too, inversely, it is always the virtue of spiritual persons to occupy themselves with heavenly realities, eternal matters, and the concerns of the Spirit.

181. The *wisdom of the flesh* is directly linked with *death* and kills those who advance and are wise according to the flesh, but the *wisdom of the Spirit* bestows tranquility of mind, *peace*, and eternal *life* on those who have it [Rom 8.6]. Those who come to possess it will trample under their feet all disturbances, every kind of vice, and even the demons themselves who strive to suggest these things. And so, since the *wisdom of the flesh* is joined to death, it is *hostile to God* [Rom 8.7]. For it is always contrary to and fighting against the will of God and his law, and makes those bound to its laws *hostile to God*.

182. Nor it is possible for the person who is in the wisdom of the flesh to keep the precepts of God and be subject to his will. As long as we are servants of pleasure, we are incapable of being servants of

---

[137]Lat. *iustificationem divinae et spiritualis legis*. We read *divinae* with BΓΔ instead of Doutreleau's *divinam*.

God. But whenever we stamp out the enticements of self-indulgence and convey our entire selves to the Spirit so that we are no longer in the flesh (that is, in the passions of the flesh), it is then that we will be subject to God.

183. Now the Apostle's text is not concerned with this flesh in which we live and in whose vessel our soul is contained, since all the saints were pleasing to God while encompassed by body and flesh. Rather, it is concerned with that which is perpetrated in human society against the precepts of God such as: *You shall love the Lord your God* [Deut 6.5] and *That which you do not like . . .* [Tob 4.15], and so forth.[138]

Interpretation of Romans 8.9: the Spirit is inseparable from the Father and the Son [184–191]

184. "But as for you," he says, undoubtedly meaning the disciples of Christ, "who have received the wisdom of the Spirit, his life, and his peace, you are not in the flesh, (that is, in the work of the flesh). For you do not perform its works, since you have the Spirit of God in you."[139] Now the Spirit of God and the Spirit of Christ are the same, leading and joining the person who has him to the Lord Jesus Christ. This is why it is written in what follows: *But if anyone does not have the Spirit of Christ, he does not belong to Christ* [Rom 8.9b]. **185.** So once again, from this text we learn of the fellowship that the Holy Spirit has with Christ and God.

[138]Lat. *Quod tibi non vis.* This is a partial translation of the LXX: ὅ μισεῖς μηδενὶ ποιήσῃς, "that which you hate do to no one." The full text in the Vulgate translation reads: *quod ab alio odis fieri tibi vide ne alteri tu aliquando facias*, "that which you hate to happen to you by another take care lest you at some time do it to another." Interestingly, both examples cited here by Didymus are prominent in the New Testament as well: Deut 6.5 is the core of the Great Commandment cited by Jesus at Mk 12.29–30 (|| Mt 22.34–40; Lk 10.25–28) and Tob 4.15 is a negative statement of the Golden Rule expressed by Jesus at Mt 7.12 (|| Lk 6.31). Both the Great Commandment and the Golden Rule are explicitly presented by Jesus as the essence of the Law and the Prophets. Hence, the scriptural citations made by Didymus here are particularly fitting.

[139]This is a paraphrase of Rom 8.9a.

186. In the epistle of Peter there is further proof that the Holy Spirit is the Spirit of Christ: he says that the Prophets whom he mentioned above[140] *investigated and inquired into what time or which circumstance was being indicated by him who was the Spirit of Christ in them, when he was bearing witness to the sufferings reserved for Christ and the things decreed to follow after; it was revealed to them that they were serving not themselves but us in those things which have now been announced to you through the Holy Spirit* [1 Pet 1.11–12].[141] **187.** The *Holy Spirit* just mentioned is also called the Spirit of God, not only in the present text,[142] but also in many other passages, such as: *No one knows the things of God except the Spirit of God* [1 Cor 2.11]. **188.** Then, following the passage which says: *But if anyone does not have the Spirit of Christ, he does not belong to Christ* [Rom 8.9b], it is added: *But if Christ is in you* [Rom 8.10a]. This demonstrates most clearly that the Holy Spirit is inseparable from Christ because wherever the Holy Spirit is, there also is Christ, and from wherever the Spirit of Christ departs, Christ also withdraws from that place.

189. *For if anyone does not have the Spirit of Christ, he does not belong to Christ* [Rom 8.9b]. If anyone were to assume the contrary of this conditional proposition,[143] he could say: "If anyone belongs to Christ such that Christ is in him, then the Spirit of Christ is in him."[144] **190.** This same logic can also be deployed likewise in the

---

[140]Prophets are mentioned in the verse (1 Pet 1.10) just before the citation that follows.

[141]This citation differs considerably from the standard Greek text and the Vulgate.

[142]I.e., Rom 8.9.

[143]Lat. *cui coniuncto si quis contrarium assumat.* In *Spir.* 189–193 Didymus employs Stoic logic. As Rom 8.9b is clearly a conditional, the term *coniunctum* most likely translates συνημμένον, the standard Stoic designation for a conditional proposition. It has the form: "if p, then q," e.g., "if it is day, then it is light." Note that according to the second-century Latin miscellanist Aulus Gellius (*Noctes atticae* 6.8.10–11), the kind of proposition known in Latin as the *coniunctum* corresponded to the Greek συμπεπλεγμένον ἀξίωμα, or conjunctive proposition, while συνημμένον ἀξίωμα, the Greek for a conditional proposition, was translated into Latin as *adiunctum* or *conexum* (*Noctes atticae* 16.8.9). Either Jerome has mistranslated συνημμένον, or by the late fourth century *coniunctum* had become an acceptable translation.

[144]The "contrary" (*contrarium*) of Rom 8.9b presented by Didymus is technically

case of God the Father: "If anyone does not have the Spirit of God, he does not belong to God." Again, one may assume the contrary of this, saying: "If anyone belongs to God, then the Spirit of God is in him."[145] This is why it is written: *Do you not know that you are a temple of God and that in you dwells the Spirit of God?* [1 Cor 3.16]. And in the epistle of John: *By this it is recognized that God dwells in certain persons, when the Spirit whom he gave remains in them* [1 Jn 3.24; 4.13]. **191.** All these passages demonstrate that the substance of the Trinity is inseparable and indivisible.

Interpretation of Romans 8.10–12: The Spirit gives us life [192–194]

192. Therefore, when he said: *But if Christ is in you, although your body is dead because of sin* [Rom 8.10a], in no way does he mean that the body is a slave to vices and wantonness. Rather, he means that when the body is made dead to sin, it will not be moved to vice and in no way will it be alive to sin. After the body has become dead to sin, Christ, who is present in those who have made their own bodies dead, manifests the Spirit of life when they do righteous works, either when they correct their deadly vices, or when they believe in Jesus Christ and live their lives according to faith in him.

193. Then the Apostle uses another conditional proposition[146] (which the dialecticians more precisely call an ἀξίωμα),[147] and

known as the contrapositive, which is the inverse of the converse. Contraposition was understood in antiquity as "conversion by negation" (ἡ σὺν ἀντιθέσει ἀντιστροφή; cf. Anon., *In Aristotelis sophisticos elenchos paraphrasis* 30.5 & 15 (M. Hayduck, *Anonymi in Aristotelis sophisticos elenchos paraphrasis*, Commentaria in Aristotelem Graeca 23.4 (Berlin: Reimer, 1884), 1–68)). Given the conditional "if p, then q," the converse is "if q, then p" and the inverse is "if not p, then not q," and the contrapositive accordingly takes the form "if not q, then not p." Didymus's reasoning is here unassailable: the contrapositive of a true conditional is always true, a basic fact about the logic of conditionals of which the ancients were surely aware, including the Stoics.

[145] Again, this is the contrapositive. See the previous note.

[146] Lat. *syllogismo coniuncto*. See n. 143 above.

[147] The Stoics recognized three other kinds of propositions (ἀξιώματα) in addi-

says: *But if the Spirit of him who raised Jesus Christ from the dead dwells in you, he who raised Christ from the dead will give life even to your mortal bodies through his Spirit who dwells in you.* [Rom 8.11]. Doesn't it seem to you that he is saying: "If the Spirit of him who raised Jesus from the dead"—that is, he who is the Spirit of the same Jesus Christ—"dwells in you, then as a consequence of this, along with your immortal souls even your mortal bodies will be given life by him who raised Jesus Christ from the dead and manifested him as the ruler and the first-born of the resurrection."[148]

194. Since the Holy Spirit has divinely granted us such a great gift as this, we are in debt to the Spirit, not *to the flesh such that we have to live according to the flesh* [Rom 8.12]. After all, whoever lives according to the flesh will die from that death which is the consequence of sin. According to James, *when sin is fully grown it gives birth to death* [Jam 1.15]. In addition, Ezekiel writes that the sinful soul dies when it is separated from the life that resides in the wisdom of the Spirit.[149]

Interpretation of Romans 8.13–17: The life the Spirit gives makes us children of God [195–196]

195. If anyone passes beyond the life of the flesh and mortifies its deeds by the Spirit, he will live a blessed and eternal life, being counted among the children of God and directed to the true path through the Holy Spirit, who is also called the Spirit of God. *For if you live according to the flesh, then you will die, but if you mortify the deeds of the body by the Spirit, then you will live* [Rom 8.13]. And then it follows: *For however many are led by the Spirit of God, they are children of God* [Rom 8.14].[150] So then, after reviving and consoling

tion to the conditional: the subconditional, the conjunctive, and the disjunctive. One suspects that the phrase "which the dialecticians more precisely call an ἀξίωμα" is a misinformed display of erudition on the part of Jerome.

[148]Cf. Col 1.18 and Rev 1.5.

[149]Cf. Ezek 18.26.

[150]Note the slightly different wording than the citation in *Spir.* 178.

them, and encouraging those to whom he spoke to hope for better things, he continues: *For you have not received a spirit of slavery leading you back into fear* [Rom 8.15a]. In other words: "You have not abstained from vices out of fear and terror of punishment, like a slave does. For the Father has given you the Spirit of adopted son-ship,[151] that is, the Holy Spirit, who is himself called the Spirit of the Son of God, the Spirit of Christ, and the Spirit of Truth and Wisdom. Now if this Spirit adopts as the children of God those in whom he has deigned to indwell, I leave it to you to infer the consequences of this power of his."

196. Furthermore, those who have this God as their Father cry out through this Spirit of adopted sonship, as the text shows: *through whom we cry out, "Abba! Father!"* [Rom 8.15b]. *The Spirit himself* adopts us as children and *bears witness* when our spirit possesses the same Spirit by participation *that we are children of God* [Rom 8.16]. In consequence of this, on the one hand, God bestows spiritual gifts upon us like a father bestows a bountiful inheritance, but on the other hand, we are *fellow heirs with Christ* [Rom 8.17], insofar as we are called his brothers through his grace and kindness. We will be *heirs of God and fellow heirs with Christ if we suffer with him in order that we may also* deserve to *be glorified together with him* through association with his sufferings [Rom 8.17].

4. THE PROPHET ISAIAH: ISAIAH 63.7–12 [197–230]

197. Now that we have discussed these matters to the extent that we could, let us examine a chapter of the Prophet which contains statements about the Holy Spirit. In this way, we learn not only from the New Testament but also from the Old Testament what we

---

[151]Lat. *Spiritum adoptionis*; Gk. Πνεῦμα υἱοθεσίας. The word υἱοθεσία literally means "adopting as a son" (υἱός), a nuance that the normal English translation, "adoption," does not capture. For Didymus and many other Greek fathers, the title "Spirit of adopted sonship" shows Spirit's intimate connection with the Father's adoption of sons in Christ.

should believe and understand about him. For we said above that
the grace of the Holy Spirit resides in all the saints, both those who
lived after the advent of our Lord, and those who lived even before
it (namely, the Patriarchs and Prophets), and that he filled them with
various charisms and powers. Just as those who raised the standard
of his righteousness both before and after his advent attained the
knowledge of truth by possessing the grace of the one God and his
Only-Begotten, so too will they possess the grace of the Holy Spirit.
For time and again we have demonstrated in many places above that
the Holy Spirit is inseparable from the Father and the Son. **198.** So
then, it is written in the Prophet:

> [7]*I have remembered the mercy of the Lord, and his power in
> all he has granted us. The Lord, the good judge of the house
> of Israel, treats us according to his mercy and according to
> the abundance of his righteousness.* [8]*And he said: "Are my
> people not my children? And will they not refrain from deal-
> ing falsely?" And he became for them salvation* [9]*from all their
> affliction. Neither a legate nor an angel, but he himself saved
> them because he loved them and spared them. He redeemed
> them and took them and raised them in all the days of the age.*
> [10]*But they did not believe and they enraged his Holy Spirit,
> and he turned to them in animosity. He fought against them.*
> [11]*And he remembered the days of the age, who led the shepherd
> of the sheep from the earth, who put the Holy Spirit on them,*
> [12]*gathering them at the right hand of Moses* [Is 63.7–12].

Interpretation of Isaiah 63.7 : God judges with mercy [199–202]

199. Frequent recipients of the blessings of God know that
they have obtained them through his grace and mercy rather than
through their own efforts. Being harmonious in mind and soul, they
all speak as one: *I have remembered the mercy of the Lord* [Is 63.7].

200. When they reflect on their frequent reception of gifts from the Lord through Moses, they give thanks. And besides his *mercy*, they also remember the manifestations of the Lord's *power*,[152] whether the wonders he repeatedly performed on their behalf among the peoples, or the soul's advancement through education in the Law, the Prophets, and the salutary precepts of Moses. After all, in the Scriptures the term "power" signifies both.[153]

201. Continuing on, they say that they remembered his mercy and powers *in all that he has granted us*, not according to his righteousness but *according to the mercy* and goodness of him who is the *judge* of both "the house that sees" and the one who sees God with a pure heart[154] [Is 63.7]. Note that the phrase "the mind that sees God" translates "Israel" from Hebrew into our language.[155] **202.** Now even though a judge sometimes brings in the rack and other instruments to torture the condemned, nonetheless when someone considers the motives for these things with deeper insight, he sees the good intentions of the one who desires to correct the sinner and confesses that he is good, saying: *He treats us according to his mercy* [Is 63.7]. For *if the Lord should mark the iniquities* of those whom he judges, *who could survive?* [Ps 129.3]. Furthermore, since *forgiveness is found with the Lord* [Ps 129.4], our Lord and Savior treats us according to his mercy by bestowing everything conducive for our salvation. In addition, when he treats us according to his mercy in rendering judgment upon us, the sentence he justly grants is mixed with the goodness of mercy.

---

[152]Cf. Is 63.7.

[153]Lat. *virtus*. The word can refer both to external manifestations of the power of God such as miracles and other prodigious acts and to internal manifestations of the power of God such as virtues of the soul which are made possible only through the grace of God. The point is that both external wonders and interior virtue are both manifestations of the same power of God. Here *virtus* translates the Greek δύναμις, which has the same range of meaning as *virtus*.

[154]Cf. Mt 5.8.

[155]The same etymology is found in Philo (*Congr.* 51, *Fug.* 208, *Abr.* 57, *Praem.* 44, and *Legat.* 4), Origen (*Princ.* 4.3.8 and *Comm. Jo.* 2.189), and Eusebius (*Praep. ev.* 11.6.32, *Dem. ev.* 7.2.36, and *Comm. Isa.* 2.45).

Refutation of a heretical interpretation of Isaiah 63.7 :
The unity of the Old and New Testaments [203–205]

203. On the basis of the present chapter, we must confront the error of those heretics who separate goodness from justice, and fabricate one God who is good and another who is just.[156] After all, you can see for yourself how in the present passage God himself is both good and judge, rewarding according to his mercy and justice, and being equally good and just. **204.** Accordingly, it is to no avail that they make a pretense of defending the wicked teaching that the God of the Gospel is good and that the God of the Old Testament is just. For in many other passages as well as in the present text of the Prophet, God is described as a "good judge." In addition, they deny that God is referred to as a "just judge" in the epistle of Paul the Apostle, who certainly is a preacher of the New Testament: *Laid up for me is a crown of justice which the just judge will award me* [2 Tim 4.8].

205. Therefore, even if they deny it, the God of the New and Old Testaments is the same, the Creator of things seen and unseen. The Savior too gives clear testimony in the Gospel that the Father is just and good: *Just Father, the world has not known you* [Jn 17.25]. And in another passage: *No one is good, except God alone* [Mk 10.18]. Furthermore, in the Old Law, in some places God is called "just" and in others "good." In the psalms: *The Lord is just and loves justice* [Ps 10.7]. And the opposite in Jeremiah: *God is good to those who endure for him* [Lam 3.25]. Again in the psalms: *How good the God of Israel is to those who are pure of heart!* [Ps 72.1]. These testimonies truly suffice to sum up our position against the heretics.

[156]This teaching was associated with Marcion and the Manichees.

Interpretation of Isaiah 63.8–9 :
Christ the Lord is our only Savior [206–211]

206. It is time for us to return to the thread intended by the Prophet, which continues in this way: *And he*—without a doubt, the Lord—*said: "Are my people not my children? And will they not refrain from dealing falsely?"* [Is 63.8]. He is saying that they will not be like those who, after being born and raised, scorned the one who begot them. *And he became for them salvation* [Is 63.8], that is, for those about whom the Lord said: *"Are my people not my children? And will they not refrain from dealing falsely?"* [Is 63.8]. Because they refrained from dealing falsely and did not despise the Father, for them he became salvation. Or because they are called children, he became for them a cause of salvation.

207. The voice of the angel affirmed to the shepherds that Christ the Lord bestows salvation, when the angel said: *Behold! I bring you tidings of a great joy which will come to all people. For to you is born today in the city of David a Savior who is Christ the Lord* [Lk 2.10–11]. He became for all who believe in him the occasion for eternal salvation.[157] He is the Savior of the world who comes to seek whatever is lost.[158] Concerning him, the choir of saints sings: *This God of ours is a God who saves!* [Ps 67.21].

208. Therefore, since it was God who bestowed eternal salvation, it was said: *Neither a legate nor an angel* [Is 63.9].[159] In other words, neither a Prophet, nor a Patriarch, nor Moses the Lawgiver saved them. For all those whom I have just listed could only serve as legates before God on behalf of their people.[160] When Moses interceded on behalf of the sinful people, he said: *If you will forgive them of their sin, forgive it* [Ex 32.32]. He begged for their forgiveness, fasting for forty days and calling upon the mercy of God in the affliction of

[157] Cf. Heb 5.9
[158] Cf. Mt 18.11 Vulgate.
[159] In *Trin.* 3.27 (PG 39.944a) Didymus cites the same verse and interprets it as he does here.
[160] Cf. 2 Cor 5.20.

his soul. For no legate from among those I listed can be the Savior since the legate himself also needs him who is the true bestower of salvation. As for angels, however many spirits there may be and to however many diverse ministries they may be sent for the sake of those who are to obtain salvation,[161] they are nonetheless not the authors of salvation. Rather, they speak for and proclaim him who is the font of salvation.

209. When it is said that *neither a legate nor an angel, but the Lord himself saved them* [Is 63.9], he saved them for no other reason than this: *because he loved them and spared them* [Is 63.9]. The phrase *he spared them* means that he spared his creatures, as we see in the passage written elsewhere: *You spare all, O Lord the lover of souls, because they belong to you. For you do not hate what you have made* [Wis 11.27+25]. **210.** For this reason and for their salvation, the Father did not spare his own Son and handed him over to death,[162] so that through his Son's death, after the destruction of the one who had the power of death (that is, the devil), he could redeem all who had been held by him in the chains of captivity.[163]

Hence it is added: *He redeemed them and took them and raised them* [Is 63.9]. For he took and raised those who had been saved and redeemed. He carried them to the heights on the wings of virtue through both knowledge and understanding of the truth. He dwells in them and with them, not for one or two days only, but for all the days of eternity. He bestows life upon them and is the author of salvation even to the consummation of the age. Enlightening their hearts for all the days of the age, he does not permit them to live in the darkness of ignorance and error. **211.** And this, I think, is the meaning of the passage: *he raised them in all the days* [Is 63.9].

---

[161]Cf. Heb 1.14.
[162]Cf. Rom 8.32.
[163]Cf. Heb 2.14.

Interpretation of Isaiah 63.10:
sinners enrage the Holy Spirit [212–214]

212. Nonetheless, since they were inconstant and willingly fell into vice, after such great kindnesses they lost faith in God, abandoned his precepts, and enraged the Holy Spirit of God, who had granted them many goods. They fell into the sin that resembles that of those who scorned their Father after being born and raised. We can be quite certain that those of whom we now speak are identical with others who were mentioned earlier. For after their sin, it was also said to them there: *You have forsaken the Lord and roused the Holy One of Israel to wrath!* [Is 1.4]. The present passage says something equivalent: *But they did not believe and they enraged his Holy Spirit* [Is 63.10]. **213.** Therefore, the present passage demonstrates the Spirit is associated with God. Whoever forsakes the Lord and loses faith provokes the Holy One of Israel to wrath and enrages his Holy Spirit. In addition, the same anger directed at sinners is ascribed to the Holy Spirit as much as it is to the Holy One of Israel.

214. Even what follows demonstrates that the Trinity has a similar bond. For Scripture says that the Lord *turned in animosity* to those who had *enraged his Holy Spirit* [Is 63.10] and that he handed them over to everlasting torment after they had blasphemed against his Holy Spirit, not in their words, but in their deeds.[164] And so, the Lord *turned to them in animosity, fought against them* [Is 63.10], and subjected them to manifold and lengthy torments, so that neither in the present time nor in the future would they attain forgiveness for their sins.[165] For *they enraged his Holy Spirit* [Is 63.10] and blasphemed against him.

---

[164]This is a reference to the Exodus story.
[165]Cf. Mk 3.29.

Interpretation of Isaiah 63.10–11.
How the Jews enraged the Holy Spirit [215–220]

215. But perhaps you want to apply this passage to the Jews who crucified the Lord Savior and accordingly enraged the Holy Spirit. If so, that which is written: *he fought against them* [Is 63.10] can be understood in this sense: they were handed over to the Romans when the wrath of God came upon them in the end. **216.** For throughout the entire earth and all regions they wander alone in foreign lands as exiles from their homeland, having neither their ancient city nor their own habitations.[166] They are recipients of what they did to the Prophets and to their Savior. Since they were bloodthirsty and continually seized by a frenzied insanity, not only did they kill the Prophets and stone those sent to them,[167] but proceeding to the pinnacle of impiety, they betrayed and crucified the Lord Savior who deigned to descend to earth for the salvation of all. For this reason they were expelled from the city which they stained with the blood of the Prophets and Christ.

217. And so, it is in this sense that we ought to understand that the Lord *fought against them* [Is 63.10]: not for a brief time, but for every age to come, even to the consummation of the world. For as we said, they wander as fugitives and captives among all nations, having neither a city nor their own region. But yet, since the one who previously fought against them is naturally kind and merciful, he grants them an opportunity for repentance, if they want to be converted for the better. **218.** This is why it is said: *And he remembered the days of the age* [Is 63.11]. For when he remembered the times to come, he partially opened to them the door that had been closed, so that after *the full number of gentiles has entered*, then *all Israel* worthy of this designation[168] *might be saved* [Rom 11.25–26].

---

[166]Cf. Ps 106.4–7. Didymus says much the same in *Zacc.* 4.185–193; 5.28–30.
[167]Cf. Mt 23.37; Lk 13.34.
[168]Cf. Rom 9.6.

219. Even though they burst out into such heedlessness that they murdered the one who was sent on their behalf, saying: *His blood be upon us and upon our sons!* [Mt 27.35], nonetheless God raised him up from the earth *in the heart of which he abided for three days and three nights* [Mt 12.40] as the shepherd of his sheep. For the text continues as follows: *he led the shepherd of sheep from the earth* [Is 63.11]. **220.** But we learn clearly in the Gospel that the shepherd of the sheep of God whom the Prophet describes in the present text is our Lord Jesus Christ. For the Savior himself testifies: *I am the good shepherd, and I lay down my life for my sheep* [Jn 10.27]. And again: *My sheep hear my voice* [Jn 10.27].

Interpretation of Isaiah 63.11–12. The Holy Spirit is given so that believers may be saints [221–225]

221. After all these passage, the Prophet continues: *Where is he who put the Holy Spirit upon them?* [Is 63.11].[169] For he is astonished that they have passed from such great happiness to so many miseries. It is as if he says: "This one who redeemed them, who raised them, who put his Holy Spirit on them, dwelling with them: where is he now? Where did he go? He forsook them because they first forsook him and provoked the Holy One of Israel to wrath. But long ago God had put the Holy Spirit on them while they were still good and striving to follow his precepts."

222. Now the Holy Spirit is only introduced to those who have forsaken their vices, who follow the choir of the virtues, and who live by faith in Christ in accordance with and through virtue. But if little by little, when negligence creeps up on them, they begin to fall into worse things, they arouse against themselves the Holy Spirit who dwells in them, and they make the one who gave him to them hostile. The Apostle wrote something like this to the Thessalonians: *For God did not call you to impurity, but rather to holiness* [1 Thess 4.7].

---

[169]Note that Didymus's citation here differs considerably from that cited above in *Spir.* 198: *who put the Holy Spirit on them.*

223. And so, he who spurns (note that "he who deals falsely with" better renders the Greek)[170] does not deal falsely with a man but with God who gave his Holy Spirit to you.[171] For in these texts, God who calls to holiness through faith, that is, who calls in order that believers may become holy, gave the Holy Spirit to them. As long as they kept the precepts of God, the Holy Spirit whom they received remained on them. But when they fell through slippery vice and lapsed into impurity, they spurned (or rather they dealt falsely with) God who gave the Holy Spirit to them to make them holy, not slaves to impurity.[172] Accordingly, those who committed such acts will pay a penalty not as if they spurned a man, but as if they spurned God.

224. So that we may know that the Holy Spirit who is given to believers is God,[173] let us learn from the utterance of the Prophet Isaiah himself when he introduces God saying to someone: *My Spirit is in you, and I gave my words to your mouth* [Is 59.21]. This text indicates that whoever receives the Spirit of God also possesses along with him the words of God (that is, words of wisdom and knowledge). And indeed in another passage of the same Prophet, God says: *I gave my Spirit upon him* [Is 42.1].

225. And so, he who puts the Holy Spirit on them remembers that Moses was sanctified *by his right hand* [Is 63.12],[174] or rather that he was an enlightened man and an initiate into the mysteries of God. Concerning him, the Lord said to Joshua the Son of Nun: *Moses is my servant* [Jos 1.13, 15], or rather, his Law written in the Old Testament. For I remember frequently reading that Moses is named in place of the Law, as here: *Even to today, when Moses is read* [2 Cor 3.15]. And Abraham said to the rich man being punished: *There they have Moses and the prophets* [Lk 16.29]. These passages are clear and

---

[170]This parenthesis is an unnecessary comment by Jerome.

[171]Cf. Is 63.8+11. Didymus refers here to the "you" of 1 Thess 4.7, just cited.

[172]Cf. 1 Thess 4.7.

[173]This is one of the rare occasions when Didymus clearly affirms that the Holy Spirit is God. See also *Spir.* 83 and 130.

[174]Note that this reference to Is 63.12 differs from that cited in *Spir.* 198 and reflects the standard text: ὁ ἀγαγὼν τῇ δεξιᾷ Μωυσῆν, "he leads Moses by his right hand."

certain proof that Moses does not signify the man mentioned above, but rather the Law.

Interpretation of Isaiah 63.12.
The right hand of God and the Lordly Man [226–230]

226. Furthermore, what is the right hand of God that guided Moses, if not our Lord and Savior? For he is the right hand of the Father and through him the Father brings salvation, raises, and triumphs, as it is said elsewhere about God: *His right hand and his holy arm have brought salvation to him* [Ps 97.1]. And again: *The Lord's right hand has triumphed; the Lord's right hand raised me; I shall not die, but I shall live and recount the works of the Lord* [Ps 117.16–17].

227. This passage is certainly the most manifest proof that this voice belongs to the person of the Lordly Man, whom the only-begotten Son of God deigned to assume from the virgin because he[175] is the right hand of God, as is written in the Acts of the Apostles.[176] He[177] was *descended from David according to the flesh* [Rom 1.3] and born of a virgin when *the Holy Spirit came upon her and the power of the Most High overshadowed her* [Lk 1.35]. David prophesied about him in the Spirit, saying that after he arose from the dead, he would be assumed into the heavens and lifted up by the right hand of God.[178] **228.** But here is how it is written in the Acts of the Apostles:

> [31]*In his foresight the same David spoke of the resurrection of the Christ, that he was not abandoned to the netherworld, nor did his flesh see corruption.* [32]*This Jesus God raised up,*

[175]I.e., the only-begotten Son of God.

[176]Cf. Acts 2.33.

[177]I.e., the Lordly Man.

[178]Cf. Ps 117.16–17. Though Didymus here starkly distinguishes the only-begotten Son of God and the Lordly Man such that they appear to be two agents, in *Spir.* 230 he affirms that the two natures of Christ belong to a single subject.

of which we are all witnesses. [33]*Therefore he was raised up
by the right hand of God, and when he had received from the
Father the promise of the Holy Spirit, he poured out this gift
on us which you yourselves see and hear.* [34]*For not even David
ascended into the heavens* [Acts 2.31–34].

After all, there can be no doubt that it was the Lord Jesus who
was raised by the right hand of God and rose again from the neth-
erworld, as he himself testifies in the text of Scripture. For he who
rose from the dead says: *I lie down to rest and I began to sleep, and I
rose again, for the Lord upholds me* [Ps 3.6].

229. And so, the word of God proclaims that he who was
assumed into the heavens was raised up by the right hand of God
(which we spoke about above), and that he received the promise of
the Spirit from the Father and poured him out on believers so that
the mighty works of God were declared in every language [Acts 2.11].
Thus the Lordly Man received communion with the Holy Spirit, as
is written in the Gospels: *Therefore, Jesus being full of the Holy Spirit
returned from the Jordan* [Lk 4.1]. And in another passage: *Jesus
returned in the power of the Spirit to Galilee* [Lk 4.14].

230. But we ought to take these statements in a spirit of piety
without any malicious criticism about the Lordly Man.[179] It is not
the case that "Lord" is one thing and "Man" another. Rather, we
must reason about one and the same subject as if he were one thing
according to the nature of God and another thing according to the
nature of man.[180] Furthermore, we must do this because God the
Word, the only-begotten Son of God, admits of neither alternation
nor increase, since he is the fullness of good things.

---

[179]At this point, several important mss. add: "who is the whole Christ, the one
Jesus, the Son of God," clearly an interpolation by a copyist concerned to bring
Didymus's archaic language in line with later Christological sensibilities.

[180]Lat. *sed quod de uno atque eodem quasi de altero secundum naturam Dei et
hominis disputetur.*

PART VI: FURTHER REFLECTIONS [231–277]

*The Spirit makes believers good and holy like
the Father and the Son do [231–237]*

231. Our discussion of the testimony of the Prophet is sufficient and more than sufficient. Let us now proceed to what remains so that we may learn that the Holy Spirit is of one substance with the Father and the Son even from this: just as the Father and the Son make believers holy and good through communion with them, so too does the Holy Spirit render believers good and holy through participation in him.

232. The following saying is addressed to God in the psalms: *Let your good Spirit guide me on a straight path* [Ps 142.10]. Now we know that in some copies it is written: "Let your Holy Spirit."[181] Furthermore, in Esdras the Spirit is called good without any ambiguity: *You gave your good Spirit to make them understand* [Neh 9.20].[182]

233. The Apostle writes that the Father sanctifies: *May the God of peace sanctify you in every way* [1 Thess 5.23]. And the Savior said: *Father, sanctify them in the Truth; your Word is Truth* [Jn 17.17]. Clearly, he is saying: "Sanctify them in me, who am your Word and your Truth, when they believe and share in me." Elsewhere God is called good: *No one is good, save one, God* [Lk 18.19].

234. We also demonstrated above[183] that the Son sanctifies, with which Paul is in agreement when he uses the same words: *For he who sanctifies and they who are sanctified are all of them from one* [Heb 2.11], signifying that it is Christ who sanctifies, and those who are sanctified can say: *Christ became for us wisdom from God and righteousness and*

---

[181]In fact, "Holy Spirit" is the reading of the Codices Vaticanus and Alexandrinus.

[182]In the early Christian period, four different books circulated under the name of Esdras (Ezra), but they were numbered differently in the Greek and Latin traditions. Here Didymus refers to Esdras III, known in the Latin tradition as Esdras II, and it corresponds to Nehemiah in our modern bibles.

[183]See *Spir.* 17 and 26.

sanctification [1 Cor 1.30]. After all, he is also called the *Spirit of sanctification* [Rom 1.4]. This is why it is also said to him: *And all the sanctified are under your hands and they are under you* [Deut 33.3].

235. Our Lord Jesus Christ is good and is begotten of the good Father. Concerning him we read: *We confess to the Lord for he is good* [Ps 117.1]. Those who *confess* are those who implore the forgiveness of their sins or render thanks to his mercy for the kindnesses he has shown.

236. The Holy Spirit also sanctifies those whom he deigns to fill, as we have already demonstrated above when we showed that he can be participated in and received by many at the same time.[184] And now the following testimony of Paul shows that he is the bestower of sanctification: *But we ought to give thanks to God always for you, brothers beloved by the Lord, since God chose us as the first-fruits for salvation through the sanctification of the Spirit and faith in the truth* [2 Thess 2.13]. Now in this passage, the gifts of God are best understood to exist in the Spirit, since one possesses faith and truth alike through the sanctification of the Spirit. **237.** Therefore, since our statements on these matters are right and pious and true, the terms "holiness" and "goodness" apply equally to the Father, Son, and Holy Spirit,

The various meanings of the term "spirit" [237–256]

The same holds true for the term "spirit." For the Father is called "spirit," as in the passage which says: *God is spirit* [Jn 4.24], and the Son is called "spirit": *The Lord is spirit* [2 Cor 3.17]. And the term "spirit" is always used to name the Holy Spirit, not because he is considered along with the Father and the Son merely on the basis of a shared name, but because a single nature possesses a single name. And since the term "spirit" has many meanings, we ought briefly enumerate the realities to which this term applies.[185]

---

[184]See *Spir.* 21–24.
[185]See Athanasius, *Serap.* 1.7–8, where he similarly enumerates the meanings of "spirit."

(1) The term "spirit" is used for the wind

238. Wind is called "spirit," as in Ezekiel: *A third part you shall scatter in the spirit* [Ezek 5.2], that is, "in the wind." In addition, if you want to understand the following passage according to the historical sense: *With a vehement spirit you shall shatter the ships of Tarshish* [Ps 47.8], then take "spirit" there as meaning nothing other than "wind." Moreover, among the many graces that Solomon received from God, he also received the gift of knowing "the tempers of the spirits,"[186] meaning by this nothing other than that he had received the gift of knowing the fierce gusts of the winds and the causes that determine their nature.

(2) The term "spirit" is used for the soul

239. The soul is also called "spirit," as in the epistle of James: *as the body is dead without the spirit,* and so forth [Jam 2.26]. For it is utterly clear that the "spirit" named here is nothing other than the soul. In this sense Stephen also called his soul "spirit": *Lord Jesus, receive my spirit* [Acts 7.59]. In addition, there is what is said in Ecclesiastes: *Who knows if the spirit of a human being ascends on high and the spirit of a beast descends below?* [Eccl 3.21]. You could also consider whether the souls of beasts are also called spirits.

(3) The term "spirit" is used for the human spirit

240. Besides the soul and the Holy Spirit, some other spirit is also said to be in a human being, about which Paul writes: *For who among human beings knows the things that belong to a human being except the human spirit that is in him?* [1 Cor 2.11]. Now if anyone wants to argue that here the term "spirit" signifies the soul, who

[186]Cf. Wis 7.20.

then is the man whose thoughts, intimate opinions, and the hidden secrets of his heart no one else knows except his spirit? Wanting to understand this passage as about the body alone is utterly foolish.

241. But if someone who maintains that these words are written about the Holy Spirit and strives through cunning deception to snatch them away, then when he carefully considers the words themselves he will stop asserting this lie. For thus it is written: *For who among human beings knows the things that belong to a human being except the human spirit that is in him? Thus also no one knows the things that belong to God except the Spirit of God* [1 Cor 2.11]. Just as human being is different from God, so too is the human spirit that is in him distinct from the Spirit of God who is in him. Now time and again we have demonstrated that the Spirit of God is the Holy Spirit.

242. But in another passage the same Apostle also distinguishes the Spirit of God from our spirit: *The Spirit himself gives testimony with our spirit* [Rom 8.16]. This means that the Spirit of God (that is, the Holy Spirit), bestows testimony on our spirit, which we have just now said is the human spirit. And to the Thessalonians: *May your spirit and soul and body be sound* [1 Thess 5.23]. For just as the soul is different from the body, so too is the spirit different from the soul, which is specifically mentioned in this passage. It is this spirit for which he prays, asking that it be kept sound along with the soul and the body. After all, it would be unbelievable and even blasphemous for the Apostle to pray that the Holy Spirit be kept sound, since he can admit of neither diminution nor increase. **243.** Therefore, as we have said, the words of the Apostle in this passage also witness to the human spirit.

(4) The term "spirit" is used for good or bad rational powers

244. The heavenly and rational powers, which the Scriptures are in the habit of designating angels and forces, are also called by the term "spirit," as here: *He who makes his angels spirits* [Heb 1.7], and elsewhere: *Are not all of them ministering spirits?* [Heb 1.14]. I think that what is written in the Acts of the Apostles should be understood in this sense as well: *The spirit of the Lord carried off Philip, and the eunuch did not see him anymore* [Acts 8.39]. In other words: "The angel of the Lord raised Philip up to the heights and conveyed him to another place."

245. The other rational creatures who fall from good into evil through their own will are called wicked spirits and unclean spirits, as here: *But when an unclean spirit departs from a man* [Mt 12.43], and in what follows: *he brings seven spirits more wicked than him* [Mt 12.45]. **246.** In the Gospels, the demons are also called spirits. But we ought to note that they are never called "spirit" without some qualification. Rather, the Gospels signify an adversarial spirit with some modifier, such as "unclean spirit" or "demonic spirit." But those spirits which are holy are called "spirits" without qualification and without any modifier.

(5) The term "spirit" is used for the human will

247. We ought to know that the term "spirit" also means the human will and the thought of the mind. **248.** After all, when the Apostle wanted a virgin to be holy not only in deed but also in mind (that is, not in body alone but also in the deep movements of her heart), he said: *Let her be holy in body and in spirit* [1 Cor 7.34]. By "spirit" he meant her will and by "body" her works. You could also consider whether what Isaiah says resonates with this: *And they who erred in spirit will discover understanding* [Is 29.24]. For those who mistake good things for bad through an error of judgment will receive *understanding* so that their error may be corrected and they may choose upright things in place of wicked things. Moreover, you could consider this: *The strength of your spirit is vain* [Is 33.11], and see whether this demonstrates the same thing.

(6) The term "spirit" is used for the understanding of Scripture

249. But above all, the term "spirit" means the deeper and mystical sense in the Holy Scriptures, as here: *The letter kills, but the spirit gives life* [2 Cor 3.6]. This says that the letter is the simple and obvious narrative in accordance with the historical sense, but that the spirit gives knowledge of what is holy and spiritual in the text read. The following is also in agreement with this sense: *We are the circumcision who serve the Lord in the spirit and place no trust in the flesh* [Phil 3.3].

250. Now there are those who do not mutilate their flesh through the letter but circumcise their heart through the spirit, removing from it everything superfluous that is attached and allied to coming to be.[187] These people are truly circumcised in the spirit, being Jews in secret and true Israelites *in whom there is no guile* [Jn 1.47]. Passing beyond the shadows and images of the Old Testament[188] and being true worshippers, *they adore* the Father *in spirit and in truth* [Jn 4.24]. *In spirit*, because they have passed beyond all bodily and lowly realities; *in truth*, because they have left behind the types, shadows, and copies, and come to the substance of Truth itself; they have scorned the lowly and bodily simplicity of words (as we said above) and attained knowledge of the spiritual law.

251. At this point, we have touched upon as many things as our meager talent allows regarding what "spirit" means. When the time is right, we will examine what each of them means, if Christ should grant it.

(7) The term "spirit" is used for the Son of God

252. Sometimes our Lord Jesus Christ (that is, the Son of God), is also called "spirit": *For the spirit of wisdom is kind* [Wis 1.6]. And

---

[187]I.e., impermanent realities that come to be and pass away.
[188]Cf. Heb 8.5. See also *Spir.* 150.

in another passage: *The Lord is spirit* [2 Cor 3.17], as we mentioned earlier when we added: *God is spirit* [Jn 4.24]. The Son is spirit not merely because of a communion in name, but also because of a sharing of nature and substance.

(8) The term "spirit" is a synonym for the Trinity

253. Now in the case of realities which are different in substance, it sometimes happens that they share the same name, and their names are called ὁμώνυμα [homonyms]. Likewise, in the case of realities which are identical in nature and substance, when they have the same name together with equality of nature, it is the practice of dialecticians to call these names συνώνυμα [synonyms]. This is why the term "spirit," and any other term ordinarily applied to the Trinity, is a συνώνυμον, for example, holy, good, and other terms similar to these upon which we touched a little before.[189]

Avoiding the danger of misinterpreting the term "spirit"

254. Furthermore, we needed to discuss these matters lest the term "spirit" be a stumbling block for us, since this word is dispersed throughout the Divine Scriptures. We should look at each instance of this word, bearing in mind the variety of passages in which it is used and the senses it has in them. And so, contemplating with all zeal and diligence the context and manner in which the term "spirit" is used, let us destroy the sophistical arguments and deceitful snares of those who claim that the Holy Spirit is a creature.

255. Because they are ignorant of the multiple senses that the term "spirit" could have in the passage: *I am the one who gives strength to thunder and who creates spirit* [Am 4.13] when they read it in the Prophet, they think that it is the Holy Spirit who is indicated

[189]See *Spir.* 231–237a.

by this term. But in this instance the term "spirit" means "wind."[190] Moreover, when they hear that God said in Zechariah that he is the one who *created the human spirit within a person* [Zech 12.1], they think that it is the Holy Spirit who is signified in this chapter, unaware that the term "spirit" can signify the soul or spirit of human being. We have already mentioned that this human spirit is third in a human being.[191]

256. Therefore, as we said earlier, we should consider the manner in which the term is used in each instance, lest perhaps through ignorance we fall into the pit of error. Now when it is a question of other matters, an error that arises through a shared use of terms brings confusion and shame to the one who made the error. But when it is a question of someone falling from the divine heights to wicked things, the error leads him to eternal punishment and the infernal regions of hell, especially if once he is deceived he chooses not to recover his senses but rather prefers to defend his error shamelessly.

An objection: Satan also fills the human heart [257–268]

257. Given the length of this volume, it would be altogether fitting to conclude our treatise. But an objection has been raised which opposes the claims we made above. We left it aside for the moment to avoid an interruption of the flow of our treatise and the insertion of impious wrangling into the middle of our pious discourse. But it is necessary, I think, to respond to this proposition and let the reader judge what he thinks about these matters.

258. So then, we argued above that the soul and mind of a human being cannot be filled with a created thing according to substance, but by the Trinity alone, since the mind is filled with created things only according to activity and the will's error or virtue.[192] In response

---

[190]See *Spir.* 66–72.
[191]Cf. *Spir.* 242.
[192]See *Spir.* 30 and 34.

to this, an objection has been put to us as if it destroyed our view on this subject. Here it is: there is a created substance called Satan in the Scriptures that enters into certain people and is said to fill their heart. **259.** For example, Peter the Apostle said to the man who kept back half of the proceeds from the sale of his field while declaring another amount: *Ananias, why has Satan filled your heart?* [Acts 5.3].[193] And the Savior himself said about Judas that *Satan entered into him* [Jn 13.27].[194] We will address both these examples, the second after the first.

260. And so, we must first concern ourselves with the Scripture: *why has Satan filled your heart?* [Acts 5.3]. How can Satan fill the mind and commanding-faculty[195] of someone without entering into him and into his mind and (so to speak) without stepping through the doorway of his heart, since this power belongs to the Trinity alone? But like a cunning, wicked, deceptive, and fraudulent imposter, by suggesting thoughts about the vices and offering incentives for them Satan draws the human soul to those desires for wickedness with which he himself is filled.

261. Next, it is written that Elymas the magician, the son of the devil, who lived a life of wickedness and malice, was full of all deceit and wickedness. Satan his father practically instilled this will in him and it became by habit like second nature. And so, when the Apostle Paul exposed and rebuked him, he said: *You are full of all deceit and all iniquity, you son of the devil!* [Acts 13.10]. Because that crafty and cunning man received in himself all deceit and fraud, he is called *the son of the devil.* The devil filled his heart and commanding-faculty with fraud and wickedness and all malice, and enticed and deceived him, so much so that one may think that Satan himself filled his soul and dwelt in him. For Satan had molded him to be his very own minister and servant of all his duplicity and perversity.

---

[193]See *Spir.* 83 and 131.

[194]Didymus is slightly inaccurate here. Neither in Jn 13.27 nor in Lk 22.3 does Jesus say that Satan entered into Judas; rather, this is a statement of the narrator.

[195]Lat. *principale cordis*, no doubt a translation of ἡγεμονικόν. This was the Stoic term for that part of the soul which was the center of consciousness and the seat of all

262. But now it is time to address the second example that we proposed, that Satan entered into Judas. **263.** When the devil noticed to which vices Judas' heart was most strongly inclined by observing his motions and what his activities signified, he discerned that he was exposed to the snares of avarice. When he found an door open to greed, he sent to the mind of Judas a strategy for obtaining the money he desired. Through this opportunity for monetary gain, he became the betrayer of his own teacher and Savior, exchanging piety for silver and receiving the reward for his crime from the Pharisees and the Jews.[196]

264. Therefore, when this thought occurred to Judas, it gave Satan the opportunity to enter into his heart and fill him with the worst kind of will. Yet he did not enter according to substance, but rather according to activity, since entering into another belongs to the uncreated nature which can be participated in by many. The devil is not capable of being participated in, seeing that he is not the Creator but a creature. For this reason too, being capable of change and alteration, he fell from holiness and virtue.

265. We said above that τὸ μεθεκτόν[197] (that is, "that which is received by participation") is incorruptible and immutable and consequently eternal, but that that which is able to be changed is made and has a beginning. In addition, that which is incorruptible is everlasting whether one looks at ages past or ages to come. Therefore, it is not the case, as certain people think, that a person is filled with the devil or becomes indwelt by him through participation in his nature or substance. Rather, we believe that he indwells the person whom he fills through fraud, deception, and malice.

---

mental states. While it is analogous to the brain as we understand it today, the Stoics located the ἡγεμονικόν in the heart.

[196]Cf. Mt 27.3–5.

[197]We read here τὸ μεθεκτόν, which seems to be the reading transliterated in B (to meteXton), C (to mettecton), and Δ (thometecton). The term τὸ μεθεκτόν is standard in philosophical contexts and is preferable to Doutreleau's τὸ μετοχικόν. Cf. Athanasius, Serap. 1.27.2.

266. The devil used this fraud of his even against the elders who turned their love for Suzanna into cruelty against her, and filled their souls with burning lust and a late-blooming passion of old age. For it is written: *Now two elders came, full of their wicked plot* [Dan 13.28]. He also filled the whole Jewish people with these snares, about whom the Prophet said: *Woe to you, a sinful nation, a people full of sin, a race of the worst kind, wicked sons!* [Is 1.4]. Now they are called a wicked race of the devil and his sons because they are wicked and full of sins.

267. If those who are called his sons in the Scriptures are not capable of receiving the devil through participation in his substance (for time and again we have shown that this is impossible for creatures), then no one else can receive him through participation in his substance, but only by adopting his most deceptive will. **268.** After all, we have said that, in the case of creatures, activity and zeal can participate in works both good and bad. But the nature and the substance of the Trinity alone is able to enter into others.

The dismissal of a foolish teaching about the Holy Spirit [269–271]

269. Quite sufficiently, I think, we have replied to the objection that was put to us. But since it seems silly and foolish to respond to idiotic matters and to want to resolve whatever the mouth of the impious may belch forth—for impiety consists in not only proposing wicked things but even more so in wanting to debate these wicked things with your opponent—therefore, I pass over in silence those assertions which they are in the habit of bandying about, proclaiming brazen sacrileges against us.[198] For they say that if the Holy Spirit is not created, then he is either a brother of God the Father or the uncle of the only-begotten Jesus Christ. Or he is either the son of Christ or the grandson of God the Father. Or he is himself the Son of

---

[198]See Athanasius, *Serap.* 1.15–17, who deals with these same heretical teachings.

God, and in that case the Lord Jesus Christ will not be only-begotten since he has a brother.

270. How wretched and pitiable are those who remain unaware that they should not discuss incorporeal and invisible realities as they would a corporeal and visible nature. As for "brother" or "uncle" or "grandson" or "son," these are corporeal names and terms that characterize human weakness. But the Trinity transcends all these names, and whenever he condescends to one of these names, he is not declaring his own nature by using our names and incongruent terms.

271. Therefore, since the only point holy Scripture makes about the Trinity is that God is the Father of the Savior and the Son is generated from the Father, we ought to think only that which is written. Once it has been demonstrated that the Holy Spirit is uncreated, we ought to understand that the one whose substance is not created is rightly joined to the Father and the Son.

CONCLUSION [272–277]

272. Given the poverty of our eloquence, what I have said on the present topic should suffice to indicate my great trepidation when I dared to speak about the Holy Spirit. **273.** For whoever blasphemes against him will receive no pardon, not only in this age but also in the age to come.[199] Nor will mercy and forgiveness be held in store for the one who has trampled on the Son of God and insulted the Spirit of grace in whom he has been sanctified.[200]

274. Indeed, this ought to be understood as holding true also in the case of God the Father. For the one who has blasphemed against him and acted impiously will be tortured without any relief, since no one will pray to the Lord on his behalf, according to the Scripture: *But if someone has sinned against the Lord God, who will pray for*

[199]Cf. Mt 12.31–32.
[200]Cf. Heb 10.29.

him? [1 Sam 2.25]. **275.** Moreover, whoever denies the Son before people will be denied by him before the Father and his angels.[201] **276.** Therefore, since no pardon is granted to those who blaspheme against the Trinity, we must take all precaution and care to avoid slipping up when we are discussing him, even in a brief and short explanation.

277. Even more, if anyone wishes to read this book, we ask that he purify himself of every evil work and all wicked thoughts, so that he may be able, once his heart is enlightened, to understand what we have said. Furthermore, being full of holiness and wisdom, he will be able to pardon us if anywhere the result of our endeavor does not fulfill our intention, and thus he can consider only the sense of what we said, not the words we used to express ourselves. For just as we confidently claim that according to our conscience we have a pious mind, so too, when it is a question of artistic prose and rhetorical eloquence and the flow and structure of the treatise, we simply confess that we fall far short of these. After all, the goal of our study when discussing the holy Scriptures was to understand piously what was written and pay no attention to our lack of skill and our limitations when it comes to speaking.[202]

[201]Cf. Mt 10.33.

[202]Ms. B, from the 12th or 13th century, has the following *explicit*: "Here ends, by God's help, the book of Didymus the Seer on the Holy Spirit, translated from Greek into Latin by Blessed Jerome, presbyter." The *incipit* of the same ms. reads: "Here begins the book of Didymus the Seer on the Holy Spirit."

Bibliography

Editions and Translations of Athanasius and Didymus

Doutreleau, Louis, ed. and trans. *Didyme L'Aveugle: Traité du Saint-Esprit*. SChr 386. Paris: Cerf, 1992.

Lebon, Joseph, trans. *Athanase d'Alexandre. Lettres à Sérapion sur la divinité du Saint-Esprit*. SChr 15. Paris: Cerf, 1947.

Montfaucon, Bernard de, ed. *S. P. N. Athanasii Epistulae IV ad Serapionem episcopum Thmuitanum*. PG 26.529–638.

Shapland, C. R. B., trans. *The Letters of Saint Athanasius concerning the Holy Spirit*. London: Epworth Press, 1951.

Sieben, Hermann Josef, ed. and trans. *Didymus der Blinde: De Spiritu Sancto/Über den Heiligen Geist*. Fontes Christiani 78. Turnhout: Brepols, 2004.

Wyrwa, Dietmar, and Kyriakos Savvidis, eds. *Athanasius Werke I/1. Die dogmatischen Schriften. 4. Lieferung. Epistulae I-IV ad Serapionem*. Berlin / New York: Walter de Gruyter, 2010.

Selected Secondary Literature

Anatolios, Khaled. *Athanasius: The Coherence of his Thought*. London and New York: Routledge, 1998.

————. *Athanasius*. London: Routledge, 2004.

Arnold, Duane W.-H. *The Early Episcopal Career of Athanasius of Alexandria*. Notre Dame: University of Notre Dame Press, 1991.

Ayres, Lewis. "Athanasius' Initial Defense of the Term Ὁμοούσιος: Rereading the *De decretis*." *Journal of Early Christian Studies* 12 (2004): 337–59.

————. *Nicaea and its Legacy: An Approach to Fourth-Century Trinitarian Theology*. Oxford: Oxford University Press, 2004.

————. "The Holy Spirit as Undiminished Giver: Didymus the Blind's *De Spiritu Sancto* and the Development of Nicene Pneumatology." Pages

57–72 in Janet Rutherford and Vincent Twomey, eds., *The Holy Spirit in the Fathers of the Church. The Proceedings of the Seventh International Patristic Conference, Maynooth, 2008*. Dublin: Four Courts Press, 2011.

_____ and Michel René Barnes. "Pneumatology: Historical and Methodological Considerations." *Augustinian Studies* 39 (2008): 163–236. Consisting of:

_____ and _____. "Introduction and Acknowledgements." *Augustinian Studies* 39 (2008): 165–7.

Barnes, Michel René. "The Beginning and End of Early Christian Pneumatology." *Augustinian Studies* 39 (2008): 169–86.

Ayres, Lewis. "Innovation and *Ressourcement* in Pro-Nicene Pneumatology." *Augustinian Studies* 39 (2008): 187–206.

_____. "*Spiritus Amborum*: Augustine and Pro-Nicene Pneumatology." *Augustinian Studies* 39 (2008): 207–21.

Barnes, Michel René. "Augustine's Last Pneumatology." *Augustinian Studies* 39 (2008): 223–34.

Ayres, Lewis, and Michel René Barnes. "Conclusions." *Augustinian Studies* 39 (2008): 235–6.

Bardy, Gustave. *Didyme L'Aveugle*. Paris: Beauchesne, 1910.

Barnes, Michel René. "Irenaeus's Trinitarian Theology." *Nova et Vetera* 7 (2009): 76–106.

Barnes, Timothy D. *Athanasius and Constantius*. Cambridge: Harvard University Press, 1993.

Beeley, Christopher A. *Gregory of Nazianzus on the Trinity and the Knowledge of God*. New York: Oxford, 2008.

Behr, John, *The Nicene Faith*. 2 vols. Crestwood: St Vladimir's Seminary Press, 2004.

Brakke, David. *Athanasius and the Politics of Asceticism*. Oxford: Clarendon Press, 1995.

Burns, J. Patout, and Gerald M. Fagan. *The Holy Spirit*. Message of the Fathers of the Church 3. Wilmington: M. Glazier, 1984; repr. Eugene: Wipf and Stock, 2002.

Casey, R. P. *Serapion of Thmuis against the Manichees*. Cambridge: Harvard University Press, 1931.

Clark, Elizabeth A. *The Origenist Controversy: The Cultural Construction of an Early Christian Debate*. Princeton: Princeton University Press, 1992.

Daniélou, Jean. *The Theology of Jewish Christianity*. Translated by John A.

Baker. London: Darton, Longmann & Todd; Chicago: The Henry Regnery Company, 1964.

Dechow, Jon. *Dogma and Mysticism in Early Christianity: Epiphanius of Cyprus and the Legacy of Origen.* Patristic Monograph Series, no. 13. Macon, GA: Mercer University Press, 1988.

DelCogliano, Mark. "Basil of Caesarea on Proverbs 8:22 and the Sources of Pro-Nicene Theology." *Journal of Theological Studies* n.s. 59 (2008): 183–90.

————. "Basil of Caesarea, Didymus the Blind, and the Anti-Pneumatomachian Exegesis of Amos 4:13 and John 1:3." *Journal of Theological Studies* n.s. 61 (2010): 644–658.

Dragüet, René. "Une lettre de Sérapion de Thmuis aux disciples d'Antoine (A.D. 356) en version syriaque et arménienne." *Le Muséon* 64 (1951): 1–25.

Egan, George A. *The Armenian Version of the Letters of Athanasius to Bishop Serapion Concerning the Holy Spirit.* Studies and Documents 37. Salt Lake City: University of Utah Press, 1968.

Fitschen, Klaus. *Serapion von Thmuis: Echte und unechte Schriften sowie die Zeugnisse des Athanasius und anderer.* Patristische Texte und Studien 37. Berlin and New York: De Gruyter, 1992.

Gwynn, David M. *The Eusebians: The Polemic of Athanasius of Alexandria and the Construction of the Arian Controversy.* Oxford: Oxford University Press, 2007.

Haas, Christopher. *Alexandria in Late Antiquity: Topography and Social Conflict.* Baltimore and London: The Johns Hopkins University Press, 1997.

Hanson, R. P. C. *The Search for the Christian Doctrine of God.* Edinburgh: T&T Clark, 1988.

Hauschild, Wolf-Dieter. "Die Pneumatomachen: Eine Untersuchung zur Dogmensgeschicte des vierten Jahrhunderts." Ph.D. diss., Hamburg, 1967.

Haykin, Michael A. G. *The Spirit of God: The Exegesis of 1 and 2 Corinthians in the Pneumatomachian Controversy of the Fourth Century.* Leiden: Brill, 1994.

Heron, Alasdair. "Studies in the Trinitarian Writings of Didymus the Blind: his Authorship of the Adversus Eunonium IV-V." Ph.D. diss., Tübingen, 1972.

_____. "The Two Pseudo-Athanasian Dialogues Against the Anomoeans." *Journal of Theological Studies* n.s. 24 (1973), 101–22.

_____. "Zur Theologie der ›Tropici‹ in der Serapionbriefe des Athanasius. Amos 4,13 als Pneumatologische Belegstelle." *Kyrios: Vierteljahresschrift für Kirchen- und Geistesgeschichte Osteuropas* 14 (1974): 3–24.

_____. "The Pseudo-Athanasian Works *De Trinitate et Spiritu Sancto* and *De Incarnatione et Contra Arianos*: A Comparison." Pages 281–98 in G. D. Dragas, ed. *Aksum-Thyateira: A Festschrift for Archbishop Methodios of Thyateira and Great Britain*. Athens and London: Thyateira House, 1985.

_____. "Some sources used in the *De Trinitate* ascribed to Didymus the Blind." Pages 173–81 in Rowan Williams, ed. *The Making of Orthodoxy: Essays in Honour of Henry Chadwick*. Cambridge: Cambridge University Press, 1989.

Hildebrand, Stephen M. *The Trinitarian Theology of Basil of Caesarea: A Synthesis of Greek Thought and Biblical Truth*. Washington D.C.: Catholic University of America Press, 2007.

Isaacs, Marie E. *The Concept of Spirit: A Study of Pneuma in Hellenistic Judaism and its Bearing on the New Testament*. Heythrop Monographs 1. London: Heythrop College, 1976.

Kannengiesser, Charles. *Athanase d'Alexandrie. Éveque et Écrivain: Une lecture des traités contra les Ariens*. Paris: Beauschesne, 1983.

Layton, Richard A. *Didymus the Blind and His Circle in Late-Antique Alexandria: Virtue and Narrative in Biblical Scholarship*. Urbana and Chicago: University of Illinois Press, 2004.

Levinson, John. "The Angelic Spirit in Early Judaism." Pages 464–92 in *SBL 1995 Seminar Papers*.

Lienhard, Joseph T. "Ousia and Hypostasis: The Cappadocian Settlement and the Theology of 'One Hypostasis.'" Pages 99–121 in Stephen T. Davis, Daniel Kendall, and Gerald O'Collins, eds. *The Trinity: An Interdisciplinary Symposium on the Doctrine of the Trinity*. Oxford and New York: Oxford University Press, 2000.

Lyman, J. Rebecca. *Christology and Cosmology: Models of Divine Activity in Origen, Eusebius, and Athanasius*. Oxford: Clarendon Press, 1993.

McGuckin, John A. *St. Gregory of Nazianzus: An Intellectual Biography*. Crestwood, N.Y.: SVS Press, 2001.

Meijering, E. P. *Orthodoxy and Platonism in Athanasius. Synthesis or Antithesis?*, 2nd ed. Leiden: Brill, 1975.

Morales, Xavier. *La théologie trinitaire d'Athanase d'Alexandrie.* Paris: Institut d'Études Augustiniennes, 2006.

Quasten, Johannes. *Patrology, Vol. III: The Golden Age of Greek Patristic Literature from the Council of Nicaea to the Council of Chalcedon.* Notre Dame, IN: Christian Classics, 1993.

Radde-Gallwitz, Andrew. "The Holy Spirit as Agent, not Activity: Origen's Argument with Modalism and its Afterlife in Didymus, Eunomius, and Gregory of Nazianzus." *Vigiliae Christianae* 65 (2011): 227–248.

Segal, Alan F. *Two Powers in Heaven: Early Rabbinic Reports about Christianity and Gnostics.* Leiden: Brill, 1977; repr. 2002.

————. "Two Powers in Heaven and Early Christian Thinking." Pages 73–95 in Stephen T. Davis, Daniel Kendall, and Gerald O'Collins, eds. *The Trinity: An Interdisciplinary Symposium on the Doctrine of the Trinity.* Oxford and New York: Oxford University Press, 2000.

Smythe, H. R. "The interpretation of Amos IV, 13 in St. Athanasius and Didymus," *Journal of Theological Studies* n.s. 1 (1950): 158–68.

Staimer, Edeltraut. "Die Schrift 'De Spiritu Sancto' von Didymus dem Blinden von Alexandrien." Ph.D. diss., München, 1960.

Swete, H. B. *The Holy Spirit in the Ancient Church.* London: MacMillan, 1912; repr. Eugene: Wipf and Stock, 1996.

Troiano, Marina Silvia. "Il *Contra Eunomium* III di Basilio di Cesarea e le *Epistolae ad Serapionem* I-IV di Atanasio di Alessandria: nota comparativa," *Augustinianum* 41.1 (2001), 59–91.

Vaggione, Richard Paul, ed. and trans. *Eunomius: The Extant Works.* Oxford: Clarendon Press, 1987.

————. *Eunomius of Cyzicus and the Nicene Revolution.* Oxford: Oxford University Press, 2000.

Weinandy, Thomas G. *Athanasius: A Theological Introduction.* Aldershot: Ashgate, 2007.

Widdicome, Peter. *The Fatherhood of God from Origen to Athanasius.* Oxford: Clarendon Press, 1994.

Index of Scripture

OLD TESTAMENT

NEW TESTAMENT

POPULAR PATRISTICS SERIES

ST VLADIMIR'S SEMINARY PRESS
1-800-204-2665 • www.svspress.com